SHAKESPEARE'S "HISTORIES"

SHAKESPEARE'S
"Histories"

MIRRORS OF ELIZABETHAN
POLICY

BY

Lily B. Campbell

METHUEN & CO LTD
11 NEW FETTER LANE · EC4

First published 1947 in the U.S.A.
Third edition 1963
First published in Great Britain 1964
Reprinted 1968
S.B.N. 416 23010 5
1.2
First published as a University Paperback 1964
Reprinted 1968
S.B.N. 416 68430 0
1.2
Printed and bound in Great Britain by
Butler & Tanner Ltd, Frome and London

CONTENTS

PREFACE

THE EDITORS of the First Folio collection of Shakespeare's plays classified them as comedies, histories, and tragedies, thus taking cognizance of history as a dramatic genre. It was a genre that grew in popularity during the last half of the sixteenth century in England, and it was as different from tragedy and comedy as they were from each other. All three of these generic names were applied to nondramatic as well as dramatic writing, and it is my belief that just as dramatic tragedy has come to be better understood since it has been considered in relation to the broad concepts of tragedy manifest not only in dramatic but in nondramatic works as well, so will history be better understood when we stop talking about it in terms of the ancient classical dramatic genres and consider it in relation to general principles of historical writing exemplified alike in dramatic and nondramatic literature.

This book is directed, therefore, to discovering the principles and methods of historiography which were current in sixteenth-century England and to demonstrating the way in which Shakespeare applied them when he wrote his histories. Shakespeare, of course, used history as story material in many of his other plays—in his Roman plays, for instance—but I am not here concerned with story material as such, whether it is derived from history or elsewhere; I am concerned solely with the kind of play listed as a history by his editors.

To cover in a single book the development of historiography in the English Renaissance and the exemplification of this theory in Shakespeare's practice has necessitated that I discard most of my notes on the background material and a goodly portion of my notes on the Shakespearean plays. I have shed these accumulations of many years with reluctance, but because of the great bulk of the material I could present just so much as might be required to make clear and to illustrate the determining ideas in sixteenth-century historical writing and Shakespeare's methods of using them.

A*

PREFACE

The limits of a readable book have also been primarily responsible for my including only studies of *King John, Richard II, Henry IV, Henry V,* and *Richard III.* This group of plays seems to me to offer ample illustration of Shakespeare's methods. However, my decision to omit *Henry VIII* has been influenced by the fact that it does not occupy an assured place in the Shakespeare canon. And I have omitted *Henry VI* because I have found it quite impossible to discuss without reviewing and reconsidering the evidence concerning the sequence and the dates of the three parts. The problem is complicated by the re-using of material which had already been altered in the *Mirror for Magistrates* to fit the times of Edward VI. I hope to publish separately a study of *Henry VI,* but it is too long and too much involved in the consideration of problems other than that of dramatic genre to be included here.

It is apparent that a broader survey of history as a dramatic genre is needed. From *Gorboduc* to Chapman there are plays unexplored from this point of view. But however enticing the opportunities, one life and one book are not enough to make much of them. I can only hope that other students of the drama will add to these beginnings by investigating plays directed to similar ends.

I have been at work upon the materials here gathered together for many years, and the research funds of the University of California provided help in securing photostats and transcribing documents before the war took away the possibilities of such services. When my work seemed bound to be terminated by the round-the-calendar teaching schedule of the war, the Huntington Library made me an affiliate member of its research staff and secured to me a few weeks in the year for completing this study. To both institutions I am grateful, as I am also grateful to my several colleagues in both institutions who have from time to time given me gleanings from their reading or have read critically bits and pieces of my manuscript. To Professors Louis B. Wright and Godfrey Davies, however, I owe special thanks, for they have read the whole.

I have used the English Arden texts throughout, and to the

PREFACE

editors of those well-edited texts of the history plays I owe a special debt. Nor do my footnotes adequately express my general obligation to E. K. Chambers' *William Shakespeare*, J. E. Neale's *Queen Elizabeth*, Camden's *Annales*, and his *Historie of the Princesse Elizabeth*, the books that have been on my desk for constant reference. It is with sincere regret that I must add that because of the difficulties of wartime transportation I was not able to procure the recently published book by Professor E. M. W. Tillyard on *Shakespeare's History Plays* before I had completed this manuscript.

Certain details of method must be explained. I have in general used the *Short-Title Catalogue* as authority for the spelling of the names of Renaissance authors. In transcribing quotations from early books I have expanded contractions and have observed modern usage in regard to *u, v, w, i*, and *j*. I have not otherwise altered the spelling or punctuation of texts save to correct obvious errors such as turned letters. I have, however, capitalized in the modern manner the important words in the primary titles of literary works while reducing the capitals in their subsidiary titles except for proper names.

LILY B. CAMPBELL

Los Angeles, California
June 1, 1945

PART ONE
HISTORY, HISTORIOGRAPHY, AND POLITICS

CHAPTER I

THE POINT OF VIEW

Professor Mark Van Doren recently wrote a book about Shakespeare based upon the comfortable postulate that Shakespeare does not "seem to call for explanations beyond those which a whole heart and a free mind abundantly supply,"[1] and he must have been discouraged when, after all his efforts to rid it of the prejudicial aura of books and learning, the friendly literary critic of the *New Yorker* magazine chose to acclaim it as a work of scholarship. For it is a heartening conviction, this, that John Doe has only to reassure himself about the wholeness of his heart and the freedom of his mind to undertake to interpret Shakespeare. Any heart and any mind will do.

Shakespeare himself has frequently been put in the Caedmon school of poets, and even Dr. Furness while dedicating himself to issuing a variorum edition of Shakespeare's works wrote in this vein:

I cannot reconcile myself to the opinion that Shakespeare ever made use of his dramatic art for the purpose of instructing, or as a means of enforcing his own views, any more than I believe that his poetic inspiration was dependent on his personal experiences.[2]

Dr. Furness' comment is as reassuring to writers as is Professor Van Doren's to critics. Personal experience and personal conviction, the contents of the mind that creates or that interprets, have nothing to do with the business of writing or of understanding, if we accept the statements of these critics. As I have said, these are comforting thoughts. They are even reassuringly democratic.

[1]*Shakespeare* (New York, 1939), p. 2.

[2]*A New Variorum Edition of Shakespeare: The Life and Death of King John*, ed. H. H. Furness, Jr. (Philadelphia and London, 1919), p. xii.

Under these rules all of us are created free and equal as critics and writers, and we stay that way.

Less comforting about the content of the critic's and the writer's mind and heart, though agreeing that Shakespeare's poetic inspiration was not dependent on his personal experiences, Professor Stoll presents another significant critical attitude, for he pictures Shakespeare's relation to the life about him as that of the mere observer, the recorder, the man who didn't take sides:

we cannot easily make out his character, his likes or dislikes, his convictions or principles. He is too fair, too tolerant, too indulgent: the creator is lost in the multitude of his creations, and, a god in his own world, he is invisible. No partisan, or satirist, no reformer or propagandist—he stays his hand, lets things be. . . . And he betrays no bias in affairs of church or state. . . . Theories and questions, creeds, problems, parties, these were not for him. Not new ideas but familiar ones interested him and served his popular dramatic purpose—pagan, Catholic, or royalist notions, for instance, not those of the newer faith. Like most of the great poets and artists he is no seer or prophet, no philosopher.[3]

To me the last two sentences do not bear the relation that Professor Stoll seems to attribute to them, for the perception of the eternal and the immutable in the ever-changing phenomena of the past and the present, rather than any hurrying to be abreast of the latest intellectual fad, seems to me to mark the great poet as seer and prophet and philosopher. But this is beside the point which I wish to make, that many critics, like Professor Stoll, regard Shakespeare as a man without intellectual or moral passion.

The voice of the historian, Professor A. F. Pollard, echoes in regard to his particular field the same judgment upon Shakespeare:

No period of English literature has less to do with politics than that during which English letters reached their zenith; and no English writer's attitude towards the questions, with which alone political history is concerned, is more obscure or less important than Shakespeare's. . . . Shakespeare himself, whose genius was less circumscribed than any other's, shuns the problems of contemporary politics. The

[3]E. E. Stoll, *Shakespeare Studies* (New York, 1927), pp. 12-13.

literature of his age was not political; and its political writings, except in so far as Hooker's *Ecclesiastical Polity* was political, were not literature.[4]

Opposed to these expounders of the literary profession there has arisen a swarm of critics who find that Shakespeare used his plays to call names. These are the identifiers. Mostly they identify Essex and Mary, Queen of Scots, but almost anyone is a candidate for high honors, the chief difficulty being that the clamor is a bit confusing which results from such clashing opinions as those which identify Armado in *Love's Labor's Lost* as the Monarcho, Antonio Perez, John Lyly, Philip of Spain, Sir Walter Raleigh, and Don John of Austria.

Finally, there are the critics who accept Shakespeare as a man of Elizabethan England who read the books that were then printed and saw the sights and knew the men and women about him. They think of him as aware of what he read and what he saw, and reflecting in his plays the modes of living and of thinking and of play writing that were current.

This group of critics of Shakespeare as represented in their approach to his historical plays found their precursor in Richard Simpson, who in two important papers in 1874 discussed "The Political Use of the Stage in Shakespeare's Time" and "The Politics of Shakespeare's Historical Plays."[5] Simpson's successors have been numerous and include many familiar names—H. B. Charlton, G. B. Harrison, Dover Wilson, E. P. Kuhl, John W. Draper, W. C. Curry, Alfred Hart, and others. These critics have made us aware that Shakespeare's plays concerning English history echoed many of the political teachings of the time. Some of them have found specific sources implied. Professor Hart, for instance, summarizes his work by saying that he "attempted to

---

[4]*The History of England, 1547-1603* (London, 1919), p. 440. See also J. B. Black, *The Reign of Elizabeth* (Oxford, 1936), pp. 239-40. For evidence combating these views see N. L. Frazer, *The Tudor Monarchy 1485 to 1588* and F. J. C. Hearnshaw, *Court and Parliament 1588 to 1688* ("English History in Contemporary Poetry," III and IV, published for the Historical Association: London, 1914 and 1926).

[5]*The New Shakespere Society's Transactions*, 1874, pp. 371-441.

show that the dramatist took his views on divine right and the mutual relation of monarch and subjects from the official book of sermons,"[6] that is, from the *Homilies* published in 1571.

But it is possible, I think, to go further than these critics have gone in relating Shakespeare to his background, to try to ascertain the general relation of his thinking to that which prevailed about him while he lived. Many of the conclusions reached by the critics whom I have described as the successors of Richard Simpson are those which I shall reach in a more roundabout way. But what I hope to show is that just as there is in the Shakespearean tragedies a dominant ethical pattern of passion opposed to reason, so there is in the history plays a dominant political pattern characteristic of the political philosophy of his age.

Perhaps it will help explain my point of view in regard to Shakespeare's plays if I venture to state my own credo. I do not believe that a poet exists in a vacuum, or even that he exists solely in the minds and hearts of his interpreters. I do not believe that he can write great poetry without conviction and without passion. I do not believe that his reflection of his period is casual and fragmentary and accidental. Rather, it seems to me the poet must be reckoned a man among men, a man who can be understood only against the background of his own time. His ideas and his experiences are conditioned by the time and the place in which he lives. He is inevitably a man of feeling. If, however, he is not merely a poet but a great poet, the particulars of his experience are linked in meaning to the universal of which they are a representative part. If he is a great poet, his feeling becomes an intense passion. It is not that he does not write out of his experience that sets him as a man apart; it is rather that he penetrates through experience to the meaning of experience. For this reason he has generally been reckoned a seer and a prophet. It is not lack of feeling but a passion for universal truth that takes his hatred and his love out of the realm of the petty and into the realm of the significant. In this sense, and in this sense only, is he impersonal. Further, the greatest poets have always in their work

---

[6]*Shakespeare and the Homilies* (Melbourne, 1934), p. 5.

been philosophers; that is to say they have developed, as they matured, consistent patterns of thought. They have seen life as a whole, not in fragments.

I hope no one will misunderstand me as saying that a poet expounds a philosophy in set words or invents a system of the universe. The poet is as much conditioned by the material he works in as by his experience. If he is a dramatist, he has to do first and fundamentally with plot. The characters may, indeed, express his philosophy or their own, but the plot is bound to express the author's philosophy; it is bound to relate particular characters and their particular actions to universal law. Macbeth may say that "Life is a tale told by an idiot," but the play of *Macbeth* is not a tale of a world run by an idiot. It is a tale of a world of clearly defined moral law, in which Macbeth and his particular actions meet with the indestructible and the universal. Poets today have another philosophy, and their plots reveal their uncertainties. But Shakespeare's plots were clear and sure because he had a definite, fundamental conception of universal law.

It is to a study of Shakespeare's historical plays from this point of view that this book is directed. The first problem involved is the definition of a history play, for that definition must lead to the background of thought and purpose which affords the basis for interpreting individual plays.

CHAPTER II

WHAT ARE "HISTORIES"?

WHEN Shakespeare's editors arranged his plays in the First Folio, they grouped them into Comedies, Histories, and Tragedies, putting the ten plays dealing with English history, and only those, into the *Histories* classification. The why of this arrangement implies definition. What was a history play in the thinking of the editors? Many scholars have discussed the genre without having agreed upon a definition.

Clearly the editors of the First Folio did not accept the authority of the titles of such plays as had already appeared in quarto editions. In the quartos the term *tragedy* had appeared in *The True Tragedie of Richarde Duke of Yorke*, *The Tragedie of King Richard the Second*, and *The Tragedy of King Richard the Third*. The term *history* had been used in the titles of *The Taming of a Shrew*, *Henry IV*, *Hamlet* (called a tragical history), and *Troilus and Cressida*, though it was perhaps used only in the sense of *story*. The more specific term *chronicle history* had, however, been used in the titles of *The Chronicle History of Henry the Fift* and the *True Chronicle Historie of the Life and Death of King Lear and his Three Daughters*. Why were these original indications of dramatic genre ignored in the First Folio?

Clearly, also, the editors did not differentiate histories from tragedies on the basis of the sources from which they were derived, for the plays listed as histories have their source in the same chronicles as *Lear* and *Macbeth* among the tragedies, and *Cymbeline* among the comedies. Most of the Shakespeare tragedies were, indeed, drawn from accepted historical sources. What,

8

then, differentiated the chosen ten in the thinking of Shakespeare's first editors?

The answer to these questions is usually vague. Many scholars have substituted description for definition in writing about Shakespeare's histories. Coleridge, seeing that the ten plays related to the history of England, and taking into account his premise that the history play should be regarded as "the transitional link between the epic poem and the drama," framed a definition to fit the facts as he saw them:

> In order that a drama may be properly historical, it is necessary that it should be the history of the people to whom it is addressed . . . It takes, therefore, that part of real history which is least known, and infuses a principle of life and organization into the naked facts, and makes them all the framework of an animated whole.[1]

It is difficult to see why Coleridge should regard plays dealing with the Wars of the Roses as "least known" to the Elizabethans, for this period was the one most frequently chronicled and made the subject of exegesis by the Tudors. But it is quite easy to see why he arrived at his definition of a true history as dealing with the people to whom it is addressed, since that apparently seemed to him the only basis upon which the ten English histories could have been differentiated from many of the others. It is evident, however, that he saw the inadequacy of his own definition, for he recognized the existence of varied types of history plays, calling *Henry IV*, for instance, a "mixed drama" and explaining:

> The distinction does not depend on the mere quantity of historical events in the play compared with the fictions; for there is as much history in "Macbeth" as in "Richard," but in the relation of the history to the plot. In the purely historical plays, the history forms the plot: in the mixed, it directs it; in the rest, as Macbeth, Hamlet, Cymbeline, Lear, it subserves it.[2]

The purpose of the history play Coleridge saw as familiarizing the people of a country with the great names from their past and

[1] S. T. Coleridge, *Literary Remains*, ed. H. N. Coleridge (London, 1836), II, 160-61.
[2] *Ibid.*, pp. 164-65.

thereby arousing "a steady patriotism, a love of just liberty, and a respect for all those fundamental institutions of social life, which bind men together."

Professor Schelling in his book on *The English Chronicle Play*, published in 1902, made probably the most effective contribution thus far to the recognition of the importance of the genre and to the history of its development. He alone recognized that the history play was more closely affiliated with historical literature than with other varieties of the drama. But he found its roots in the tide of patriotism which swept England at the time of the threat from the Spanish Armada, and he saw it withering with the "un-English prince," King James of Scotland, on the throne of England. Professor Schelling would recognize two groups of history plays: those centering about history and historical personages, and those dealing with legendary history, or at least involving a more or less conscious deviation from history.

Professor Tucker Brooke in his small volume on *The Tudor Drama*, published in 1911, devoted a chapter to the history play[3] which has been the basis for a good deal of the teaching of the subject to college students. He isolated two main causes as accounting for the popularity of the history play during the last years of Elizabeth: "an unusual public interest in the matters treated in such plays; and particular stage conditions which . . . greatly stimulated the demand for dramas constructed on the loose and facile pattern usual to this type." Professor Brooke recognized the great interest of the Elizabethans in the history of foreign lands as well as their own, but he did not analyze the nature of the "matters treated in such plays" which interested them. Inevitably, like his predecessors, he found difficulty in defining the history play and chose to describe its various forms rather than to confine it in any formula. He listed plays of mixed type, biographical plays, histories of tragic type, romanticized treatments of history, and a most important group which he described as

Plays *par excellence* of national feeling or national philosophy, where

[3]Chap. ix, pp. 297-351.

the normal interest in *dramatis personae* is more or less absorbed either in the expression of patriotic sentiment or in the interpretation of problems of government and statecraft. It is this class which gives to the Elizabethan history play its individuality as a dramatic species.[4]

The many noble utterances of patriotic fervor which occur in Shakespeare's histories have led most students to think of the plays as patriotic plays, and the fact that the most notable of the plays were produced in the ten or twelve years immediately following the defeat of the Armada has led to the very common acceptance of a *post hoc, ergo propter hoc* explanation. But the descriptions of the history play as essentially the expression of the great patriotic ardor which centered about the victory of 1588, as resulting from the "triumphant exhilaration" of the Armada year, as exhibiting "exuberant nationalism," and as being "jubilant in pride of country and of race," ignore, strangely enough, the fact that with the exception of *Henry V* and perhaps *Henry VIII*, Shakespeare's plays were written, not about the admirable rulers of England and their times, but rather about those rulers who had sowed the wind and reaped the whirlwind. We should hardly expect that in the United States a great spirit of exuberant nationalism, a proud jubilation in victory, would result in plays centering about Presidents Buchanan and Harding. It seems just as unlikely that the desire to celebrate the greatness of England should result in plays about Richard II, who was deposed for his sins; or Henry IV and his rebel-ridden kingdom; or Richard III, infamous for his tyranny; or Henry VI, who "lost France, and made his England bleed." Surely, the implied definition of patriotism, limiting it to its prideful and jubilant aspects, is too narrow to cover Shakespeare's loyal but searching study of England's past.

August Wilhelm Schlegel long ago provided a key to the meaning of the Shakespeare histories when he said that they, as a series, furnish "examples of the political course of the world, applicable to all times,"[5] though he did not use his key to unlock

---

[4]P. 303.

[5]*Lectures on Dramatic Art and Literature*, trans. John Black (London, 1889), pp. 419 *et seq.*

the specific significance of the individual plays in relation to the times in which they were written.

When in 1929 Professor H. B. Charlton published his lecture on *Shakespeare, Politics, and Politicians*,[6] he went further with the statement that a better name for the history plays would be political plays, "for they are plays in which the prevailing dramatic interest is in the fate of a nation." Very disappointingly he then defined the political purpose of the plays as "exercising and fostering patriotism" and gave the old description of the England of the Armada:

A wave of exuberant national sentiment cried out for such stimulus as visible reminders of England's past could give it.

The way in which the history play answered this need, according to Professor Charlton, is reminiscent of the travesty on the teleological conception of the universe which proved a divine providence by the fact that men actually had two legs in a world that proffered trousers, for he says of Shakespeare:

His tragedies are glimpses of individual man as a nursling of immortality, his vision of the ways of God with man: his comedies are his imaginative experience of the same individual in his domestic and social relationship with other members of civilized society. But by *pure chance* there was in Shakespeare's day a type of theatrical entertainment which was neither tragedy nor comedy, neither focused mainly on the life eternal, nor on the life private, domestic, and social. There was the so-called History or Chronicle Play.[7]

However, Professor Charlton did face squarely the dilemma of patriotic plays written about the nation's rulers who are least to be emulated:

But what ultimately will distinguish the history-play from tragedy is beginning to appear. Comedy and tragedy are concerned with the eternal or ephemeral fate of individual men. The history play is concerned with communities of men, and primarily with nations. The real hero of the English play is England.

[6] (The English Association, Pamphlet 72: 1929).

[7] The italics are mine.

12

WHAT ARE "HISTORIES"?

Having taken the important step of recognizing the plays as political, and having defined the interest in history as an interest in nations, he was thus led to a conclusion which seems to me utterly without justification, that England is the hero of the plays. Accepting England as the hero but fully aware of the far from noble conduct of the English heroes who act for the hero England, he was forced to the decision that national politics are to be judged on general Machiavellian principles, for even in *Henry V* there is

> the sense that not only is politics a nasty business, but that a repugnant unscrupulousness is an invaluable asset in the art of government. That is the burden of the English History Plays, jubilant as they are in pride of country and of race.

J. A. R. Marriott anticipated Professor Charlton in considering the plays as political plays in his *English History in Shakespeare* and in his more important paper on "Shakespeare and Politics,"[8] where he examined the plays to find what was said

> upon "Politics" as properly understood: upon the science of government and the art of statesmanship; upon man's place in the πολις; upon the reciprocal obligations of ruler and ruled; upon the relation of the citizen and the commonwealth.

It is in distinguishing between Shakespeare's continually derogatory references to *politicians* and his constant concern with *politics* in the true meaning of the word that Marriott made his most significant contribution, but he went further than this in stating certain premises necessary to the understanding of Shakespeare's history plays. First, he stressed what no critic should ever forget—that Shakespeare was above all a playwright, "possessed of pre-eminent skill in delineation of character by means of dialogue," and that we must be wary of "identifying Shakespeare's sentiments with those of his puppets." Second, he insisted that Shakespeare's approach to contemporary problems in politics or religion was an indirect approach, for he was too great an artist "to allow contemporary problems in politics or religion to ob-

---

[8]*English History in Shakespeare* (2d ed., London, 1918); the paper is in the *Cornhill Magazine*, CXXXVI (1927), 678-90.

trude themselves directly into his drama," and that if he wanted to teach the ecclesiastical controversies of the time, he would do it not by reference to the "Jesuit mission" but by picturing the relations between King John and Pope Innocent III. Third, he said, Shakespeare as a dramatist was of necessity only incidentally a philosopher, politician, or historian. Finally, he reaffirmed the "law of the universal" as the law to which Shakespeare like every great artist must conform, so that his appeal may always be to humanity at large and not merely to any one nation.

Having oriented the discussion by his definition of politics and his premises as to Shakespeare the artist, Marriott concluded that the theme of Shakespeare's history plays is the evil of civil dissension, domestic discord, and unnatural controversy as set forth by Edward Halle in the first sentence of his chronicle, that he pictures in *King John* the peril to the State of internal divisions, in *Richard II* the political amateur, in *Henry IV* the professional politician, in *Henry V* saintly strength, and in *Henry VI* saintly weakness. In the plays concerning the Wars of the Roses, "Shakespeare, with unerring dramatic instinct, turned aside from political philosophy and seized upon the personal aspects of the disorders of that day."

But because the premises are in general so eminently sound and so universally held, it does not follow that the conclusions are equally acceptable. It seems necessary, then, to detour from the matter of definition to discuss them briefly. That Shakespeare was first of all a playwright and skillful in the portrayal of character by dialogue, and that his characters did not necessarily utter the author's sentiments, is a statement to which with most other critics I can but say "Amen." But a dramatist is more than a portrayer of character by dialogue. His most important business is with plot, if we agree with Aristotle that his drama is or should be the representation of an action. In his interpretation of the individual plays Marriott has indicated that Shakespeare "turned aside from political philosophy and seized upon the personal aspects of the disorders of that day," a logical result of this omission of plot from the business of the dramatist. Perhaps Richard II does appear as an amateur politician, but it does not

follow that the play of *Richard II* is a play concerned with amateur politics. Our concern should be to ask what the plot says.

That Shakespeare's approach to any contemporary problem of
politics or religion must, because he was an artist, have been an
indirect approach cannot be disputed if taken to mean only that
Shakespeare did not use his plays as polemical tracts. But the use
of the word *indirect* ignores the fact that, as I shall try to show
in succeeding chapters, the chief function of history was considered to be that of acting as a political mirror. The idea of
holding the mirror up to nature (or to politics) pervaded the
whole conception of art during the Elizabethan period, but to
identify the conception of the mirror with indirection seems to
me inaccurate.[9]

That Shakespeare as a dramatist was only incidentally philosopher, politician, or historian is a contention that takes us back
almost to the question of whether the egg or the hen comes first,
but it is a fundamental question in the criticism of all the arts,
reminiscent as it is of the theory of "art for art's sake." Marriott
quoted the wise words of Sir Walter Raleigh (the second)
reminding us that Shakespeare "had a meaning even while Drama
was his trade," though I would suggest that *medium* is a better
word than *trade*, for if we are considering Shakespeare as an artist
rather than a craftsman, it is more fitting to consider the creator
or interpreter of life in relation to his medium of expression.
Certainly Shakespeare did not, so far as we know, write a treatise
on moral philosophy or a political discourse or a history of England. His medium was the drama, and through the drama he
said what he had to say. His medium made concrete what another
man might say of philosophy or political theory in a treatise
dealing with abstractions or generalizations. He represented an
action with its causes and its results, so that it had a beginning,
a middle, and an end. The action was put into being by concrete
and specific persons on the stage; as living beings they spoke and
did their deeds of good or evil, and as living persons they hated
and loved and feared and rejoiced. But because Shakespeare

[9]See below, pp. 107-8.

used the medium of the drama to express what he had to say, there is no reason for denying to him a moral and a political philosophy which motivated first the choice of story and second the plotting of that story.

To return, then, after this detour, to the main question: What is a history play? The Elizabethans expected any work of history to act as a political mirror, to be concerned with *politics* in the sense in which Marriott defined the term. And a history play must be regarded as a literary medium for history. If it is understood that a history play is concerned with politics, furthermore, the point of its divergence from tragedy becomes clear, for the divisions of philosophy known as *ethics* and *politics* were familiar from the very titles of Aristotle's works and represented the accepted approaches to the study of human conduct. For instance, the popular orations of the much revered Isocrates, translated into English as *A Perfite Looking Glass for All Estates*,[10] opened with an "Oration of Morall Instructions . . . : contayning a perfite description of the duetye of every private person," which was followed by an "Oration of Morall Instructions as Touching the Dutie of Princes and Magistrates and the Well Governing of a Commonweale." Spenser, writing the great Tudor epic, proposed to organize his poem about this dual concept, and he pointed out the fact that he was following the examples of Homer and Virgil and Ariosto and Tasso in so doing. He called the divisions of philosophy *Ethice* and *Politice*, the one concerned with the private moral virtues, the other with the public or political virtues.[11] What Professor W. D. Ross said of Aristotle could be equally well said of Shakespeare:

he does not forget in the *Ethics* that the individual man is essentially a member of society, nor in the *Politics* that the good life of the state exists only in the good lives of its citizens.[12]

[10]"Translated by Hieronimus into Latin and now into English by Thomas Forrest" (London, 1580).

[11]See Spenser's letter to Raleigh, published with the 1590 ed. of the first three books of the *Faerie Queene*. See also below, p. 307.

[12]*Aristotle* (London, 1930), p. 186.

Nevertheless, the dividing line is there, and it is to this distinction between private and public morals that we must look for the distinction between tragedy and history. Tragedy is concerned with the doings of men which in philosophy are discussed under *ethics;* history with the doings of men which in philosophy are discussed under *politics.*

To understand why this was so and why it had to be so in Elizabethan England we must turn to the aims and purposes and methods which the history plays shared with all other forms of historical writing, and these can be understood only by surveying the course of the writing and the interpreting of history as it developed in Tudor England during the sixteenth century.

CHAPTER III

THE HUMANISTIC REVIVAL OF HISTORY

ISTORY, like God, bears the stamp of its creator. And just as we speak of an anthropomorphic conception of God, we may speak of an anthropomorphic conception of history which men have fashioned in their own image. The scorn of most historians today for the sixteenth-century chronicles is matched by the distrust of the scientific age in the fundamentalist's conception of God. But whether or not we can learn much about God from the fundamentalists, we can learn much about the men who wrote that God into theology by studying their concepts of him. And whether or not we can learn much about the facts of history by studying the sixteenth-century chronicles, we can learn much about the sixteenth century by studying the concepts of history which determined the nature of these chronicles.

Shakespeare's wide reading in history is in no need of proof to any student of his dramas, as I have said, for his tragedies, his histories, and even some of his comedies bear the indelible mark of their sources. And Shakespeare's interest in history was shared by his age. The number of histories written, translated, and printed under the Tudors is amazing: histories of England and of foreign countries; translations of the works of Greek, Roman, Jewish, and continental historians; poeticized versions of history. The rise of a drama using the materials and subserving the purposes of history was inevitable, for the stage has never failed to mirror the interests of the world about it.

To understand this phenomenal flood of historical works, it must be remembered that *history written as a continuous narrative and integrated by creative minds* was in the modern world a development of the Renaissance. The forces which introduced what Professor Huizinga has described as "an imposition of form upon the past"[1] can, of course, be studied here only in the most general way, for one life would be all too short to compile a complete account of the translating, writing, reading, and criticizing of history during the long period of the spreading Renaissance. As the late Professor Lathrop pointed out, "It would be easy to fill a volume with the praise of history from the prefaces of scholars in the Renaissance."[2] But such prefaces are but a part of the evidence of the concern of scholars, and indeed, men of all sorts, with history and historical theory, for there are also to be considered a substantial number of works on historiography, the very existence of which has been generally unnoticed or unmentioned by English historians, but which give real evidence not only as to the widespread interest in history but also as to the reasons for this interest. These *artes historicae* have recently been studied helpfully though incompletely by Dr. John L. Brown as background for his work on Bodin.[3] Their variety and universality are well illustrated in a two-volume collection of eighteen works published in Basle in 1579 by Wolfius.[4]

The whole story of the development of historiography during the Renaissance and particularly during the sixteenth century, however, will perhaps be best understood if it is viewed as the product of the two great intellectual movements of the time: the first, the revival of humanism through the renewed knowledge of the classics; the second, the Reformation. Both movements were interested in history, but for different reasons.

The way in which the revival of humanism motivated the

---

[1] Johan Huizinga, "A Definition of the Concept of History," trans. D. R. Cousin, in *Philosophy & History: Essays Presented to Ernst Cassirer*, ed. R. Klibansky and H. J. Paton (Oxford, 1936), p. 5.

[2] H. B. Lathrop, *Translations from the Classics into English from Caxton to Chapman, 1477-1620* (Madison, 1933), p. 80.

[3] *The Methodus ad facilem historiarum cognitionem of Jean Bodin* (Washington, D.C., 1939). See especially chap. iii, pp. 46-85. A list of these "arts" is given by J. E. Spingarn, *Critical Essays of the Seventeenth Century* (1908), I, 238-39, in a note on Bolton's *Hypercritica*.

[4] *Artis historicae penus* (enlarged from the 1576 ed.). A complete list of the contents is given in J. L. Brown, p. 48, note.

interest in history can be clearly discerned by reading the apologies with which the translators of the ancient histories regularly adorned their dedications and prefaces. These defenses repeat over and over again certain fundamental tenets as justification for the writing and the reading of history.

First, and of the utmost importance in a world newly roused to nationalism, oblivion seemed to have descended upon those nations which had no histories written to perpetuate their fame; on the other hand, the Jews, the Greeks, and the Romans lived eternally in their histories. The men of the Renaissance were eager searchers for fame for themselves and for their native countries.

Second, history explained the rise and fall of nations, and the Renaissance echoed the question of Polybius as to whether anyone could be so indifferent or so slothful as not to want to know by what policies and government almost the whole of the civilized world was brought under the dominion of the one city of Rome within a period of fifty-three years.

Third, history embodied the past experience of men and of nations and consequently was the best of teachers, especially for the prince or magistrate, who was never secure from flatterers and selfish advisers. History was, indeed, a storehouse of exempla. It could make young men wise, while old men without it were but as children in their innocence and ignorance. But it must be noted that private men were not the concern of ancient history, and the exempla were helpful to men as rulers or as subjects.

Fourth, history manifested the fickleness of fortune and at the same time enabled men to rise above fortune and be indifferent to it.

Fifth, because human nature remained the same, like causes produced like results. Thucydides said he wrote for those who wanted a true picture of the events that had happened and of those "like events which may be expected to happen hereafter in the order of human beings," and a modern scholar gives him credit for having shown how far generalization about human action on the basis of the past can be legitimately used to prognosticate the future. Also, it should be noted that Plutarch's

Parallel Lives of the Greeks and the Romans demonstrated a sort of corollary to this theory. There was a deal of searching of history for practical purposes—for help in building fortifications and in planning military campaigns, for instance—but these five uses of history may be said to cover all such specific instruction.

The materials of history these Renaissance salvagers of the past found to be variously esteemed. While Thucydides wrote only of what he himself had seen or what he had heard from reliable witnesses, Polybius argued for a general history, saying that one might as well hope to get an idea of the body from seeing its several parts as to get the history of the whole from separate histories of isolated episodes.

Thucydides was especially commended for putting into the mouths of his characters the very speeches which they were supposed to have uttered, though his method would scarcely be accepted from a modern historian, for he said that his practice was to have the speaker utter "the sentiments proper to the occasion, expressed as I thought he would be likely to express them, while at the same time I endeavored, as nearly as I could, to give the general purport of what was actually said."[5] But on the other hand, opinion was divided about the admissibility of the theatrical episodes and emotional scenes ruled out by Polybius as fit not for history but for drama.

The ancient historians most read during the Renaissance recorded a sequence of events in such a manner as to offer an understanding of the relation between causes and results, and they were commended for doing so. History proper came to be recognized as *a continuous, selective, and integrated narrative* and to be distinguished from mere records of fact, such as annals. Truth was universally reckoned the objective of the historian, and impartiality the most necessary of his virtues.

The slow progress of translation in England as compared with the Continent, particularly France, can be followed in Professor Lathrop's important *Translations from the Classics into English*, and it is no part of my purpose to repeat the record here. But it

---

[5]Thucydides, *The Peloponnesian War*, trans. Benjamin Jowett in *The Greek Historians* (New York, 1942), I, 576.

must be remembered that, though lagging behind France, England did see the work of translating the classical historians continuing *from Caxton to Chapman* (to borrow the rest of Professor Lathrop's title).[6] Many of the translations from the Greek were made by way of the French, and much of the philosophy of history found in the prefaces of English historians was inherited from the Continent, but it was finally made English in word and thought. And the influence of the ancient writers was a persistent and all-pervasive one.

[6]A complete list of translations from the classics is given by Lathrop, pp. 311-18. Particular comment on the translations of the classical histories will be found on pp. 80-91, 168-74, 178-93, 234-55.

CHAPTER IV

CLASSICAL RHETORIC AND HISTORY

THE NUMBER of editions and translations of the works of the ancient historians is in itself indicative of the tremendous interest of the men of the Renaissance in history. But from ancient writers on rhetoric and oratory they also derived ideals of historical writing which were to motivate and direct their own endeavors. From ancient histories they determined the purposes and principles of historical writing, but treatises on rhetoric and oratory reinforced many of their conceptions of the methods and the qualities of the historian.

The traditional acceptance of rhetoric as a means to win the reader or the hearer to belief made it inevitable that the political writer or orator should be advised to use history for political ends. Thus Aristotle in his *Rhetoric* recommended for those engaged in making laws "so much *Politicall*, or *Civill Philosophy* as to know what are the severall kindes of Governements; and by what meanes, either from without or from within, each of those kinds is preserved, or destroyed." Such knowledge, he said, is acquired "partly by observing the severall governments, in times past by *History*; and partly by observing the government of the times present, in severall Nations by *Travell*."[1]

Thomas Wilson, "Doctor of the Civill Lawes," and author of *The Art of Rhetoric*, published in 1570 the translation of seven orations of Demosthenes on which he had been working since 1556, stressing in his preface the fact that the orator was much indebted to Thucydides, whose history he had eight times copied out in his own hand, and from whom he borrowed whole sentences. Wilson's preface described Demosthenes as "chiefe Orator among the Grecians," and his orations as "most nedeful

---

[1]Aristotle, *A Briefe of the Art of Rhetorique* (Thomas Hobbes, 1637?).

to be redde in these daungerous dayes, of all them that love their Countries libertie, and desire to take warning for their better avayle, by example of others." His dedication of the work to Sir William Cecil suggests further that Demosthenes was a counsellor in his country as Cecil is in England, wherefore "he is your glasse I am well assured whereupon you do often loke, and compare his time, with this time: Countrie with Countrie: neighbours with neighbours: and King with King." Pollard refers to a story published in the *Literary Magazine* for 1758 that Wilson was employed by the government to translate Demosthenes with a view to rousing national resistance to Spain. At any rate, Wilson records that Cardinal Bessario used one of the orations when he went to ask Louis XI of France to make peace with Charles of Burgundy and turn his war against the Turks, and that since, as Thucydides said, "like time bringeth forth lyke examples, so long as the world lasteth, and the course of nature remaineth," Demosthenes must continue to be similarly useful:

For never dyd glasse so truely represent a mans face, as Demosthenes doth shewe the worlde to us, and as it was then, so it is now, and wyll be so still, tyll the consummation and ende of all things shall be.[2]

Quintilian summed up this contribution of history to oratory in one of the most favored quotations of Renaissance historiographers: "History, also, may provide the orator with a nutriment which we may compare to some rich and pleasant juice."[3]

[2]See Wilson's Preface. Professor A. F. Pollard, writing on Wilson in the *Dictionary of National Biography*, comments on this book: "The preface contains 'a remarkable comparison of England with Athens in the time of Demosthenes,' the part of Philip of Macedon being filled by Philip of Spain (Seeley, *British Policy*, 1894, i, 156); it is similar to the 'Latin treatise on the Dangerous State of England,' on which Wilson speaks of being engaged on 13 Aug. 1569 (*Lansd. MS.* xiii, art 9) and which is now extant in the Record Office (*State Papers*, Dom. Eliz. cxxiii, 17) being dated 2 April, 1578, and entitled 'A Discourse touching the Kingdom's Perils with their Remedies.' To this is to be attributed the curious story contributed probably by Dr. Johnson to the 'Literary Magazine' (1758, p. 151) to the effect that Wilson was employed by the government to translate Demosthenes with a view to rousing a national resistance to Spanish invasion (*Addit. MS.* 5815, f. 42)." I do not recognize the "remarkable comparison" here spoken of, and I have been unable to see the *Literary Magazine*.
[3]Quintilian, *Institutes*, Bk. X (Loeb Classical Library), IV, 19.

But it was Cicero who furnished the motto emblazoned on every banner waved by the apologists for history, a motto so much quoted that Sidney made it the theme of the egotistic burbling of the historian who entered the scene to advance the claims of history over philosophy and poetry:

Historia vero testis temporum, lux veritatis, vita memoriae, magistra vitae, nuntia vetutatis, qua voce alia, nisi oratoris, immortalitati commendatur?[4]

Cicero made a contribution to historiography, however, which went far beyond this distillation of praise when he scorned the idea that it was enough for a man not to be a liar in order to write history and stressed the responsibility of the orator to historical writing. One of the speakers in his *De oratore* is, indeed, made to summarize the requirements for a writer of history, and these requirements were so basic to the sixteenth-century theorists and practitioners that I propose to recapitulate them here. The historian must tell the truth and the whole truth without partiality or malice. But beyond this, "the completed structure rests upon the story and the diction." History demands "chronological arrangement and geographical representation." It chronicles important events and should indicate what actions and results are approved. It demands an account not only of what was done and said but also of the manner in which it was done and said. It must consider causes "whether originating in accident, discretion, or foolhardiness" in estimating consequences. The individual actors of events of importance must be described in detail. And he adds:

Then again the kind of language and type of style to be followed are the easy and the flowing, which run their course with an unvarying current and a certain placidity, avoiding alike the rough speech we use in Court and the advocate's stinging epigrams.[5]

Of special significance, too, was a statement attributed by Cicero to the same speaker:

in Greece the most eloquent were strangers to forensic advocacy,

[4]Cicero, *De oratore*, Bk. II (Loeb Classical Library), I, 222.
[5]*Ibid.*, p. 245.

and applied themselves chiefly to reputable studies in general, and particularly to writing history.[6]

In proof he instanced Herodotus, Thucydides, Xenophon, Callisthenes, and Timaeus. Here is a basis for the Renaissance belief of the so-called rhetorical school that history is a phase of rhetoric.

Viewing history as a form of creative expression, the writers on rhetoric and oratory provided the Renaissance also with the materials upon which to base their understanding of different literary forms by their differentiation of history and poetry, history and tragedy, history and oratory. The famous passage from Aristotle's *Poetics* was the subject of almost endless exegesis during the Renaissance, and for the English reader was amplified in Sidney's *Defence of Poesie*. Aristotle said:

The distinction between historian and poet is not in the one writing prose and the other verse—you might put the work of Herodotus into verse, and it would still be a species of history; it consists really in this, that the one describes the thing that has been, and the other a kind of thing that might be. Hence poetry is something more philosophic and of graver import than history, since its statements are of the nature rather of universals, whereas those of history are singulars.

And Aristotle also said:

It is evident . . . that the poet must be more the poet of his stories or plots than of his verses, inasmuch as he is a poet by virtue of the imitative element in his work, and it is actions that he imitates. And if he should come to take a subject from actual history, he is none the less a poet for that; since some historic occurrences may very well be in the probable and possible order of things; and it is in that aspect of them that he is the poet.[7]

Elsewhere he explained further that while a drama, and ideally also an epic poem, must be based on a single, complete action, a history deals, not with one action, but with one period, no

[6]*Ibid.*, p. 239.

[7]Aristotle, *De poetica*, 1451[b] in *The Works of Aristotle translated into English*, ed. W. D. Ross (Oxford, 1910-31), Vol. XI.

matter how many concurrent but disconnected events may have to be included.[8]

Along with Aristotle and Cicero, Quintilian is to be reckoned among the most influential writers and the most familiar in the Renaissance. He, too, discussed history at length and insisted that, while the orator made use of history, his function was distinct from that of the historian:

For history has a certain affinity to poetry and may be regarded as a kind of prose poem, while it is written for the purpose of narrative, not of proof, and designed from beginning to end not for immediate effect or the instant necessities of forensic strife, but to record events for the benefit of posterity and to win glory for its author. Consequently, to avoid monotony of narrative, it employs unusual words and indulges in a free use of figures. . . . It is, however, occasionally permissible to borrow the graces of history to embellish our digressions. . . .[9]

Of special interest also is his discussion of history as one of the three kinds of narrative:

First there is the fictitious narrative as we get it in tragedies and poems, which is not merely not true but has little resemblance to truth. Secondly, there is the realistic narrative as presented by comedies, which, though not true, has yet a certain verisimilitude. Thirdly there is the historical narrative, which is an exposition of actual fact. Poetic narratives are the property of the teacher of literature. The rhetorician therefore should begin with the historical narrative, whose force is in proportion to its truth.[10]

While ancient history thus brought to the Renaissance an awareness of the usefulness of history and provided models for historical writing, ancient orators and rhetoricians reinforced example by precept. Above all, they influenced the concept of history as a form of creative writing, opposed to the idea of history as a set of records. Furthermore in viewing it as a part of rhetoric they made possible the inference that like rhetoric it could be an effective instrument for capturing men's interest and directing their wills.

[8]*Ibid.*, 1459ᵃ.
[9]Quintilian, *Institutes*, Bk. X, Vol. IV, p. 21.
[10]*Ibid.*, Bk. II, Vol. I, p. 225.

CHAPTER V

RENAISSANCE CONCEPTIONS OF HISTORY

THAT the Renaissance owed many of its ideas of historiography to the Revival of Learning, which had restored to the modern world an acquaintance with ancient histories and with ancient theories of historical writing, is at once apparent to anyone who reads his way among the multitudinous histories, prefaces to histories, defenses of history, treatises on politics and law and rhetoric, and all the varied writing which discussed history during the sixteenth century. I have chosen to suggest the multiple Renaissance approaches to the whole subject, however, by discussing the work of four men as representing perhaps the most important schools of thought in regard to history which developed during this period.

The first is Niccolo Machiavelli, who demonstrated to the sixteenth century the political significance of history. It is not certain whence the idea came to Machiavelli of using history as a basis for the exposition of political theory, but certainly his reading of classical histories was to a great extent responsible for his conviction that "he who would foresee what is to happen should look to what has happened: for all that is has its counterpart in time past." Because man remains the same, history repeats itself. His experiment was based upon the work of an ancient Roman historian. It appeared as *Discorsi . . . sopra la prima deca di Tito Livio*, first printed in Rome in 1531. A Latin edition was published in London in 1584, but there was no translation into English until 1636. Machiavelli's preface explains why he decided to use the first decade of Livy as the basis for political discourses. He had, he says, noted that while his countrymen were eager to rescue a piece of ancient statuary to adorn a house and to stimulate others to copy it, yet they neglected the records of the ancient virtues of kingdoms, of commonwealths, of rulers, and of citizens as set forth in histories. This he wondered at the more because all legal cases were determined by ancient decisions, "for the civill laws are nothing else, but the opinions given by ancient Lawyers, which since having bin reduc'd to a Method, direct our Doctors of the Law now a dayes, in giving of their judgments." And he continues:

yet for all this in the ordering of Commonwealths, in the maintenance of States, in the government of Kingdomes, in ordeining of military discipline, in waging of warre, in giving judgment upon the subjects, in amplifying of the Empire, there are neither Princes, nor Republiques, Commanders, nor Citizens who ever seeke after any of these ancient patternes.

To correct this omission he wrote his discourses on Livy concerning matters "conformable to moderne and ancient affairs" that his readers might "reape that profit, for which end the knowledge of historie ought to be sought after."[1]

Machiavelli was the pioneer, but the most important contributor to the development of the study of history for its political usefulness was Jean Bodin, who in his *Methodus ad facilem historiarum cognitionem*, first published in 1566, formulated the problems of the relationship between history and politics as they were to be recognized during the next century. He discussed many questions: the nature and the kinds of history, the proper order for reading histories, the formulation of topics under which aspects of history may be considered, the qualifications of the historian, the relation of geography to history, the organization of the history of states to show their rise and fall in relation to historical events, and Daniel's prophecy of four kingdoms for the world. The concluding section is given over to a plan of historical study, of collecting and ordering history and histories. For the purpose of this review, however, the most important aspect of his contribution to the idea of the usefulness of history is that summarized by Professor Allen:

[1] *Machiavels Discourses upon the First Decade of T. Livius*, trans. Edward Dacres (London, 1636), Preface.

The chief use of history is to subserve politics; to help us to understand the meaning and the function of the state; its needs and its structure, the causes of its prosperity or decline. The business of the historian is, above all, to explain the revolutions, the profound and radical changes, through which human societies pass. From a sufficiently wide study of history it should be possible to draw accurate conclusions as to the laws governing human society and to determine the best form of government and the best form of law under given conditions.[2]

It is interesting to note that the introductory epistle to Thomas Heywood's translations of Sallust's *Catiline* and *Jugurtha*, published in 1608-9, has been identified by Professor Lathrop as a translation of the fourth chapter of this work, the identification having been suggested by Heywood's marginal reference, "Bodin."

Bodin's greatest influence on the thinking of his day came through his *Six livres de la république*, first published in 1576 and translated into English in 1606, but the *Methodus* was the herald of his coming ideas, and it was the *Methodus* that popularized many of his ideas concerning the importance of historical studies. It was perhaps the most popular of the sixteenth-century *artes historiae* and perhaps also the most important in affirming the relation of history and political theory.[3] It will be remembered that Bodin accompanied the Duc d'Alençon to England in 1581 on his visit to promote the marriage with Queen Elizabeth.

One of those who had been laying foundations upon which Bodin and others were to build was François Baudouin (or Baldwin), who may for this brief review of continental forces represent the special contribution of those who developed the idea of the mutual interdependence of law and history and the necessity for combining the study of the history of law with other

[2]J. W. Allen, *A History of Political Thought in the Sixteenth Century* (London, 1928), pp. 405-6. See also B. Reynolds' translation, *Method for the Easy Comprehension of History* (New York, 1945).

[3]See John L. Brown, *The Methodus . . . of Jean Bodin;* Henri Baudrillart, *J. Bodin et son temps* (Paris, 1853), pp. 145-67; Jean Moreau-Reibel, *Jean Bodin et le droit public comparé dans ses rapports avec la philosophie de l'histoire* (Paris, 1933).

historical studies. Baudouin was French, for a part of his life he was a Calvinist, and he was deeply concerned with the reception of Roman law. He illustrates in his own work a variety of influences, for while he showed the effect of his Reformation leanings by his insistence upon history as manifesting the government of God and by stressing the necessity for the study of universal as well as national history, he also showed his acquaintance with Greek and Latin authors by recapitulating classical teaching in regard to history, particularly that of Cicero, and in his comparison of history and poetry. He saw history as interpreting the past for the benefit of the present and as prophetical of the future. But his chief contribution was in relating history and jurisprudence both in theory and practice, and it will be remembered that in the history of law the century saw the conflict between Roman and common law, with the common law gradually emerging as legal precedent rather than as merely a set of examples.[4]

Of the great so-called rhetorical school of historical writing, Robertello may be chosen to represent those who viewed the writing of history as a part of rhetoric. Annals Robertello excluded from consideration, since they have no method or system, but he argued that the historical faculty found in such writers as Thucydides arises from the rhetorical faculty, for they describe the mores and the speech of men. Men are themselves the material for history, he said, not as human beings who move or live or reason, for all that belongs to philosophy, but in so far as they act and speak in public affairs. The historian does not concern himself with private affairs, with humble affairs, or with the matters of daily intercourse. History is thus differentiated from philosophy [ethics]. It is also differentiated from poetry in that it is concerned with truth as opposed to verisimilitude, and with particulars as opposed to universals. In method too it is distinguished from poetry in that it follows the course of events in time as they happened, while poetry may plunge *in medias res*. Requiring vast knowledge of many subjects, the writing of

[4]F. Balduinus, *De institutione historiae universae et ejus cum jurisprudentia conjunctione* in *Artis historicae penus.*

history truthfully, clearly, elegantly, and correctly, Robertello thought, should be judged one of the most difficult parts of rhetoric.[5]

Inadequate as any such arbitrary and highly selective account of the Renaissance approaches to history must be of necessity, it illustrates three important truths: the Renaissance theories of history were to a great extent the outgrowth of the study of ancient classical historians and rhetoricians; the approaches to the study of history were diverse, and the uses to which it was put were manifold; the political usefulness of history was common to the thinking of all the commentators.[6]

I have already mentioned the influence of Reformation theories of history on Baudouin, and indeed the Reformation has to be considered a joint influence with the Revival of Learning on the whole period. But the men I have discussed here are primarily representative of the humanistic approach to historical studies. The contribution of the Reformation I have reserved for a separate chapter.

[5]F. Robertellus, *De historia* in *Artis historicae penus.*

[6]For an account of the Renaissance writers see Eduard Fueter, *Histoire de l'historiographie moderne*, trans. Emile Jaumarie (Paris, 1914). For the most complete account of Italian historians see Girolamo Tiraboschi, *Storia della letteratura italianna* (Milan, 1824), Tomo VII, Parte 3, cap. 1.

CHAPTER VI

HISTORY AND THE REFORMATION

CONCURRENT with the new sense of nationalism which marked the sixteenth century was a conflict within the church which led to the decentralization of Christendom, and which had a profound effect on the writing of history. The movement which we know as the Reformation found history necessary to the establishment of the positions toward which it was moving. Any argument concerning either theology or church government had, of necessity, to invoke history, and gradually both secular and ecclesiastical history became important to the theses of the Reformers. History, indeed, became one of their major concerns.

No account of the Reformation conceptions of history can, however, fail to record the influence of Saint Augustine's *City of God*. Vives dedicated a commentary on this work to Henry VIII in 1522, but it was not until 1610 that the original work and the commentary were published in an English translation. The influence of the work was, however, not dependent upon translation, for it had long since provided many of the foundation stones for the building of a Christian interpretation of history.[1] In four ways especially Saint Augustine may be reckoned a pre-

[1] The *Catholic Encyclopedia* in the article on Saint Augustine of Hippo says that Augustine was concerned with answering the pagans who attributed the fall of Rome to its rejection of pagan deities, and it comments: "Considering this problem of Divine Providence with regard to the Roman Empire, he widens the horizon still more and in a burst of genius he creates the philosophy of history, embracing as he does with a glance the destinies of the world grouped around the Christian religion, the only one which goes back to the beginning and leads humanity to its final term." The most complete treatment of the subject is J. N. Figgis' *The Political Aspects of S. Augustine's "City of God"* (London, 1921).

cursor of the Reformation writers about history. First, he used an account of universal history to justify the ways of God to men. Second, he accepted, though without great clarity, the four kingdoms of Daniel's prophecy as a basis for the division of history. Third, he set the ideal for the Christian prince or ruler in the famous passage often referred to as "The Mirror of Princes."[2] Fourth, and of most importance from the point of view of this study, he provided in certain other chapters of Book V the foundation on which was built the conception of history as a manifestation of the judgments of God, for he wrote (in the words of the 1610 translation) that it is incredible that God "would leave the kingdomes of men, and their bondages and freedomes loose and unconfined in the laws of his eternal providence," in which laws he had included heaven and earth, man and beast, tree and herb.[3] More explicitly he wrote also:

the true God that giveth the heavenly kingdome onely to the godly, but the earthly ones both to good and bad, as himself liketh, whose pleasure is all justice; he is to have all power of giving or taking

[2]See Bk. V, chap. xxiv: "For wee Christians doe not say, that Christian Emperors are happy, because they have a long reigne, or die leaving their sonnes in quiet possession of their Empires, or have beene ever victorious, or powerfull against all their opposers. These are but gifts and solaces of this laborious, joylesse life; Idolators, and such as belong not to God (as these Emperors doe) may enjoy them: Because God in his mercy will not have these that know him, to beleeve that such things are the best goods hee giveth. But happy they are (say wee) if they reigne justly, free from being puffed up with the glozing exaltations of their attendance, or the cringes of their subjects, if they know themselves to bee but men, and remember that: if they make their power their trumpetter, to divulge the true adoration of Gods Majestie, if they love, feare and honor him: if they long the most for that Empire where they need not feare to have partners: if they be slack to avenge, quick to forgive: if they use correction for the publick good, and not for private hate: if their pardons promise not liberalitie of offending, but indeed onely hope of reformation: if they counterpoyse their enforced actes of severitie, with the like waight of bounty and clemencie, if their lusts bee the lesser because they have the larger licence: if they desire to rule their owne affects, rather then others estates: and if they do all things, not for glory, but for charity, and with all, and before all, give God the due sacrifice of prayer, for their imperfections; Such Christian Emperors wee call happy, here in hope, and hereafter, when the time wee looke for, commeth indeed."

[3]Chap. xi.

away soveraignty, ascribed unto himselfe alone, and no other, . . .

And of war he said in a chapter proving "That the originalls and conclusions of warres are all at Gods dispose":

So likewise doth he with the times and ends of warre, be it his pleasure justly to correct, or mercifully to pitty mankind, ending them sooner or later, as he willeth.[5]

The use thus made of history by the Church Father who was to influence the thinking of those who wandered far from the later Catholic church is important.

The acceptance of the historical books of the Old Testament both as divine precedent and the source of fundamental material for the writing of history must also be considered as of prime importance in considering the interpretation of the purposes and methods of history by the Reformation historians and educators. But these men knew too the ancient classical historians and orators, and they imposed the specialized Christian philosophy upon the humanistic ideas of historiography instead of creating a rival learning.

Again I have chosen to discuss the contributions of the Reformation to the writing of history by discussing the work of a few representative writers whose books were most familiar in England. As early as 1520 it is said that Luther was advocating the inclusion of history in the education of a Christian youth,[6] but it is generally agreed that it was Melanchthon who advanced the study of history to a science in the thinking of the Reformers, and who showed most clearly its place in the movement.[7] Menke-Glückert has made the most thorough analysis of Melanchthon's

[4]Chap. xxi.

[5]Chap. xxii.

[6]Frederick Eby, *Early Protestant Educators* (London and New York, 1931), pp. 45 *et seq.*

[7]E. Menke-Glückert, *Die Geschichtschreibung des Reformation und Gegenreformation* (Leipzig, 1912), p. 11. I quote the most important passage as translated by Professor Gustave Arlt, of the University of California at Los Angeles: "Obviously it is just as great a violation of historical truth as Luther's description of German Imperial history as the deception of the simple German people by the cunning pope. But just as Luther's inquiry had unexpected

influence and has restudied the evidence for his authorship of the work published as that of Johann Carion.[8] I am not concerned here with this vexing problem, and it must suffice to say that the work of Carion gave expression to Melanchthon's ideas on history. It was Englished by Walter Lynne and published in 1550 as *The Thre Bokes of Cronicles*, gathered from "the beste Authours that have written in Hebrue, Greke or Latine." It was dedicated by its translator to Edward VI and offered as containing "all that is nedefull to be knowen, concernyng thynges done in tymes passed."

This work of Carion was first of all a universal history. Furthermore, it contained a preface which advanced the Reformation theses concerning history, and—of primary importance—it advanced the claim of both "heathen" and Bible histories as the supreme teachers, particularly for princes, since both teach political and moral virtues:

> For besyde that, the holy scryptures do make mentyon of the wyll of God and of hys worde, and also of Christes spyrytual kyngdome, they teache also of polityke administration, and set forth manye notable examples, whych are necessary to be knowen in the governaunce of a commune weale, and by the whych, the myndes of Prynces may be sturred and inflamed to the endevour of ryght pryncely vertues.
>
> The hystoryes of the Heythen, declare of the ofsprynge and begynnynge of great realmes, and for what causes alteracyons and great chaunges do befall in realmes: besides that, they do conteine

---

secondary results, namely the discovery of sources of ecclesiastical history and a sharper scrutiny of historical proofs, so also Melanchthon's manner of approach becomes significant. It assigns to history an independent value on a par with theology; it contains the admission that the examples of Holy Writ are not sufficient. It leads to the secularization of history and it forms the preliminary step to the crudest form of scientific observation, namely comparison. If present-day institutions have their prototypes in former ones then it is worth while to examine both in relation to their greater or smaller degree of similarity. Particularly since history, as Melanchthon asserts, deals with state constitutions, the study of state institutions appears as a logical subject. Through the Reformation, therefore, history becomes a science. Melanchthon himself lectured on history and the first professorships of history were established in Protestant universities."

[8]*Ibid.*, chaps. i-iii.

also preceptes of vocatyons and powres, by the whych commune weales be stablyshed and preserued. . . .

Seinge now, that it is necessary that every man had nede of two maner of powers, namely, the politike or external, and beside this by the faith and drede toward God, the examples of either of them are propoundid and set before us in the histories.

Specially it emphasizes the dangers to the state of any change of government and the threats to its very existence of conspiracies. Reading of such things in history is therefore valuable to rulers, and Thucydides' argument is brought in as proof:

that thereby they maye learne to beware in theyr governaunce, lest any such lyke do befall: For such cases do dayly befall. Yea though the persons do sometyme chaunge in commune welthes, neverthelesse so much as is concernynge the qualytye of mattiers, the worlde is and alwayes abydeth lyke to hym selfe.

Private persons can also learn from history lessons fundamental in a theocracy—and very popular in England:

The magistrate must be obeyed. They, which rebelled against the higher powers, were never unpunished, as Absalon, Catalina, Brutus, Cassius and such like that were therefore punished.

Carion's *Chronicle*, it must be noted, was the basis of the work of Thomas Lanquet, whose chronicle was seemingly but a less flowing translation and perhaps a less selective one than Lynne's. Lanquet's chronicle was left unfinished at his death and was extended by Thomas Cooper and later also by Robert Crowley. It is generally referred to as Cooper's *Chronicle*. Lanquet retranslated and extended the Carion preface into a lengthy discourse "Of the Use and Profite of Historyes, and with what Judgement They Ought to be Redde," indicating in no way his debt to Carion. The chronicle has often been praised, but so far as I am aware, the indebtedness to Carion has not been noted. I note it here because of the importance of realizing how widely the Reformation treatises were disseminated in England.

A second writer on history who was of particular importance

in England during the Reformation was Simon Grynaeus.[9] His relationship with Erasmus made it natural to send to him the five books of Livy which he discovered. Recommended by Erasmus, Grynaeus came to England, probably in 1531, to search for manuscripts, and was welcomed and also, it would seem, somewhat suspiciously watched by Sir Thomas More.[10] Henry VIII called upon Grynaeus for help in considering the matter of his divorce.[11] But in the history of English historiography his preface "Concerning the Profite of Readyng Historyes" which was apparently first published at Venice in the 1538 Latin edition of Trogus Pompeius was of greatest significance. It appeared in Golding's translation of Trogus published in 1564 and again in 1570 and 1578. It appeared likewise somewhat abridged and adapted to its use as a dedicatory essay in the Wilkins translation published in 1591. With slight modifications and with no indication of its origin Thomas Lodge appropriated it as his own address to the Courteous Reader "As Touching the Use and Abuse of Histories" prefixed to his translation of the works of Josephus.

Grynaeus advised all men to read histories. As his words were translated by Golding he said:

> For what can be thought more pleasaunt or profitable, than sytting as it were in the Theatre or Stage of mans life . . . to be made ware and wyse at the perilles of other men, without any daunger on his owne behalfe: to take ensample of all sortes, the which a man may apply to his owne behoofe and utilitie in every thyng: and at suche time as he shall chaunce to be present amonge gret men, when with greatest advisement they do debate most weighty affaires, to be able to discusse the ende and sequele of the same. . . .

Grynaeus thought that the chief interest in history was in the interpretation of cause and effect. It is not enough for the reader to learn what has been, to enjoy the stories recorded, to bask in

---

[9]Pierre Bayle's *General Dictionary* (1734-41) gives a good account of him and his friendship with Melanchthon, More, and others. See also Pierre Larousse, *Grand Dictionnaire Universel*.

[10]R. W. Chambers, *Thomas More* (New York, 1935), p. 282.

[11]See *Letters and Papers, Foreign and Domestic, of the Reign of Henry VIII*, ed. James Gairdner (London, 1862-1910), 1531, Nos. 145 and 287.

past glory, for "an historiographer is but the interpreter of thinges done," and it is his interpretation that must be the goal of the reader. Neither the reader nor the writer of histories can be free from sin if he is guilty of prejudice or prejudgment in viewing history. The great lesson of history for Grynaeus, however, was that the providence of God governs over all. By the policy of men things are put into execution, but the final outcome of events is determined by God. Man proposes but God disposes, and history shows his handiwork.

The work of Johann Sleidan [Joannes Philippson] has received more respectful attention from modern historians than has the work of most of the chroniclers of the Renaissance because of his nearer approach to modern ideals in the care which he bestowed upon selecting his materials and scrutinizing his authorities,[12] but for the purposes of this study his most significant emphasis is upon the importance to Christian thinking of secular as well as Biblical history. In the preface to *A Briefe Chronicle of the Foure Principall Empyres*, his most important work, translated into English in 1563, he explained:

among us, who make profession of the name of Christe, the Bible obtaineth first place amongest suche kindes of writtinges, the which in deducting the originall beginning of mankynd, doth both declare unto us the will of god, and also give unto us many examples as well of the mercye, as of the yre and wrath of God. After the Bible it consequently behoveth to know all that which is writen of other nations. For nothing almost can come to passe but thereof is, and a great while agone hath bene, set out some resemblance. Wherein the governours of common weales have great ayde and succour, provided that they be not careles in this kind of instruction.

Like Melanchthon and Carion he went back to the prophets of the Old Testament for the basis of his division of history. Some of these writers of the Reformation had recognized the triple division of history as that which represented the world under the law of nature, then under the law of Moses, and finally under the

---

[12]An interesting tribute to Sleidan's care and accuracy is seen in the prefatory address of John Daus, translator of *A Famouse Cronicle of Oure Time, called Sleidanes Commentaries*, published in 1560.

law of Christ, but others, like Sleidan, accepted Daniel's prophecy of the four empires, in the last of which periods they were living.[13] It should be recalled that Sleidan was regarded as the official historian of the Reformation and received a pension from Edward VI while he was in England to carry on his work.[14]

Joseph ben Gorion was the name which appeared as that of the author of another book the popularity of which was attested by the fact that it went through nine editions in England alone between 1558 and 1615. This book was Englished by "Peter Morwyng of Magdalen College in Oxford," and its 1558 title reads:

A Compendious and Most Marveilous History of the Latter Tymes of the Jewes Commune Weale, beginnynge where the Bible or Scriptures leave, and continuing to the utter subversion and laste destruction of that countrey and people.[15]

The history of the Jews could teach Christians useful lessons, the prefatory address to the reader pointed out:

Every man deliteth to behold the pictures of auncient persons, as of *Hercules, Hector, Julius Caesar, Arthur,* and reverenceth them as thoughe they were halfe Gods: how much more pleasure should it be to behold the lively images of their mindes which appeare in their actes and dedes whyle thei were here in this life, whereby we shoulde learne to knowe good from evil, and by the appliyng of their dedes unto our maners, with considering the event and successe they had of their actions, we maye take ether an example or some admonicion, or occasion to amend our lives, wherein besides pleasure, is also profit. As when thou seest the Jewes here afflicted with divers kinds

---

[13]Melanchthon apparently used both divisions. For their exposition in English see *The Exposicion of Daniel the Prophete, gathered oute of Philip Melanchton, Johan Ecolampadius, Chonrade Pellicane & out of Johan Draconite, etc.* by George Joye in 1545 and printed at Geneva.

[14]On his work in this connection see Fueter, *Histoire de l'historiographie,* p. 248.

[15]According to the *Dict. Nat. Biog.,* Peter Morwen (or Morwinge) was expelled from his fellowship at Magdalen College, Oxford, in 1553 for his protestant beliefs. The years until Elizabeth's accession and his return were spent in Germany, where apparently he undertook the translation of Joseph ben Gorion's work. This history was popularly thought to be by Josephus.

of misery, because they fell from God: then maist thou be admonished hereby to see the better to thine owne waies, least the like calamities light upon thee, unlesse thou be so fond to thinke God will more spare thee, which art but a wild Olive and but grafted into the stock of faith, if thou bring either noughty fruit or no fruit, then he did the natural braunches which sprang naturally of the rote itself. Thou shalt read here of terrible and horrible eventes of sedicion and rebellion . . . ; in so muche that nothing hastened their destruction so greatlye as their own doggidnesse and intestine hatred. Be thou warned therefore by their harmes, and take hede thac thou maist avoid the like.

It will be seen, I think, from this brief account that the Reformers accepted history, both Biblical and profane, both ecclesiastical and secular, as an important part of learning. They emphasized the value of universal history in showing the relation of God to men and nations. They recognized the particular place in political teaching which history occupied. With Thucydides they believed that "like time bringeth like examples, so long as the world lasteth and the course of nature remaineth," but God the eternal played an important part in their thinking of the persistent laws of cause and effect. And, as will be seen more clearly later, they found the truth of history an antidote to the popular fiction of the time.

CHAPTER VII

THE INFLUENCE OF CONTINENTAL THEORIES
IN ENGLAND

THE HISTORY of English historiography during the sixteenth century has not yet been written. Literary historians have in recent years made valuable contributions to a possible future synthesis by studying the work of individual writers such as Polydore Vergil, More, Halle, Bacon, and Raleigh, but the task is hardly begun. I can, therefore, try here only to illustrate and not to summarize the English reception of the Renaissance and Reformation theories. I have, however, read a large number of the prefaces to the translations of foreign histories, ancient and modern, and I have studied many of the histories written in England to determine the purposes they served and the methods they employed. I have also consulted books written during this period which were only partially or incidentally concerned with history to find what was said on the subject. The instances which I offer as illustrative are chosen because I believe them to be representative. First, in this chapter, I propose to cite typical statements of historical theory devised in England or adopted from continental writers, and in the next chapter to discuss the actual writing of English history during the period.

I have already indicated how the *artes historiae* of Carion, Grynaeus, and Bodin were appropriated for prefaces by English writers. There were probably many other prefaces than those I have mentioned which were merely lifted from continental works, but even in apparently original work the ideas were obviously derivative. For example, there is the dedication addressed to Thomas Duke of Norfolk by Alexander Barclay in offering his translation of Sallust's *Jugurtha*. This was, according to Professor Lathrop, probably the first of the classical histories to be translated into English, having been published sometime between November, 1520, and November, 1523.[1] The dedication is a mosaic of the most familiar passages from ancient authorities, as can be seen in the following extract:

But great is the laude and many be the commodities and utilities of histories. An hystorie is the recorder of tymes passed: the lyght of veritie: the maistres of mannes lyveng, the presydent of memorie: the messanger of antiquitie. And (as Titus Livius recordeth in his prologue) the knowledge of hystories among other thinges is most holsome, necessary, and profitable. For every good example which in them is writen: is set for a warnyng and monycion unto princes and governours thereby to rule and order themselfe: and a commonwele. And every example of miserable fortune of tyrannes, is set as a monicion for the same governours nat to be of tyrannous behavour, lest at last they may fal into lyke miserable ruyne and calamite. And also (as sayth Cicero) a man to knowe nothing of that which was done before his tyme and remembrance: that is as who sayeth alway to be a chylde. . . . lykewyse as unto aged men is more credence and auctorite gyven, than to yong men: bycause of experience of many thyngs. So such noble and diligent mynds as delyteth in redynge hystories: may have knowledge nat only of the dedes of one mannes lyfe: but also of the dedes most famous of al tymes syth creation of the world . . . princes shall fynde writen in bokes before their eyen ryght many thyngs concernyng their wele, honour, and fame: which theyr frends dare nat be bolde to tell them for drede of dysplesure: fathermore without the knowledge of hystories never man coude become good oratour. For (as affermeth Quintilian) hystories be of such myght and effect that they may norisshe the speche of an oratour with soft and swete lycour.

By way of summary Barclay concludes that history shows the laws of God and man maintained, vice and vicious men corrected, virtue and virtuous men rewarded and exalted. And he adds that the reading of history seems to aid in bringing men to a knowledge of and a contempt for the transitory pleasure and the misery of this uncertain life.

Such prefaces as were affixed to the translations of continental

[1]Lathrop, *Translations from the Classics*, pp. 81-84.

works were generally, like this of Barclay, mere compendia of quotations or paraphrased passages from ancient or modern continental works, but many of the foreign treatises were introduced into England intact, as I have already indicated in discussing Reformation historiography. One reason was that the English translators of the classics very often used intermediary translations as the bases for their own Englishing of the texts, and inevitably they Englished along with the original texts the comments of the intervening translators as they found them in appended dedications and prefaces. A revealing example of the way in which a cumulative set of these theorizings about history came into English literature is found in the 1550 edition of Nicolls' Thucydides. The work had been translated from Greek into Latin by Laurentius Valla and dedicated to Pope Nicholas V, who is known to have given definite impetus to the movement to study ancient history. Claude De Seyssel,[2] Bishop of Marseilles and later Archbishop of Turin, turned Valla's Latin into French and dedicated his work to Louis XII. James Colyn, secretary to Francis I, added another French preface. Thomas Nicolls, "cytezene and Goldsmith of our Cytie of London," translated the accumulated wealth of this French translation into English, dedicating the whole to Sir John Cheke.

The work received special attention from Edward VI, for there is prefixed "The tenoure of the Kynges Majesties most gracyous Privelege for Seven yeares" which prescribes as penalty the forfeiture of all pirated books and a fine of twenty pounds should anyone attempt to defraud Nicolls of his rights. Edward's words indicate, too, that he expected Nicolls to continue his work of translation:

Thomas Nicolls, Cytezene and Goldsmith of our Cytie of London, hath not onely translated the hystorye, wryttone by Thucidides the Athenyan of the warres that were amonge the Grekes, chiefly betwene the Peloponesians and the Athenyans out of Frenche into Inglish, but also intendeth contynuing in that his vertuous exercyse,

<hr>

[2]See p. 58 below for discussion of De Seyssel's visit to the court of Henry VII. See also Lathrop, p. 86.

thereby to reduce and bring other profytable hystories out of Frenche and latenne into our sayd maternall language, to the generall benefyt, comodytie and profyt of all our loving Subjects, that well shall digeste the same: . . .

And the King "Myndyng to relieve and helpe our sayd subjecte in hys labours and study," demanded that all possible encouragement and assistance should be given to Nicolls by publishers and others who had to do with the book trade, explaining his royal intervention in the translator's behalf by describing himself as "We, who from oure tender yougth have loved and embrased Godly and vertuous learnyng." History was "Godly and vertuous learnyng" to those favoring the Reformation, and it was to Sir John Cheke, King Edward's tutor, the close friend of the foreign Reformers then in England, and famous Greek scholar, that Nicolls modestly addressed his work.

The three rather extensive defenses of history prefaced to the text of Thucydides clearly made further discussion by Nicolls a work of supererogation, and he was content with a simple dedication, though he did contribute a short comment on rhetorical ornament in historical writing. All of the translated prefaces drew from the common store of the praises of history, but each has some points of special interest. Valla in writing to Pope Nicholas V justified translation in general by affirming that if the Bible had not been translated from the Hebrew and the Greek into Latin, "we other latyn men shulde not have hadde any knowelayge of God." De Seyssel, who had previously translated into French for Louis XII the works of Xenophon, Diodorus, Appian, and Trogus, as well as certain ecclesiastical histories, explained his labors as occasioned by the king's desire for practical guidance in political affairs, instruction as to how to conduct himself in governing his own realm and others that God committed to his care, both in time of peace and time of war. James Colyn, addressing Francis I, in typical Reformation fashion opposed the goods of history to the evils of fiction: a knowledge of Pericles, Hannibal, and Scipio to a knowledge of "Tristrams, Girons and Lancelotes and other, which do fylle bookes wyth dreames." But the core of the teaching is found in a quotation from Philippe de Comines:

Wyth thys, the Civile and warly learnynge, the constitucions of laws and Royalmes, the facyons, whereby they are acquired and maygteyned, the meanes whereby they fall into decaye, and agayne whereby they are reestablyshed and restored: all these thynges be onely conteygned in the descryption of good hystoryes and none where els.

In 1553 John Brende translated the history of Quintus Curtius, "conteyning the Actes of the greate Alexander," using, according to Lathrop,[3] the edition of Christopherus Bruno which had been printed at Basle in 1545 and basing his dedication on that of Bruno. This translation was published eight times by 1614 and was one of the best known of Elizabethan histories.[4] Brende dedicated it to John Dudley, Duke of Northumberland, in whom he found a worthy parallel to the great Alexander. The dedication illustrates the blending of Reformation and Renaissance teaching in regard to history, emphasizing from both points of view its value in giving political guidance, as can be seen in the following passage:

the same beyng counted the most excellent kynde of knowledge, the chiefest parte of civyl prudence and the mirrour of mans lyfe. There is required in all magistrates both a fayeth and feare in God, and also an outwarde policye in wordly thynges, whereof as the one is to be learned by the scryptures, so the other must chiefly be gathered by readyng of histories. For in them men may see the groundes and begynnynges of commenwealthes, the causes of their encrease, of their prosperous mayntenaunce, and good preservation: and againe by what meanes they decreased, decayed, and came to ruyne. There the vertues and vices of men do appeare, how by their good doynges they florished, and by their evil actes they decayed. How they prospered so long as they mainteyned justice, persecuted vice, used clemencye and mercye, were liberal, religyous, vertuous, and voyde of covetousnes. And contrariwise, howe they fell into manifold calamityes, miseries, and troubles, when they embraced

[3]Lathrop, p. 87.

[4]See pp. 304-5 below.

46

vyce and forsoke vertue. In historyes it is apparent how daungerous it is to begin alterations in a commenwealth. How envy and hatredes oft risying upon small causes, have ben the destruction of great kyngdomes. And that disobeyers of hygher powers and suche as rebelled agaynst magystrates, never escaped punyshment, nor came to good end.

For those who did not read Greek and Latin, familiarity with ancient authors had to come through translation. Elizabeth, like the other children of Henry VIII, did not depend upon translations, for she read both the Greek and the Latin authors daily even when her duties as queen had become exacting, as her old tutor, Roger Ascham, tells us. But Elizabeth followed in the footsteps of her father and grandfather when she encouraged the translations of the classics, and it was to her royal favor that Sir Thomas North offered his translation of Amiot's French translation of the work most important to the study of Shakespeare, *The Lives of the Noble Grecians and Romanes, compared together by the grave learned philosopher and historiographer, Plutarke of Chaeronea.*

North declared that no other "profane" book popular in his day taught so much obedience and devotion to rulers as did Plutarch's *Lives.* He compared philosophy and poetry with history and concluded:

All other learning is private, fitter for Universities than cities, fuller of contemplacion than experience, more commendable in the students themselves, than profitable unto others.

But for the fuller understanding of history North referred the reader to the preface of Amiot, which he translated along with the French translation of Plutarch. The preface is long—eight large folio pages—but it must be reviewed in outline, because here is one book we know to have been well thumbed by Shakespeare.

Histories, Amiot said, are the best teachers

bicause an historie is an orderly register of notable things said, done, or happened in time past, to mainteyne the continuall remembrance of them, and to serve for the instruction of them to come.

History is a storehouse, a public storehouse to be compared

with the memory of the individual man. It is the most ancient form of writing and indeed antedates writing itself. It is a monument more durable than triumph or pillar or sepulchre. It is rightly called by Horace the mother of truth and uprightness:

For it is a certaine rule and instruction, which by examples past, teacheth us to judge of things present, and to foresee things to come: so as we may knowe what to like of, and what to follow, what to mislike, and what to eschew.

It is better than moral philosophy as a teacher because it teaches by example rather than by precept and hence teaches more effectively. It is to be preferred to poetry because unlike poetry it is not concerned with enriching of truth for delight but is content with truth itself. Furthermore, it is more universal than any other kind of learning, for its examples show the way to both private and public virtue. It can make the young and the untraveled wise, being a substitute for hardly gained experience:

> A happie wight is he that by mishappes
> Of others, doth beware of afterclappes.

Amiot answers those who object to history because writers are partial by saying that history cannot be blamed for a writer's prejudice. The historian ought to be free from envy and hatred and a desire to flatter. He ought to choose carefully what he sets down:

forasmuch as his chiefe drift ought to be to serve the common weale, and that he is but as a register to set downe the judgements and definitive sentences of Gods court, whereof some are geven according to the ordinarie course and capacitie of our weake naturall reason, and other some goe according to Gods infinite power and incomprehensible wisedome, above and against all discourse of mans understanding, who being unable to reach to the bottome of his judgements, and to finde out the first motions and groundes thereof, do impute the cause of them to a certaine fortune . . .

Though history is delightful and profitable to all, yet it is of special value to princes and kings,

seeing the ground of stories is, to treat of all maner of high matters of state, as warres, battells, cities, contries, treaties of peace and alliances, and therefore it seemeth more fit for them, than for any other kinde of degrees of men: . . .

Furthermore, reading histories is the one method by which great men can be instructed in the truth, for princes are generally surrounded by flatterers from whom it is impossible that they should learn the truth.

As to the kinds of history, Amiot distinguishes only between histories and lives:

The one which setteth downe mens doings and adventures at length, is called by the common name of an historie: the other which declareth their natures, sayings, and maners, is properly named their lives.

It must indeed be apparent to anyone who reads the classical and continental works of history which flowed from the printing presses of sixteenth-century England that they brought with them in their dedications and prefaces theories of historiography which by the time that Shakespeare wrote his historical plays had become commonplaces. The great documents of Renaissance historiography were incorporated in whole or in part in these prefaces and dedications, ideas were appropriated, and it is clear that England accepted with practical unanimity the humanistic theories of history as they were modified by the Reformation. The independent publication of treatises on historiography was, however, slow and scattered in England, like the publication of treatises on literary criticism. The first of these independently issued treatises was Thomas Blundeville's *The True Order and Methode of Wryting and Reading Hystories, according to the precepts of Francisco Patricio, and Accontio Tridentio,* published in 1574. As is apparent from the title this was a telescoping of the translation of two works from the Italian. Dr. Hugh Dick has recently published this work with an account of the authors, pointing out the relation of Blundeville to the group of Italians at court, one of whom was Giacomo Concio (Latinized into Jacobus Acontius).[5] The patronage of the Earl of Leicester, in-

---

[5]*Huntington Library Quarterly,* III (1940), 149-70. See also the same writer's "Giacomo Concio: A Renaissance Exile" in *Modern Language Forum,* XXVI (1941), 12-18.

voked by Concio when he dedicated his original work, was again invoked by Blundeville in dedicating his translation, and it is important to note the interest which Leicester displayed or was said to display in history. Blundeville offered his work,

Knowynge youre Honor amongst other good delyghtes, to delyght moste in reading of Hystories, the true Image and portrature of Mans lyfe, and that not as many doe, to passe away the tyme, but to gather thereof such judgement and knowledge as you thereby be the more able, as well to direct your private actions, as to give Counsell lyke a most prudent Counseller in publyke causes, be it matters of warre, or peace: . . .

He mingles selections from Patricio's ten dialogues on history with parts of Concio's essay to create a new whole. From Concio, he selects the purposes served by studying history:

First, that we may learn to acknowledge the providence of God;

Second, that we may learn how to act wisely in public and in private affairs, both in time of peace and in time of war;

Third, that we may learn by example to follow the good and flee the evil.

In elaborating these statements he makes it clear that history deals with nations:

As touching the providence of God, we have to note for what causes and by what meanes hee overthroweth one kingdome and setteth up another . . . And though he suffreth the wicked for the most part to live in prosperitie, and the good in adversitie: yet we maye see by many notable examples, declaring as well his wrath, and revenge towardes the wicked, as also his pittie and clemencie towardes the good, that nothing is done by chaunce, but all things by his foresight, counsell, and divine providence.[6]

From Patricio, Blundeville records the various advantages which derive from history, since

Every Citie or Countrye standeth upon three principall poynts, unto one of which all publique actions doe appertaine, that is, peace, sedition and warre . . .[7]

[6]Blundeville, *op. cit.*, fol. F2v-3v.
[7]*Ibid.*, D3r.

And again he draws from Patricio when he defines history specifically:

Hystories bee made of deedes done by a publique weale, or agaynst a publique weale, and such deedes, be eyther deedes of warre, of peace, or else of sedition and conspiracie.[8]

But he recognizes that those deeds which affect the public weal are done by specific persons at specific times for specific causes by specific means, and he would include the economic, geographic, and political survey of the country in the study of its history.[9]

As for that part of history which is given to chronicling the lives of individuals, Blundeville thinks that those who can offer examples for following virtue or eschewing vice are worthy of record, and if these were public personages, they should be considered in relation to the kind of government with which they were concerned. The lives of princes are, however, especially worth recording in order that the student of history may know how affairs have been governed under every kind of ruler, good and bad. The approach to such biographical study, it is significant to note, should in Blundeville's estimation be made with due awareness that man's fate is controlled both by outside force or destiny and by his own character:

And whatsoever enterprise any man taketh in hand, he doth it being mooved and provoked thereunto, eyther by some outwarde principle, or by some inwarde principle, if outwarde, it is eyther by destinie, by force, or by fortune, if inwarde, then it is eyther by nature, by affection, or by choyse and election, and such election springeth eyther of nature, or of some passion of the minde, of custome, or else of the discourse of reason.[10]

In Blundeville's amalgamation of the works of Patricio and Concio there is thus evident the familiar mingling of humanistic and Reformation theories of historiography with due emphasis on the primary purpose of history as the demonstration of the providence of God over all.

[8]*Ibid.*, A4ᵛ.
[9]*Ibid.*, B1-2.
[10]*Ibid.*, C3ᵛ.

Francis Bacon in 1605 considered both Biblical and secular history in his work *Of the Proficience and Advancement of Learning, Divine and Humane*, accepting history as one of the three parts of learning along with poetry and philosophy.[11] Of human learning he says:

> For CIVILE HISTORY, it is of three kindes, not unfitly to be compared with the three kinds of Pictures or Images: for of Pictures or Images, wee see some are Unfinished, some are parfite, and some are defaced: So of Histories, wee may find three kindes, MEMORIALLS, PARFITE HISTORIES, and ANTIQUITIES: for MEMORIALLS are Historie unfinished, or the first, or rough draughts of Historie, and ANTIQUITIES are Historie defaced, or some remnants of History, which have casually escaped the shipwrack of time.
>
> MEMORIALLS or PREPARATORY HISTORY are of 2 sorts, whereof the one may be tearmed COMMENTARIES, and the other REGISTERS; . . . [12]

He adds to these definitions:

> HISTORY which may be called JUST and PARFITE Historie, is of three kinds, according to the object which it propoundeth, or pretendeth to represent: for it either representeth a TIME, or a PERSON, or an ACTION. The first we call CHRONICLES, the second LIVES, and the third NARRATIONS, or RELATIONS.[13]

Bacon repeats here as elsewhere many of the praises of history which had become commonplace, and in his plea to the new king for a more adequate history of Britain, and particularly Scotland, he reviewed English history by way of demonstrating the providence of God manifest in the period from the uniting of the houses (of York and Lancaster) to the uniting of the kingdoms (of England and Scotland).

Recently Dr. Leonard F. Dean has studied in some detail Bacon's ideas of historiography and has ranked him among the followers of Polybius, whom he has described justly:

They associated history-writing with political theory rather than

[11]Bacon, *op. cit.*, fol. 10ᵛ.

[12]*Ibid.*, fol. 12.

[13]*Ibid.*, fol. 11ʳ.

with oratory or research, and they studied the past not so much to find examples with which to enforce conventional morality as to learn what is politically expedient. History to them, was a form of didactic literature concerned with the difficult art of political administration.[14]

One of the few independent works on historiography written in England during the Renaissance was salvaged by an eighteenth-century antiquarian. This was Edmund Bolton's *Hypercritica; or a rule of Judgment for writing or reading our History's*,[15] an early seventeenth-century work which gains significance because of its author's translation of Florus' *Abridgment of Livy*. Bolton did not contribute any new ideas to historiography, but his criticism of pagan and Christian historians is revealing. He criticized the "Ethnicks" for omitting in general the "Part of the heavenly Providence in the Actions of Men," and the Christian authors for too easily shuffling up events "in briefly referring all causes immediately to the Will of God," and generally neglecting "to inform their Readers in the ordinary means of Carriage in human Affairs."[16] He ranked Livy the best of ancient writers because he was the most religious and Tacitus the worst as judged by this standard. Of Christian writers he found Philippe de Comines and Sir Thomas More the best because they respected "as well the superior, as the inferior Efficients of Operations in the World." He found that modern historians often erred by reading into historic events "the Jealousies, Passions, and Affections of their own Time."[17] Yet even while he was urging Bodin's dictum that history ought to register things done and leave the reader to pass judgment, he weakened and

[14]"Sir Francis Bacon's Theory of Civil History-Writing" in *ELH*, VIII (1941), 161-83.

[15]Reprinted in Joseph Haslewood, *Ancient Critical Essays* (London, 1811-15), and in J. E. Spingarn, *Critical Essays of the Seventeenth Century* (Oxford, 1908).

[16]Haslewood ed., p. 224.

[17]*Ibid.*, p. 232.

added: "howsoever in some rare Cases it may be lawful to lead the same."[18]

But the proof of the pudding is in the eating and not in the recipe from which it is compounded, and the proof of the acceptance of the theories of historical writing which had gradually been set down during the Renaissance and Reformation period must be found in the actual writing of history in England during that period.

18*Ibid.*, p. 233.

CHAPTER VIII

ENGLISH HISTORY IN THE SIXTEENTH CENTURY

C L. Kingsford terminated his study of *English Historical Literature in the Fifteenth Century* at 1485, appending a chapter on the sixteenth-century histories. No more adequate work has appeared, and the several general histories of historiography which have been published in recent years give very spare accounts of the Tudor histories.[1] Professor Harry Elmer Barnes, for instance, in one of the latest of these works gives just a little over one page to the subject of "humanist historiography in England," and he mentions—and barely mentions—only Polydore Vergil, Sir Thomas More, Sir Walter Raleigh, William Camden, and Francis Bacon. Fueter in his more comprehensive survey of modern historiography devotes twelve pages to the English Renaissance and is the only one of these writers to link English historical writing to various movements on the Continent. But to the histories which are perhaps most important to the study of the literature of the period and certainly most important to the study of Shakespeare he gives only one short paragraph (I have the French translation before me):

Les nombreuses Chroniques (de Hall, Holinshed, Grafton, Stow, etc.), parues dans le cours du xviᵉ siècle sont sans aucune importance

---

[1]The latest is J. W. Thompson, *A History of Historical Writing* (New York, 1942). The best for this period and the only one much concerned with the philosophy of history is that of E. Fueter (*Histoire de l'historiographie*), referred to many times in these pages. Conyers Read, *Bibliography of British History: Tudor Period, 1485-1603* (Oxford, 1933) is here as always in Tudor studies a trustworthy guide. Bishop W. Nicolson in his *English, Scotch and Irish Historical Libraries* (London, 1776) made an interesting beginning, which is yet useful. See also L. B. Wright, *Middle-Class Culture in Elizabethan England* (Chapel Hill, 1935), Chap. ix.

pour notre histoire. Elles correspondent à peu près aux nouvelles éditions contemporaines des *Grandes Chroniques* de France et sont comme elles informes et sans critique. Elles étaient destinées à la bourgeoisie et á la petite noblesse; elles étaient loyalistes, comme le souhaitaient ces deux classes, qui avaient tiré le plus grand profit du gouvernement fort des Tudors, et qui étaient peu sensibles aux besoins intellectuels. La plupart ne sont pas de vrais ouvrages d'histoire, mais de grossières compilations, des produits fabriqués pour les masses, souvent d'ailleurs confectionnés non par des écrivains de profession, mais par des libraires.[2]

There are undoubtedly two reasons for this neglect of the popular and influential English chronicles. In the first place, the historian of history is dependent on a mass of detailed scholarship which is not yet available concerning these English works. In the second place, he is usually intent upon detecting the emergence of new ideas and especially the emergence of those new ideas which have prevailed and which are now accepted. Like most of the literary critics who are today giving allegiance to "the history of ideas," he is trying to trace the source from which today's ideas have come. That is to say, he is primarily interested not in discovering what succeeding generations thought about history or how they wrote history, but in tracing the origins of what we today hold worthy or even of what he himself today holds worthy.[3] The literary historian, on the other hand, approaches the study of history, as he does that of any other form of writing, from the past rather than from the present. He tries to see what were its purposes and its methods in succeeding generations. It is solely from this point of view, then, that I propose to examine the histories of England published and written during the Tudor period. It is needless to say, I hope, that a review of these works in a single chapter presents merely a sampling of the whole. But

[2]Fueter, *op. cit.*, p. 203.

[3]Preserved Smith, for instance, in his *Age of the Reformation* (1920) said: "It is hard to see any value, save occasionally as sources, in the popular English chronicles of Edward Hall, Raphael Holinshed, and John Stow. Full of court gossip and of pageantry, strongly royalist, conservative and patriotic, they reflect the interests of the middle-class cockney as faithfully as does a certain type of newspaper and magazine today."

there is so much that is common to all as far as method and purpose are concerned that it does not seem necessary to eat the
whole firkin in order to judge the butter.

The Tudor sovereigns were responsible, directly and indirectly, for much of the determination to write anew the history of
England during their reigns. However, the printing press, still
new when Henry VII was crowned, had already made and continued to make certain histories of an older period available. The
Polychronicon of Higden in Trevisa's translation, first published
in 1482, contains a "Proheyme" particularly interesting as showing what may be called the continuity of historical theory, for
it calls history a perpetual conservator of the past, the giver of
immortality to both good and evil, fame and infamy. It praises
history as the mother of philosophy and the nurse of good learning, and argues that though poets have by their fables undertaken
to inflame the "courages" of men, though laws and institutions
have tried to punish men into goodness, it is history that has
proved the most effective teacher. And significantly, it parallels
two undertakings, this history of a secular kind, and the *Golden
Legend* with its accounts of the lives, miracles, passions, and
deaths of divers holy saints.

But our concern here is with the histories published or written
under the Tudors, and since, as Kingsford says, the chronicle of
Fabyan is to be regarded as the last of the fifteenth-century
histories rather than the earliest of the sixteenth century, I propose to begin with the *Chronicle* of John Hardyng, first published
in 1543 with a continuation in prose by Richard Grafton.[4] The
preface recites many of the commonplaces concerning history,
but I call attention to one stanza particularly which records the
divine endorsement of history:

> Wherfore Goddes woorde and holy scripture
> Which abandoneth all maner vanitee
> Yet of Chronicles admitteth the lecture

[4] For an account of the two variant editions by Grafton in the same year
and the history of Hardyng's manuscript versions see C. L. Kingsford, "The
First Version of Hardyng's Chronicle," in the *English Historical Review*,
XXVII (1912), 462-82.

> As a thing of great fruite and utilitee
> And as a lanterne, to the posteritee
> For example, what they ought to knowe
> What waies to refuse, and what to folowe.

The "Proheme" to "My lorde of Yorke" points out the general lessons of history taught therein. The comment on Henry IV, for instance, calls attention to one of the divine laws to be expounded at length by Raleigh much later:

> For when Henry the fourth first was crouned
> Many a wyseman, sayd then full commenly
> The third heyre shuld not joyse but be uncrouned
> And deposed of all regalitee
> To this reason they dyd there wittes applye,
> Of evill gotten good, the third should not enjoyse
> Of longe agone, it hath bene a commen voyce.

But new works were to be written, and the first Tudor king, Henry VII, set himself to the task by engaging the services of two foreigners, Bernard André and Polydore Vergil. Dr. William Nelson in his recent study of the scholars whom Henry VII brought to his court stresses the king's recognition of history as "the princely subject *par excellence*" and offers an illustration:

Claude De Seyssel, the French ambassador, could find no more appropriate gift for Henry VII than a French translation of Xenophon, royally inscribed on vellum. In the dedication De Seyssel says that King Henry has a splendid library and enjoys both hearing and reading histories and other matters fit for a wise and noble prince. He is an experienced ruler, both in peace and in war, and will therefore recognize the value of the practical advice and warnings to be found in Xenophon's *Anabasis*, a work which, in the opinion of King Louis XII of France, should be divulged only to princes and to great personages.[5]

This work had been given to Louis XII, who, Dr. Nelson says, wished to be the sole possessor of such a rare treasure, but Henry's kindness to De Seyssel was so great that a second copy was made.

---

[5]"The Scholars of Henry VII" in *John Skelton: Laureate* (New York, 1939), p. 23.

I have already spoken of De Seyssel in connection with the translation of Thucydides by Nicolls,[6] but it must be emphasized here that King Henry VII, anxious as he was to bring England abreast of the new learning on the Continent, could scarcely have failed to be impressed by the interests of the French ambassador, who was to his own king a sort of translator-general of the ancient histories.

Bernard André had been teaching at Oxford before he was appointed tutor to the king's eldest child, Prince Arthur, and the thorough grounding in history which the young prince received is evidenced in André's statement that by the time he was sixteen Arthur "had either committed to memory or read with his own eyes and leafed with his own fingers" Thucydides, Livy, Caesar, Suetonius, Tacitus, Pliny, Valerius Maximus, Sallust, and Eusebius.[7] After four years as tutor André was appointed to write the life of Henry VII and was generously rewarded, apparently on a yearly basis. He kept records of current events in the form of annals.

But it was Polydore Vergil's appointment to write a history of England that was for English historiography the most important event of the reign of Henry VII.[8] Vergil came to the English court about 1501 as a papal envoy, but for fifty years he remained in England, where he gained preferment and ultimately was naturalized. When he appointed Vergil to write a history of England, Henry VII was, as the Tudors continued to be, much concerned with finding King Arthur on the family tree. However, Vergil's work was not published until 1534, when Henry VIII had succeeded his father, and instead of bolstering the Tudor claims,

[6]See above, pp. 44-45.

[7]Nelson, *op. cit.*, p. 15.

[8]The basis for most modern accounts of Vergil is the preface of Sir Henry Ellis in his edition of *Three Books of Polydore Vergil's English History* (London, 1844) published for the Camden Society (Vol. XXIX). Other accounts will be found in Kingsford, Fueter, Thompson, etc. Of special interest is the article by E. A. Whitney and P. P. Cram, "The Will of Polydore Vergil," in the *Royal Historical Society Transactions*, Fourth Series, XI, 117-36, where a list of editions with some account of Vergil's influence on later English writers is to be found.

it attacked the historicity of Arthur. The result was a battle of books which has been the subject of much recent scholarship,[9] and a defamation of Vergil's character which has not yet received adequate unprejudiced appraisal. But these matters are not of importance here. What is important is that Vergil was the first of the humanist historians to write the history of England. As Kingsford pointed out, he is regarded as the first to break public-ly in England with the long tradition of a purely annalistic form of history. On the positive side, Sir Henry Ellis said of his work:

It was the first of our histories in which the writer ventured to com-pare the facts and weigh the statements of his predecessors; and it was the first in which summaries of personal character are introduced in the terse and energetic form adopted in the Roman classics.[10]

But it must be remembered that Vergil wrote in Latin, and that the nine editions of his work to 1651 were all published on the Continent. It made a knowledge of English history accessible to readers outside England, but it did not provide the mass of Eng-lish people directly with a history of their own land.

Indirectly, by furnishing Halle and later English writers with much of their material, Vergil contributed greatly to the writing of English history for popular consumption. He wrote history as a connected, unified narrative, relating cause and effect, inter-preting events, generalizing their significance so that they might serve as useful lessons ever capable of new application, and in so doing he set the pattern for the popular chronicles. I quote from the sixteenth-century translation of his work (which was not published until the nineteenth century), by way of illustrating these characteristics. In chronicling the terrible dream of Richard III on the night before the battle of Bosworth Field, for instance, he comments:

But (I beleve) yt was no dreame, but a conscyence guiltie of haynous offences, a conscyence (I say) so muche the more grevous as thof-

---

[9]The pioneer study was made by Edwin Greenlaw in a paper on "The Battle of the Books," published in *Studies in Spenser's Historical Allegory* (Baltimore, 1932). See also C. B. Millican, *Spenser and the Table Round* (Cambridge, Mass., 1932).

[10]*Op. cit.*, p. xxviii.

fences wer more great, which, thowght at none other time, yeat in the last day of owr lyfe ys woont to represent to us the memory of our sinnes commyttyd, and withall to shew unto us the paynes immynent for the same, that, being uppon good cause penytent at that instant for our evell led lyfe, we may be compellyd to go hence in heavynes of hart.[11]

Again, telling how Edward IV won protection in York by promising under oath to treat the citizens well and to be an obedient and faithful servant of King Henry VI thenceforth, even as he was plotting to deprive that king of his throne, Vergil moralizes:

Thus oftentimes as well men of highe as of low cawling blynded with covetousnes, and forgetting all religyon and honesty, ar woont to make promyse in swearing by thimmortal God, which promyse neverthelesse they ar already determynyd to breake before they make yt. Of this matter yt shall not yrk me to make mentyon in the lyfe of king Richerd the third . . . , wher perchaunce yt may be well conceavyed that thissew of king Edward did partycypate also the fault of this perjury.[12]

And when he describes the murder of the little princes by Richard III, he repeats the moral and enlarges upon it:

What man ys ther in this world, who, yf he have regard unto suche noble children thus shamefully murderid, wyll not tremble and quake, seing that suche matters often happen for thoffences of our ancestors, whose faults doo redownd to the posterytie? That fortunyd peradventure to these two innocent impes because Edward ther fathyr commytted thoffence of perjury, . . . and for that afterwardes, by reason of his brother the duke of Clarence death, he had chargyd himself and his posterytie before God with dew desert of grevous punysshement.[13]

Thus Vergil found occasion to speak of rebellion, treason, war, good government and bad, all of the matters that go to the making and unmaking of kingdoms, and he spoke as one who in the vicarious experience of history had learned well the political lessons which are needful.

[11]*Ibid.*, p. 222.
[12]*Ibid.*, p. 139.
[13]*Ibid.*, pp. 189-90.

By way of contrast to Vergil's attack upon the reliability of Geoffrey of Monmouth it is interesting to note the attitude of John Rastell in his *Pastime of People*. Rastell seems to have doubted Geoffrey as much as did Vergil, but he considered the end more important than the means. Therefore, while acknowledging that he did not wish his readers precisely to believe what he rehearsed out of Geoffrey, he proceeded with the story as given by that author because he found there many examples of princes who governed well,

and also a man reding in the same shall see how the stroke of God fell ever uppon the people, other by battell, darth, or deth, for their vice and misleving; and also how divers princis and grete men, exaltid in pride and ambicion, using tiranny and cruelte, or ells being neclygent in governyng of theyre people, or giffing them self to vicious liffing, were ever by the stroke of God punished for the same.[14]

That Henry VIII, like his father, took a personal interest in the writing of history is very evident. Lord Berners, translating Froissart at the king's command, as he tells us, added a preface in which he quoted Cicero, praised history as defying oblivion, being the best teacher, and constituting the only everlasting monument. Grynaeus, recommended by Erasmus, was given permission by the king to come to England to search for ancient monuments. But of far more importance was the appointment of John Leland to recover the antiquities of England, backed by the royal authority which was necessary. Holinshed records two Latin epigrams made in honor of the king and his bounty by Leland, who apparently was expected to offset the doubting Vergil.[15] We learn a good deal about the historian and his methods and purposes from the report which he made in 1546 to Henry VIII and which was published in 1549 with annotations and a new dedication to Edward VI by John Bale as *The Laboryouse Journey and Serche of Johan Leylande for Englands Antiquities*. Bale says that Leland prepared himself for his task:

[14]In the reprint by T. F. Dibdin (London, 1811), p. 7.

[15]He published his reply in 1544, *Assertio Inclytissimi Arturii Regis*. It was translated into English in 1582 by Richard Robinson.

as for all authors of Greke, Latyne, Frenche, Italian, Spanyshe, Bryttyshe, Saxonyshe, Walshe, Englyshe, or Scottyshe, towching in any wyse the understandynge of our Antiquitees, he had so fullye redde and applyed them, that they were in a maner graffed in hym as of nature. So that he myght well cal him selfe *Antiquarius*.[16]

Bale argued that want of access to the ancient records of Britain had caused Caxton, Fabyan, Hardyng, and now Vergil to err as they had in many points.

And .ii. thynges chefely have caused them (Leylande sayth) so longe to be witholden from us. The one is the slacknesse of em- pryntynge . . . An other is the want of ornature, that they have not bene changed into a more eloquent stile, to the full satisfyenge of delycate eares and wyttes.[17]

And we have the expansion of these ideas in Leland's own re- port that he had collected, both for the royal libraries and his own, ancient authors which had lain "secretely in corners" and remained unknown because they were not printed, and because they had not been "clothed in purpure." Since we have in this latter reason Leland's recognition of the claims of the humanist rhetoricians, his words are important:

And also because men of eloquence hath not enterprised to set them fourth in a floryshynge style, in some tymes past not com- menly used in Englande of writers, otherwise wele learned, and nowe in suche estymacyon, that except truth be delycately clothed in purpure her written verytes can scant fynde a reader.[18]

The works which Leland projected it is not here in point to recount in detail; but it should be noted that he proposed to establish the antiquity and the originality of the English church, the claims of Englishmen to greatness through the ages, the historical greatness of England, shire by shire, and the true rela- tion of England to ancient Rome. Most of the proposed work he did not live to complete, but his records and papers were

[16]Fol. B5r.
[17]Fol. C3v.
[18]Fol. C3r (wrongly numbered C5).

used by many of the succeeding generation of historians.[19]

Bale was inclined to think the "purpure" of fine writing might be dispensed with, but he looked upon Leland's work as fulfilling the duty of Englishmen both as Christians and as patriots to write history. He especially recommended histories to Christian governors as mirrors wherein the cause and the reformation of abuses might be seen, and he linked Biblical and secular history together in his praise.

Though he did not fail to repeat the usual humanistic arguments for history, Bale stressed the Reformation special pleading: that the prophecies of the Bible will by history be understood, that the fallacies of papistical teaching will be undermined, that the history of the English church as well as of the English nation will be brought to light. And he urged noblemen and rich merchants to pay for printing one by one the works of antiquity. A single "belly banquet" foregone would pay for the printing of three important works and would contribute to winning new respect for England from France and Italy. Also he begged that there be saved for posterity the great works left unfinished at the death of their authors. In this connection he praised Thomas Cooper for completing the work of Lanquet and the one who was responsible for printing the chronicle of Edward Halle.

But before I can continue the discussion of the work of the historians mentioned by Bale, I must return to the writer who along with Polydore Vergil is ranked highest by all historiographers. Sir Thomas More is important because he wrote *The History of Richard the Third* with such theatrical effectiveness that no one has yet been able to change or to qualify in the popular mind the picture which he presented of the usurping tyrant and his dreadful end. Fueter compares his work to that of the school of Leonardo Bruni (Aretine) in Italy:

Il partage leurs défauts comme leurs qualités, leur recherche de l'arrangement théatral et de la peinture sentimentale, la rhétorique

---

[19]An early account of the peregrinations of Leland's papers is given in [William Huddesford], *The Lives of those Eminent Antiquaries John Leland, Thomas Hearne, and Anthony à Wood* (Oxford, 1772), I, 26-29. *The Laboryouse Journey* is reprinted in this work also.

dans les discours insérés, et aussi l'art de bien grouper les récits, le soin minutieux de l'expression, l'urbanité relative de la polémique.

He also notes critically his political bias:

L'obligation de distribuer l'ombre et la lumière d'aprés des considér-
ations politiques a empêché Morus de nous donner de ses figures une franche analyse psychologique. Il fit des efforts remarquables pour caractériser plus à fond qu'on n'était habitué à le faire dans l'historiographie rhétoricienne; mais partout il se heurtait aux barri-
ères que rencontre toujours un écrit de parti.[20]

It was Roger Ascham who most truly saw the place of More in the history of English historical writing, for recalling his dis-
cussions about history with Sir Robert Asteley, and questioning the *what* and the *why* and the *how* of history, he formulated as clearly as any one in England basic standards of judgment. When he wrote of More to Asteley, he judged him by these careful standards:

Syr Thomas More in that pamphlet of Richard the thyrd, doth in most part I beleve of all these pointes so content men, as if the rest of our story of England were so done, we might well compare with Fraunce, Italy, or Germany in that behalfe.

The points he set out are in reality an outline of humanistic theory and are so important that, though I am keeping Ascham's words, I am separating them from their enveloping text for emphasis:

1) to write nothyng false,
2) to be bold to say any truth,
3) to marke diligently the causes, counsels, actes and issues in all great attemptes,
4) of euery issue, to note some generall lesson of wisedome and warines, for lyke matters in time to come,
5) [to use diligence] to kepyng truly the order of tyme,
6) [to describe] lyvely, both the site of places and the nature of persons not onely for the outward shape of the body: but also for the inward disposition of the mynde.

And Ascham added concerning the appropriate style:

[20]Fueter, *op. cit.*, pp. 198-99.

The stile must be alwayes playne and open: yet sometime higher and lower as matters do ryse and fall: for if proper and naturall wordes, in well joyned sentences do lyvely expresse the matter, be it troublesome, quyet, angry or pleasant, a man shal thinck not to be readyng but present in doyng of the same.[21]

More's adherence to the truth and the time order is not of so much interest here as is his realizing of the other ideals set down by Ascham. He did record, not merely deeds, but also all the causes, counsels, acts, and issues from which they resulted; his long analysis of Richard's choice of exactly the right moment to seize the crown is a case in point.[22] His history is full of general lessons "for lyke matters in time to come." Thus, after describing Richard's coronation, he moralizes: "And as the thing evil got is never well kept, through all the time of his reign never ceased there cruel death and slaughter, till his own destruction ended it." And after telling of the murder of the two little princes, he comments that "God never gave this world a more notable example, neither in what unsurety standeth this worldly weal, or what mischief worketh the proud enterprises of an high heart, or finally, what wretched end ensueth such dispiteous cruelty."

He described the physical appearance of his characters so that they could walk on the stage, and the "inward disposition of the mind" so vividly that it could be dramatized. I quote one brief passage by way of illustration, the passage describing Richard after the murder of the princes:

For I have heard by credible report, of such as were secret with his chamberers, that after this abominable deed done, he never had quiet in his mind, he never thought himself sure: where he went abroad, his eyes whirled about, his body privily fenced, his hand ever on his dagger, his countenance and manner like one always ready to strike again; he took ill rest o' nights, lay long waking and musing,

[21]"R. Ascham to John Asteley" prefixed to Ascham's *Report and Discourse . . . of the Affaires and State of Germany* (London, 1570?). Written in response to a letter from Asteley dated October, 1552.

[22]Sir Thomas More, *The English Works*, ed. W. E. Campbell (London and New York, 1927-1931), I, 433.

sore wearied with care and watch, rather slumbered than slept, troubled with fearful dreams, suddenly sometime started up, leaped out of his bed and ran about the chamber, so was his restless heart continually tossed and tumbled with the tedious impression and stormy remembrance of his abominable deed.[23]

Furthermore, like Thucydides, he made his characters speak real speeches as though recorded by a stenographer at the time. This habit, too, contributed to the dramatic quality of the writing and made the transition from narrative to dramatic presentation easier.

The effect of More's *Richard* upon the chronicles which we have specially to consider as the sources of Shakespeare's historical plays can scarcely be overestimated. As is well known, it was first published with Hardyng's *Chronicle* in 1543 as a part of the extension by Richard Grafton derived from "diverse and sondry autours that have writen of the affaires of Englande."[24] Grafton finished out the story of Richard in the same general style that More had used. But Grafton showed the influence of the Reformation in putting in God as more conspicuously the stage manager of the worldly events he recorded. More wrote like a humanist, though like a Christian humanist. Grafton wrote like a Reformation humanist.

More's work was printed for the second time though still with certain inaccuracies in the chronicle of Edward Halle, posthumously issued by Richard Grafton in 1548,[25] and it lived on in the succeeding chronicles which built one upon another.

Halle's history is organized about the lives and reigns of eight kings, seen in the table of contents:

[23]*Ibid.*, pp. 451-52.

[24]The collations of the various texts of More's history are to be found in the Campbell edition, the work of W. A. G. Doyle-Davidson, pp. 229-317. R. W. Chambers in an essay on "The Authorship of the 'History of Richard III'" (pp. 24-53) gives an account of the publication of the various editions.

[25]Concerning the supposed 1542 edition of Halle's work and the general history of the publishing of the chronicle, see A. F. Pollard, "Edward Hall's Will and Chronicle," in the *Bulletin of the Institute for Historical Research*, IX (1932), 171-77.

An introduction into the devision of the two houses of Lancastre and Yorke.
  i. The unquiet tyme of kyng Henry the fowerth,
  ii. The victorious actes of kyng Henry the v.
  iii. The troubleous season of kyng Henry the vi.
  iiii. The prosperous reigne of kyng Edward the iiii.
  v. The pitifull life of kyng Edward the v.
  vi. The tragicall doynges of kyng Richard the iii.
  vii. The politike goveraunce of kyng Henry the vii.
  viii. The triumphant reigne of king Henry the viii.

His chronicle was undoubtedly written to serve the political purposes of Henry VIII, being directed to teaching political lessons in general and one imperative lesson in particular, the destruction that follows rebellion and civil dissension in a realm. Dr. W. Gordon Zeeveld would, indeed, place it as the most ambitious of the inspired works of propaganda of the first half of the sixteenth century, "whose purpose was to scotch such dormant subversive elements in the kingdom as dared to raise their heads."[26] The very title of Halle's work is political:

The Union of the Two Noble and Illustre Famelies of Lancastre and Yorke, beeyng long in continual discension for the croune of this noble realme, with all the actes done in bothe the tymes of the Princes, bothe of the one linage and of the other, beginnyng at the tyme of kyng Henry the fowerth, the first aucthor of this devision, and so successively proceadyng to the reigne of the high and prudent prince kyng Henry the eight, the undubitate flower and very heir of both the sayd linages.

His theme is sounded in the opening passage:

What mischiefe hath insurged in realmes by intestine devision, what depopulacion hath ensued in countries by civill discencion, what detestable murder hath been committed in citees by seperate faccions, and what calamitee hath ensued in famous regions by domestical discord and unnaturall controversy: Rome hath felt, Italy can testifie, Fraunce can bere witnes, Beame can tell, Scotlande maie write, Denmarke can shewe, and especially this noble realme of Englande can apparantly declare and make demonstracion.

[26]"Richard Morison, Official Apologist for Henry VIII," *PMLA*, LV (1940), 413 and note 52.

And as he speaks of the particular horror of the wars caused by the dissension between the houses of York and Lancaster, he adds pertinently:

> For what noble man liveth at this date, or what gentleman of any auncient stocke or progeny is clere, whose linage hath not ben infested and plaged with this unnaturall devision.

Halle's dedication of his work to the king showed him a master of the familiar humanistic doctrines concerning history, as do the many stock-in-trade defenses of history or historical method scattered throughout his work. He quoted Cicero when he once more defined history as "the witnesses of tymes, the light of trueth, and the life of memory."[27] He saw history as the only means of fighting "the cancard enemie," "the suckyng serpent," "the dedly darte," "the defacer"—Oblivion.[28] Only Gildas and Geoffrey of Monmouth had rescued England's ancient history, and after Froissart, who ended his history at the beginning of the reign of Henry IV, Halle says, no one but Fabyan and "one without name, which wrote the common English Chronicle," had written in the English language of the seven kings who followed Richard II. Of these two later writers he comments that they were "men worthy to be praysed for their diligence, but farre shotyng wide from the butte of an historie."

With complete disregard of the anachronism involved in his doing so, the ghost of the Earl of Worcester is made to comment in the *Mirror for Magistrates* upon the relative merits of Fabyan and Halle, showing what "the butte of an historie" should be:

> Unfruytfull Fabyan folowed the face
> Of time and dedes, but let the causes slip:
> Whych Hall hath added, but with double grace,
> For feare I think least trouble might him trip: . . .[29]

The same prophetic ghost forecast the banning of Halle's work. In the history of sixteenth-century history writing in England,

---

[27] Fols. ccli and cclii of the section on Henry VIII.
[28] In the dedication to Edward VI.
[29] *The Mirror for Magistrates,* ed. L. B. Campbell (Cambridge, 1938), p. 198.

Halle is actually of great importance for three reasons. First, though he is proved by modern scholars to have incorporated in his work many facts and views taken from Vergil, often merely acting as translator,[30] he was still the first of the sixteenth-century writers to write in English in the fashion of the Renaissance a history of England covering a considerable period of time. Like Vergil, whose work he used, and like More, whose *Richard III* he incorporated as a whole in his chronicle, he described the physical appearance of men and places, he analyzed psychological conflicts and their issues, he probed for the causes of events, he emphasized the end of the action and the manner of a man's death as revealing the judgment finally imposed in a moral universe.

Second, he wrote with an avowed political aim, and like both Vergil and More, he made the lessons drawn from history both explicit and capable of general application. Pre-eminent, as I have said, was the lesson of the danger to a nation when civil discord and rebellion were allowed to raise their ugly heads.

Finally, and of special interest in this study, Halle presented a period of English history, from the beginning of the trouble between Richard II and Henry Bolingbroke to the end of the conflict between the houses of York and Lancaster, which was to be the period most dealt with in the literature of the time. The *Mirror for Magistrates* was confessedly based primarily upon Halle, and it moralized his history into its many tragedies. Daniel dealt with this period in his *Civil Wars*, and there were many dramas and poems written about it, because its lessons were pertinent in Tudor times. But above all, Shakespeare chose to write his greatest historical plays about this period, and he opened his *Richard II* at the exact point at which Halle begins his history. Because of the way in which one of the English chroniclers incorporated the work of another, only to be himself used by the next, it is impossible to distinguish the indebtedness of poets and dramatists to specific historians, but the debt of literary men of the English Renaissance to Halle was very great.

[30] See Note 8 above.

It was Richard Grafton, famous above all for the large part he played in making the Bible in English accessible to his countrymen, who incorporated More's life of Richard III in his extension of Hardyng's chronicle and printed both works for the first time. It was Grafton who published Halle's chronicle after the author's death. Quite logically a man who had salvaged so much historical writing began to compile from "sundry authors" his own account of English history. A preliminary work was published in 1562 with the title of *An Abridgement of the Chronicles of England*, and it was dedicated to Lord Robert Dudley, afterward the Earl of Leicester, as one who had prepared himself for a part in government by reading histories. Grafton recited to his patron the traditional praises of history, reaching his climax with the Reformation addition: "But the principall commoditie in the highest respecte is the settynge foorth of the course of Godds doinges."

This preliminary chronicle was followed in 1565 by *A Manuell of the Chronicles of England* and in 1568 and 1569 by his great work,[31] the two-volume history of the world which served to orient England's history, as is indicated in the title:

A Chronicle at Large and Meere History of the Affayres of England and Kinges of the Same, deduced from the creation of the worlde, unto the first habitation of this islande: and so by contynuance unto the first yere of the reigne of our most deere and sovereigne lady Queene Elizabeth: collected out of sundry aucthours, whose names are expressed in the next page.

The dedication to Cecil includes interesting criticism of historical writing in England:

For among so many writers, there hath yet none to my knowledge, published any full, playne and meere Englishe historie. For some of them of purpose meaning to write short notes in maner of Annales, commonly called Abridgementes, rather touch the tymes when things were done, then declare the maner of the doyngs, leaving thereby some necessitie of larger explication, and referring the de-

---

[31]The second volume is dated 1568, the first 1569. It is probable that the STC 12146 is not a separate edition of the whole work but the first edition of the second volume.

sirous Reader to a further serch and study. Other have dealt but with the reignes of a few kings, and yet thereof have made long bookes, with many tedious disgressions, obscure descriptions and frivolous dilations: which forme of writing if it should not be reformed, coulde not in the whole be folowed without pestering the Reader with importable Volumes. Other have intermyngled the affaires of other foreyne Nations with the matters of Englande, yea, even where the one had no concurrencie or dependaunce of the other.

As might be expected, the man responsible for the publication of the work of More and Halle followed their way of writing history, though his plan was much larger. He makes history theatrical. He analyzes and describes. He universalizes particular events by pointing out their significance. He relates cause and effect. He sees history, however, even more definitely as exhibiting the judgments of God. Yet he does not fail to quote Cicero and to show his familiarity with humanistic theory and practice in writing history.

Grafton's importance as a source for Shakespeare has not yet been adequately recognized, I think, but it is impossible here to take time to prove it, for we must pass on to the one chronicler universally accepted as having furnished Shakespeare with much of the material for his history plays. The chronicles of England, Scotland, and Ireland which are known as Holinshed's *Chronicles* were, however, actually a group project arranged by the printer Reginald Wolfe, who had inherited much of Leland's material. Wolfe died in 1573, and Holinshed became what I suppose we would call the co-ordinator.[32] The first edition was published in 1577, a second edition enlarged and continued in 1587. It is to this second edition that Shakespeare seems to have been most indebted. There are seven separate dedications of separate parts of the three volumes, but only one of them approaches the dignity of an *ars historica*, that of John Hooker to Sir Walter Raleigh.[33] Hooker began in the orthodox fashion:

[32]See Holinshed's dedication to Cecil of the 1577 edition, which became the dedication to Volume III in the 1587 edition.

[33]This dedication is prefixed to the Irish history in *The First and Second Volumes of Chronicles*.

Among all the infinit good blessings, . . . I thinke none more expedient and necessairie, than the use and knowledge of histories and chronicles: which are the most assured registers of the innumerable benefits and commodities, which have and dailie doo grow to the church of God, and to the civill goverment throughout all nations.

He discoursed of the antiquity of history; of its pre-eminence in teaching what is to come by lessons from the past as witnessed by Thucydides, Cicero, Augustine, Melanchthon, and others. He proclaimed that English kings as well as ancient rulers like Alexander and Caesar were interested in the preservation of records and added pridefully:

No realme, no nation, no state, nor commonwealth throughout all Europa, can yeeld more nor so manie profitable lawes, directions, rules, examples and discourses, either in matters of religion, or of civill government, or of martiall affairs, than doo the histories of this little Isle of Britaine or England.

But so much could not be said for Ireland with whose affairs he had been loath to meddle, until upon deeper consideration,

I began . . . to behold the too great and woonderous workes of God, both of his severe judgement against traitors, rebels, and disobedient; and of his mercie and loving kindnesse upon the obedient and dutifull. Whereof, though there be infinite examples both in the sacred histories and humane chronicles: yet I find none more apparent and effectuall, nor more fit for us, and for this our time and age, than the histories of our owne nation, which yeeld unto us most infinite examples, how yoong princes rebelling against the kings their fathers, noble men against their sovereignes, and the commons against the kings and rulers, some by the mightie hand of God swallowed up in the seas, some devoured with the sword, some by martiall and some by civill lawes executed to death; and few or none which have escaped unpunished.

Holinshed himself in dedicating his chronicle to Cecil was content to recount the history of the whole project, and in addressing the readers to explain his methods and apologize for his limitations. One fact concerning his method should, however, be specially noted. Where his authorities disagreed, he said, he tried to give their varying accounts and let the reader choose between them rather than himself to select which was most trustworthy. In the course of his work, if not in any prefatory essay, nevertheless, Holinshed did insert from time to time passages in the contemporary vein of historical theory. But of much more significance than any of the numerous inserted praises of history is Holinshed's demonstration of the precepts of Renaissance historiography. In his text and in his eye-catching marginal comments he made clear his understanding of cause and effect in human actions and of the vengeance exacted by God for sin, working out with arithmetical accuracy the relation of each sin to the divine vengeance. Thus when Shakespeare read the history of Richard III in Holinshed, he found not only in the text but also in the marginal comment the morals with which Holinshed adorned the tale, such morals as "The Just judgement of God severalie revenging the murther of the innocent princes upon the malefactors," and "The outward and inward troubles of tyrants by means of a grudging conscience."

At the end of the account of the reign of each king, Holinshed sums up his character and his achievements. To read these summaries is to see the heart of Holinshed's political philosophy and to discover how definitely it represented Tudor thinking. By way of illustration I quote first from the judgment passed on Richard II:

His chance verelie was greatlie infortunate, which fell into such calamitie, that he tooke it for the best waie he could devise to renounce his kingdome, for the which mortall men are accustomed to hazard all they have to atteine thereunto. But such misfortune (or the like) oftentimes falleth unto those princes, which when they are aloft, cast no doubt for perils that maie follow. He was prodigall, ambitious, and much given to the pleasure of the bodie. . . . How then could it continue prosperouslie with this king? against whom for the fowle enormities wherewith his life was defamed, the wrath of God was whetted and tooke so sharpe an edge, that the same did shred him off from the scepter of his kingdome, and gave him a full cup of affliction to drinke: as he had doone to other kings his predecessors, by whose example he might have taken warning. For it is an heavie case when God thundereth out his reall arguments either upon prince or people.[34]

In spite of this common judgment on Richard II, however, Holinshed, while acknowledging the young king's dissolute living and his choice of advisers in whom the people did not have confidence, blamed both commons and nobles for their ingratitude toward him. And of Bolingbroke, whom he represents as intent on avenging the death of the Duke of Gloucester, he says that "he wanted moderation and loialtie in his dooings, for the which both he himselfe and his lineall race were scourged afterwards, as a due punishment unto rebellious subjects."[35]

When he comes to sum up the life of Henry IV in his turn, Holinshed writes:

But yet to speake a truth, by his proceedings, after he had atteined to the crowne, what with such taxes, tallages, subsidies, and exactions as he was constreined to charge the people with; and what by punishing such as mooved with disdeine to see him usurpe the crowne (contrarie to the oth taken at his entring into this land, upon his returne from exile) did at sundrie times rebell against him, he wan himselfe more hatred, than in all his life (if it had beene longer by manie yeares than it was) had beene possible for him to have weeded out and remooved. And yet doubtlesse, woorthie were his subjects to tast of that bitter cup, sithens they were so readie to joine and clappe hands with him, for the deposing of their rightfull and naturall prince king Richard, . . .[36]

The relation of Shakespeare to Holinshed is so well established that it is important to recognize Holinshed's conformity to the pattern of historical writing which had been established during the century and to consider how impossible it would have been for Shakespeare to read Halle and Grafton and Holinshed or any of the other historians of the period in the manner of a modern historian looking for facts and ignoring all the general significance of the facts. It was to show the significance of the facts and to establish by them general moral and more especially general political laws that the historians were writing.

[34]*Op. cit.*, III, 507-8.
[35]*Ibid.*
[36]*Ibid.*, III, 541.

John Stow is another important figure in the annals of historical writing in sixteenth-century England, but his great work, *A Survay of London*, is outside our immediate field of interest. Stow assisted in the salvaging of several of the older chronicles of England and helped many of his contemporaries in compiling their historical works. He bought part of Leland's papers after Reginald Wolfe's death and contributed by the loan of books and papers to the continuation of Wolfe's work under Holinshed. He became a rival to Grafton when he published his *Summarie of English Chronicles* in 1565, and the charges and counter-charges which the two historians exchanged have long contributed their dash of acrimony to literary gossip.[37] The *Summarie* was expanded in 1580 to become *The Chronicles of England*, and the *Chronicles* were in turn recast and enlarged to become *The Annales of England* in 1592. This is the work which Shakespeare may have used. In spite of its basic organization as annals, it was written as a connected narrative in the humanistic tradition. And Stow offers the usual praises of history. History gives immortality to men and events worthy of remembrance. It records "wise handling of weightie affaires, diligently to be marked and aptly to be applied." It encourages the nobility to noble feats, discourages unnatural subjects from "wicked treasons, pernitious rebellions, and damnable doctrines." Professor Conyers Read comments interestingly on Stow's close connection with the government that "It might even be asserted that the Government made use of his various *Chronicles* in something like the way in which modern governments make use of the press to influence public opinion."[38] Like his predecessors Stow apparently actually tried to make his history serve the purposes which he set forth in theory as its proper objectives.

One of the friends of Stow who profited from his possession of Leland's papers was William Camden, but Camden's great

[37]The authoritative account of Stow is found in C. L. Kingsford's introduction to his edition of *A Survay of London* (Oxford, 1908), especially pp. ix-xxv.

[38]In *Mr. Secretary Walsingham and the Policy of Queen Elizabeth* (Cambridge, Mass., 1925), III, 455.

sixteenth-century work, the *Britannia*, like Stow's *Survay* lies outside our field of interest here. His *Annales*, first published in 1615, was also written in Latin and spoke English for the first time when it was translated by Abraham Darcie in 1625 from a French translation of the Latin original. It covered only the years of Elizabeth's reign, and it was organized, as its title indicates, to give a year-by-year account. Nevertheless it was written as a continuous narrative though in a plain, unrhetorical style, and it has continued to furnish all students of the Elizabethan times a basic knowledge of people and events.

Camden has been held in repute by modern historians because of the care which he gave to searching for facts and the impartiality with which he recorded them. In his preface he indicates his sources: records of the privy council, letters from ambassadors, parliamentary records, acts and statutes and proclamations, and above all the papers preserved by William Cecil, Lord Burghley. But in spite of his quite modern interest in sources, Camden declared history to be primarily concerned with matters military and political, and sometimes perforce ecclesiastical. The dignity of history, he said, demanded that it deal only with important events, but he added some "small things," and he did not fail to search out reasons and causes. Among histories, he explained,

That of Polybius pleaseth me exceedingly, If you take out of History WHY, HOW, To WHAT END, and WHAT IS DONE, and whether the Actions answer the intents, that that remaines is rather a mocking than an instruction; and for the present may please, but will never profit Posteritie.

Camden is in theory and purpose a Renaissance historian, and his first translator offers a preface so clearly summarizing the tradition that I quote here the first paragraph by way of emphasizing the persistence of that theory into the seventeenth century:

Learned Cicero, that King of Oratorie, who telleth us, that the course of this mutable life is inconstant, and the worldly fortunes of mortals truely vaine and variable, doth very eloquently commend History, calling it The witnesse of times; intimating, that wee could not attaine to the knowledge of severall actions, done at sundry seasons, but by her helpe, and how much the science of Histories prófits, is proved, in regard they are the handmaids to Prudence and Wisdome, the which may be easily and truly purchased out of the deeds and examples of others, there written. How much it conduceth to the good governement of Common-wealths to have the examples of Councels before our eyes, it appeareth, in regard of the general respect the wisest men have had to them. Neither are true Histories a little commodious for shunning of horrible alterations and calamities; for they recite the examples of all times, for the punishments of Seditions, Treasons, and such other abominable Crimes, the which escape not unpunisht, no not in this life: Out of which examples we may collect most wholesome instructions, for the good using of our both private and publike Offices, that such Evils may be shunned in us, which were punished in others; the which is true wisedome, according to that in the Proverbe:

> Other mens harmes
> are wise-mens armes.[39]

Reference has already been made in an earlier chapter to Francis Bacon's theories of history, but Bacon was also a practising historian. His famous *Historie of the Raigne of King Henry the Seventh* was not published until 1622, after the death of Shakespeare, and hence falls outside the limit arbitrarily set for this study. But Spedding printed from a Harleian manuscript an earlier work undertaken during the reign of Elizabeth but left incomplete, *The History of the Reigns of K. Henry the VIII, K. Edward, Q. Mary, and part of Q. Elizabeth.*[40] Here Bacon has explained the basis of his choice of a period about which to write. He found no adequate accounts of the Tudor reigns, the records of the period were available, and there were no times which had produced greater actions, "nor more worthy to be delivered to the ages hereafter." For, he argued, the rehearsal of wars and conquests does not make "profitable and instructive history":

[39]Abraham Darcie in the 1625 translation.

[40]Francis Bacon, *Works*, ed. J. Spedding, R. L. Ellis, and D. D. Heath (Boston, 1900), XI, 32 *et seq.* It had been printed inaccurately, Spedding noted, in the *Cabala* (1663 ed., pp. 254-56).

but rather times refined in policies and industries, new and rare
variety of accidents and alterations, equal and just encounters of
state and state in forces and of prince and prince in sufficiency, . . .[41]

Further, he found in this period from Henry VIII to Elizabeth
an incomparable variety, of a king raised to an absolute sovereign, a minor king, a queen married to a foreigner, and finally
a queen who ruled without marriage and without the help of
any powerful kinsman, and he continued:

Besides there have not wanted examples within the compass of the
same times neither of an usurpation, nor of rebellions under heads
of greatness, nor of commotions merely popular, nor of sundry desperate conspiracies (an unwonted thing in hereditary monarchies),
nor of foreign wars of all sorts; invasive, repulsive of invasion, open
and declared, covert and underhand, by sea, by land, Scottish,
French, Spanish, succors, protections, new and extraordinary kinds
of confederacies with subjects.[42]

Much of this argument was repeated in his later work, and both
Schlegel and Goethe seem to have adopted its principles as the
basis for their praise of English history as peculiarly adapted to
universal teaching. But my concern here is merely to note in
passing the similarity of Bacon's motive for choosing the Tudor
period and that of Halle and others for choosing the period of
the Wars of the Roses, for instance. History continues to be
considered useful as a political mirror.[43]

The culminating document of Renaissance historiography
in England was Sir Walter Raleigh's great preface to his *History
of the World*, published in 1614, only two years before the death
of Shakespeare.[44] In this preface Raleigh did for historiography

[41]*Op. cit.*, p. 34.

[42]*Ibid.*, p. 35.

[43]Both Fueter and Dean comment on Bacon as different from those that
preceded him, making him a political historian veering to the Florentine school.
In purpose he seems to me no more political than his predecessors.

[44]It should be noted that Raleigh apparently intended to do much as Grafton
did, to orient the history of England to the history of the world. Another
work, *Tubus Historicus*, published in 1636, indicated his interest in the Reformation type of universal history.

what Sidney did for literary criticism in his *Defence of Poesie*. He gathered all the theories of the Renaissance and the Reformation into a new whole, and as a great artist he fashioned a masterpiece which superseded all that went before. To see the great tradition in its fullest and most inspired expression it is necessary only to read this one document; but to understand the preface as the culmination of a tradition and not as the personal creation of one man it is necessary to read it in the light of what had gone before.

The very title page indicates the completeness with which it summarizes its two-fold inheritance. The most quoted passage in Renaissance historiography, Cicero's description of history, is here translated into visual symbolism. The figure of History as *Magistra Vitae*, even as she tramples upon *Mors* and *Oblivio*, supports a globe which is touched on one side by a winged and laurel-wreathed *Fama Bona*, and on the other by a winged but foully-spotted *Fama Mala*. To the left of the central figure of History is *Experientia* between the pillars of *Testis Temporum* and *Nuncia Vetustatis;* to her right is a naked *Veritas* between the pillars of *Lux Veritatis* and *Vita Memoriae*. But over all is the eye of *Providentia*, admitting the Christian interpretation of history.

The explanatory poem, said to be by Ben Jonson, interprets the symbolism:

> From *Death* and darke *Oblivion* (neere the same)
> The *Mistresse of Mans life*, grave Historie,
> Raising the *World* to good, or *Evill* fame,
> Doth vindicate it to Æternitie.
>
> *High Providence* would so: that nor the good
> Might be defrauded, nor the Great secur'd
> But both might know their wayes are understood,
> And the reward, and punishment assur'd.
>
> This makes, that lighted by the beamie hand
> Of Truth, which searcheth the most hidden springs,
> And guided by *Experience*, whose streight wand
> Doth mete, whose *Line* doth sound the depth of things:

> Shee chearefully supporteth what shee reares;
> Assisted by no strengths, but are her owne,
> Some note of which each varied *Pillar* beares,
> By which as proper titles she is knowne,
>
> *Times witnesse, Herald of Antiquitie,*
> *The light of Truth, and life of Memorie.*

The preface is a very personal one, written out of the bitterness and disillusion, the patience and philosophic endurance of Raleigh's years in prison. But the lessons of history, the platitudes of historiography, were living realities to Raleigh, and he clothed them in the impassioned language of deep conviction. The first of the preface repeats the teachings of the title page. It rehearses the claims of history to being the oldest kind of learning and the true victor over time, so that "wee may gather out of History a policy no lesse wise than eternall; by the comparison and application of other mens fore-passed miseries, with our owne like errours and ill deservings." In history "the infinite eye and wisedome of GOD doth pierce through all our pretences," and makes our own consciences our accusers. History declares the judgments of God, but it is impossible to repeat all the infinite examples of God's justice, and history deals only with the great of the earth:

The markes, set on private men, are with their bodies cast into the earth; and their fortunes, written onely in the memories of those that lived with them: so as they who succeed, and have not seen the fall of others, doe not feare their owne faults. GODS judgments upon the greater and greatest, have beene left to posterity; first, by those happy hands which the Holy Ghost hath guided; and secondly, by their vertue, who have gathered the acts and ends of men, mighty and remarkeable in the world.

"But the judgementes of GOD," Raleigh said, "are forever unchangeable; neither is he wearied by the long processe of time, and won to give his blessing in one age to that which he hath cursed in another." And in order to prove the eternal and universal sameness of God's judgments he turns to a review of the history of the various nations. His summary of the history of

England is, because of its very compactness and brevity, the clearest demonstration of the way in which the theories of historiography may be applied and the most explicit working out of history as presenting the judgments of God, that the English Renaissance produced. I propose, then, to follow in some detail his account of that period of English history with which Shakespeare was most concerned.

Raleigh begins with Henry I, but I pass on to his discussion of the way in which the cruelty of Edward III was paid for by his grandchild, Richard II:

> For Richard the second . . . alwaies tooke him-selfe for over-wise, to bee taught by examples. The Earles of *Huntington* and *Kent*, *Montague* and *Spencer*, who thought themselves as great polititians in those daies, as others have done in these: hoping to please the King, and to secure themselves, by the Murder of *Gloucester;* died soone after, with many other their adherents, by the like violent hands; and farre more shamefully then did that Duke. And as for the King him-selfe (who in regard of many deedes, unworthy of his Greatnesse, cannot bee excused, as the disavowing him-selfe by breach of Faith, Charters, Pardons, and Patents) He was in the Prime of his youth deposed; and murdered by his Cosen-germane and vassal, *Henry* of *Lancaster;* afterwards *Henry* the fourth.

But God's vengeance was poured upon Henry IV in his turn, so that his reign was troubled, and his grandchild, Henry VI, paid the full price:

> This King, whose Title was weake, and his obtaining the Crowne traiterous: who brake Faith with the Lordes at his landing, protesting to intend only the recoverie of his proper Inheritance; brake faith with *Richard* himselfe; and brake Faith with all the Kingdome in Parliament, to whom he swore that the deposed King should live. After that he had enjoyed the Realme some few yeares, and in that time had beene set upon on all sides by his Subjects, and never free from conspiracies and rebellions; he saw (if Soules immortall see . . .) his Grand-childe *Henrie* the sixt, and his Sonne the Prince, suddenly, and without mercy, murdered; the possession of the Crowne (for which he had caused so much blood to bee powred out) transferred from his race; and by the Issues of his Enemies worne and enjoyed: . . .

Now for *Henrie* the sixt, upon whom the great storme of his Grandfathers greevous faults fell, as it formerly had done upon *Richard* the Grand-childe of *Edward*: ... Hee drew on himselfe and this Kingdome the greatest joynt-losse and dishonor that ever it sustained since the *Norman* Conquest.

But the new sovereigns of the House of York only brought the divine vengeance upon themselves through their sins when they followed the House of Lancaster, for Edward IV allowed the slaughter of Henry VI's son, Prince Edward, and the execution of his own brother, Clarence. In instructing Richard, Duke of Gloucester, to kill his predecessor, Henry VI, Edward taught him how to kill his successors, the young princes. And this Richard, "the greatest Maister in mischiefe of all that forewent him," was brought to a shameful end, the third and last of the House of York to reign:

And what successe had *Richard* himselfe after all these mischefes and Murders, policies, and counter-policies to Christian religion: and after such time, as with a most mercilesse hand hee had pressed out the breath of his Nephews and Naturall Lords; other than the prosperity of so short a life, as it tooke end, ere himselfe could well looke over and discerne it? the great outcrie of innocent bloud, obtayning at GODS hands the effusion of his; who became a spectacle of shame and dishonor, both to his friends and enemies.

It is in rehearsing the judgment of God upon the Tudors, however, that Raleigh is most interesting, for he makes the fate of the House of Tudor another link in the terrible chain of crime and punishment, and shows the eternal justice executed on the Tudors as the same which determined that the houses of Lancaster and York perish. In cutting off Richard III, Henry VII "was therein (No doubt) the immediate instrument of GODS justice," yet

the taking off, of *Stanles* head, who set the Crowne on his, and the deathe of the young *Earle* of *Warwick*, sonne of *George* D. of *Clarence*, Shews, as the successe also did, that he held somewhat of the errors of his Ancestors, for his possession in the first line ended in his grand children, as that of *Edward* the third and *Henry* the fourth had done.

Upon Henry VIII Raleigh heaped his wrath, saying that "if all the pictures and Patternes of a mercilesse Prince were lost in the world, they might all againe be painted to the life, out of the story of this King." And at the end "it pleased GOD to take away all his owne, without increase," so that the crown has now descended to one whom Henry had cut off from consideration. Of this living king, James I of England, Raleigh affirms that he received the crown at God's hand, and that he stayed the time of putting it on in spite of provocation to hasten that time.

Though Raleigh denied that he wrote of the eldest times in order to "taxe the vices of those that are yet living, in their persons that are long since dead," he took pains in his preface to review English history and to point out the repetition of the historical pattern which began with the seizing of a throne and which ended with its loss by the third heir or the third generation. The throne that Edward III gained, his grandson Richard II lost; the throne that Henry IV gained, his grandson Henry VI lost; the throne that Edward IV gained, the third heir lost; the throne that Henry VII gained passed from the Tudors with the death of his grandchild Elizabeth. Such was the pattern of God's vengeance worked out in detail, but it was a pattern which had been the common theme of history from Hardyng onward. Whether Raleigh used the past to tax the vices of the present, at least he showed that the Tudors were judged by the same unchangeable justice of God as were their predecessors.

CHAPTER IX

HISTORY VERSUS POETRY IN RENAISSANCE ENGLAND

IN ORDER to understand the place of history in the English Renaissance we must turn to the attacks made upon poetry[1] and especially secular poetry, first by the adherents of the Reformation and later by the Puritans, for the attackers of poetry were the defenders of history. And it must be remembered that *poetry* was a more inclusive term then than now, covering drama and much of that which we call creative literature.[2] These attacks upon poetry are not today so well known as are the defenses of poetry and particularly the great defense offered by Sidney. Nevertheless, the defenses of poetry cannot be fully comprehended unless we remind ourselves that defense is always organized to resist attack.

In the intellectual conflicts of men, as well as in their physical conflicts, the issues over which any battle is fought are to a great extent determined by the forces which attack, and the defense of poetry in the Renaissance was largely based upon Aristotle's *Poetics*, which was framed about the issues raised by Plato in his attacks upon the arts of imitation, particularly in the tenth

---

[1]On this subject see J. E. Spingarn, *A History of Literary Criticism in the Renaissance* (New York, 1899), pp. 3-23.

[2]The clearest exposition of the term was given by Sidney in his *Defence of Poesie*, where he makes it clear that "it is not riming and versing that maketh a Poet . . . But it is that fayning notable images of vertues, vices, or what els, with that delightfull teaching, which must be the right describing note to know a Poet by: . . ." As is well known the two editions of the same work were published in 1595 under the alternate titles of *The Defence of Poesie* and *An Apology for Poetry*. Here and elsewhere I quote from G. Gregory Smith's reprint of the work in *Elizabethan Critical Essays* (Oxford, 1904), I, 150-207. See on this subject K. O. Myrick, *Sir Philip Sidney as a Literary Craftsman* (Cambridge, Mass., 1935), p. 118.

book of the *Republic*. Plato accused poetry, first, of being merely an imitation of an imitation of an idea and hence thrice removed from the truth. The poet he saw, not as the creator, but merely as the copier of a copy of an idea. To the poet, then, he ascribed the inferiority of an imitator and an imitator not of reality but of appearance. Second, he attacked poetry because it "feeds and waters the passions instead of drying them up," because its appeal is to the passions rather than to the reason. Thus the poet is also inferior in that he is concerned with the inferior or animal part of the soul. Aristotle's defense of poetry had of necessity to meet these two fundamental charges, and his *Poetics* did meet them, first, by explaining the nature of imitation, and second, by projecting his theory of catharsis which contended that the rousing of the passions by art was not destructive but rather eminently healthful in purging the forces of destruction.

Ironically, the arguments and the authority of the pagan Plato were incorporated in the early Reformation opposition to the arts as they were being fostered by the revival of pagan learning, and later into the Puritan attack upon poetry, especially upon drama; while the Aristotelian defense was developed into the basic premises of the ethical aesthetics expounded by such Christian apostles of the arts as Sidney. Reformers and Puritans, calling Plato and his Christian spokesman Saint Augustine to witness for them, attacked poetry primarily as lying and as licentious. Inevitably they defended history as true and as rational. With them history and philosophy (including Christian philosophy and theology) took precedence over poetry as teachers and guides to what was "useful to States and to human lives."

Literary criticism as it evolved during the sixteenth century was thus, by reason of the attacks upon poetry, preoccupied with the business of defending poetry as a moral teacher, though in its more ample documents it became involved in discussions of definitions, rules, and devices, which were primarily the business of rhetoric. Any consideration of literary criticism during the Renaissance must, therefore, recognize the compelling necessity which made it primarily a defender of poetry and only secondarily an expounder of techniques.

In considering the defense of poetry as a moral teacher, then, it must be remembered that the attack upon poetry was based upon the two fundamental charges: that it was only an imitation thrice removed from reality, and that it pandered to the passions. But Horace's familiar words, "By at once delighting and teaching the reader, the poet who mixes the sweet with the useful has everybody's approval," offered an opportunity to add a third charge, that the poison of poetry was the more dangerous because of the honey of the container. In Puritan terminology the charges meant that, as Stephen Gosson summarized them in his *Apologie of the Schoole of Abuse*, the "auncient Poetes are the fathers of lies, Pipes of vanitie, and Schooles of Abuse."[3]

Those who attacked poetry defended history upon the chosen issues. History dealt with truth rather than fiction; real people and real events were its material. Its appeal was to the reasonable soul of man, not to the passions of the animal soul. Truthfulness and impartiality were the prime requisites for the historian. Furthermore, history was the most ancient form of writing, they said; it was concerned with important events, public events; and it manifested the workings of divine law in the world.

This opposition between history and poetry is again and again emphasized in the many defenses of history, from some of which I have already quoted. Even those who were in no sense unaware of the excellence of poetry found history the more worthy. Thus Meredith Hanmer in dedicating the second edition of his translation of *The Auncient Ecclesiastical Histories* to the Earl of Leicester wrote on December 15, 1584:

Wherefore (my good Lord) seeing that as *Plato* sayeth running wittes are delighted with poëtrie, as *Aristotle* writeth, effeminate persons are ravished with musicke, and as *Socrates* telleth us histories agree beste with staide heades: I present unto your honour these histories agreeing very well with your disposition, and being the fruites of my travell and studie.

---

[3]Printed with *The Ephemerides of Phialo* (London, 1579). Reprinted with *The Schoole of Abuse* in Arber's English Reprints (London, 1869). The quotation is given on Cicero's authority.

Hanmer adds that whereas at the court of Elizabeth "the Christian is no rare Phoenix, the godly is no blackeswanne," yet

Many now adayes had rather reade the Dial of Princes, where there is much good matter: the Monke of Burie, full of good stories; the tales of Chaucer, where there is excellent wit, great reading and good decorum observed: the life of *Marcus Aurelius*, where there are many good Morall preceptes: the familiar and golden Epistles of *Antonie Gwevarra*, where there is both golden wit and good penning: the stories of King *Arthur*: the monstrous fables of *Garagantua*: the Pallace of pleasure, though there follow never so much displeasure after: Reinard the Fox: *Bevis* of Hampton: the hundred mery tales: *Skoggan*: *Fortunatus*: with many other infortunate treatises and amorous toies written in English, Latine, Frenche, Italian, Spanishe, . . .

The foundations of the attack upon poetry were carefully rebuilt in a work first published in England in 1569 and then again in 1575, *Henrie Cornelius Agrippa, Of the Vanitie and Uncertaintie of Artes and Sciences, Englished by Ja. San. Gent.*, and dedicated to Thomas Duke of Norfolk. Sanford's address to the reader tended to compromise with the opposition by affirming that all learning, like a diseased body, is not to be cast off but made well again. The author of the work showed no such tendency to compromise, however. His chapter "Of Poetrie" declares without equivocation:

Poetrie, as *Quintilian* writeth, is an other parte of Grammar, not a little prowde in this thinge onlie, that in times paste, the *Theaters*, and *Ampitheaters*, the goodliest buildings of men, were erected not by Philosophers, not by Lawiers, . . . but with exceding great expenses, by the fables of Poetes, an Arte, that was devised to no other ende, but to please the eares of foolishe men, with wanton Rithmes, with measures, and weightinesse of sillables, and with a vaine jarringe of wordes, and to deceive mens mindes with the delectation of fables, and with fardels of lies. Wherefore, shee dothe deserve to be called the principall Authoure of lies, and the maintainer of perverse opinions: and as touchinge that whiche doth appertaine to furie, and drunckennesse, and to impudencie, and boldenesse, wee pardon it, what is he that is able to endure with a quiet minde, that unfeareful boldenesse of lieinge: for what place wil shee leave voide of pevishe trifles, and fables?[4]

Agrippa in a later chapter very interestingly describes the acting of stage players (which he classifies according to classic precedent as dancing) as "the Arte of Imitation, and Demonstration," paying tribute to its effectiveness:

This Arte dothe so much excell, that there neede no interpretours, for it dothe so aptly represent with pleasaunt gesture an olde man, a boye, a woman, a servaunt, a handmaide, a drunkarde, an angrie person, and the differences and passions of all persons, that also the beholder standinge aloofe of, not hearinge the Enterlude maie perceave the argument thereof by the onely motions of the Plaier.[5]

But in spite of the excellence of the players' representations, Agrippa frowned upon their art because of the unworthy objects which they presented to the public view.

As for history, Agrippa recognized its claims to pre-eminence:

An Historie is a declaration of thinges done with praise, or dispraise, whiche, as it were in a certaine lively picture, doth set before our eies the Counsailes, Deedes, and Endes of great things, the Enterprises of Princes, and Noble menne, with the order, and discription of times, and places: and therefore all menne, for the moste parte, calle it the Mistresse of life, and verie profitable to the framinge thereof, because that with the examples of many thinges, she dothe partelye enflame moste excellente menne, for the immortal glorie of praise and renowme, to all woorthye enterprises, partely, because for feare of perpetual infamie, shee letteth all wicked and naughtie men from misdooinge:[6]

but he added cynically, since some men prefer a great rather than a good fame, "this thinge oftentimes hathe chaunced otherwise." Furthermore, he suggests that even historians have written lies, such as those they have rehearsed concerning the beginning of the world, the universal flood, and the building of Rome. Even in regard to more nearly ascertainable facts, historians have

[4]*Op. cit.*, chap. iv.

[5]*Ibid.*, chap. xx.

[6]*Ibid.*, chap v.

had to depend on uncertain recitals of events which they did not witness. Finally, Agrippa says, "Historiographers enter-meddle lies with the truthe, for delectations sake," so that both wisdom and harm can come from histories.

Nashe made this attack of Agrippa the occasion for his well-known defense of poetry and particularly of plays, in spite of the fact that, according to McKerrow, Nashe was indebted to Agrippa's work for most of his display of classical learning.[7] He said of the work:

As there be those that rayle at all men, so there be those that raile at all Arts, as *Cornelius Agrippa, De vanitate scientiarum,* and a Treatise that I have seene in dispraise of learning, where he saieth, it is the corrupter of the simple, the schoolemaister of sin, the store-house of treacherie, the reviver of vices, and mother of cowardize; alledging many examples, how there was never man egregiously evill but he was a Scholler: . . .[8]

The popularity of the work was very great, and McKerrow called attention to the testimony afforded by Barnabe Riche's *Allarme to England* to the fad among would-be courtiers for studying Agrippa and other authors in order to be, as Riche said, "curious in their cavilling."

The most direct attack upon poetry as lying with which I am familiar was, however, that made in Coignet's work which was published in London in 1586 in a translation by Sir Edward Hoby as *Politique Discourses upon Trueth and Lying.*[9] The dedication was to Sir William Cecil, but the instigator of the work was Thomas Digges, who prefaces the translation with "A commendation of this worke," in which he advances the familiar

[7] Thomas Nashe, *Works,* ed. R. B. McKerrow (London, 1910), V, 118-19 and note. Other scattered references.

[8] Nashe, *Pierce Penilesse his Supplication to the Divell* in *op. cit.,* I, 191. Sir John Harington in his Preface to the translation of *Orlando Furioso* noted particularly Agrippa's attack on poetry as lying and made a long defense of it against this charge (G. G. Smith, *Elizabethan Critical Essays* [Oxford, 1937], II, 199-206).

[9] The author was Matthieu Coignet, but his name in the English translation is given as Sir Martyn Cognet. For an account of this work and of the French attack upon poets as liars see Robert J. Clements, "Pléiade Censure of Classic Mendacity," *PMLA,* LVI (1941), 633-44.

argument that princes and great estates are always in danger because of the lack of faithful friends who will tell them the truth,
being subject to the flatterers who surround them:

And therefore have the wise Philosophers admonished Emperours,
Kinges, Princes, and other great and honourable persons, that
swymme in the Seas of felicitie, by reading Histories and morall
politicke discourses to enforme themselves of such matters, as their
Parasites will not, and honest servantes or friendes many times dare
not reveale unto them, thereby to escape the dangerous downefall
of impendant calamities, whereunto the greatest Princes are much
more subject than the most inferiour private persons.

Three chapters of Coignet's work are of special interest here,
Chapters 17, 35, and 36. Chapter 17 argues on the conventional
lines the general proposition that "It is needfull to read histories,"
advancing the claim of history over that of philosophy, and inevitably quoting Cicero. But at the moment our concern is with
his argument that we should read nothing but histories:

And if that which *Plinie* writeth be true, that all that time which is
not imployed to the study or exercise of good things is lost: and
that which *Seneca* hath written, that they are all fooles, that in this
great scarcetie of time which is bestowed of them, learne but matters superfluous: Wee ought much to lament, that the desire which
the common sort have to histories, is an occasion that they give
themselves to fables and old wives tales, which is nought els but a
vaine delight without anie profite: whereas in histories, besides
pleasure, there is great learning, to teach us not to undertake uppon
the fiske and flying, either any warre that is not necessary, or any
quarrels, suites in law, or other affaires of importaunce.

Furthermore he emphasizes the dispassionate ideal of history, for
those historiographers "who have had least passions, and parti-
alitie," are those who will not "set out fables and lies."

Chapter 35,[10] devoted to the arguing of the bald assertion
"That lying hath made poets and painters to be blamed," is an
almost complete recapitulation of all the charges advanced by
the attackers of poetry. It begins:

[10]This chapter is reprinted in G. G. Smith, *op. cit.*, I, 341-44.

Plato wrote that Poetrie consisted in the cunning invention of fables, which are a false narration, resembling a true, and that therein they did often manifest sundrie follies of the gods; for this cause he banished and excluded them out of his common wealth, as men that mingled poyson with honie. Besides thorough their lying and wanton discourses they corrupt the manners of youth, and diminish that reverence which men ought to carrie towards their superiors, and the lawes of God, whom they faine to be replenished with passions and vice. And the principall ornament of their verses are tales made at pleasure, and foolish and disorderly subjectes, cleane disguising the trueth and historie, to the end they might the more delight; and for this cause have they bin thrust out of sundry cities. Among other, after that *Archilocus* came into *Sparta*, he was presently thrust out, as soon as they had understood, how he had written in his poems, that it was better to lose a mans weopens then his life, and forbad ever al such deceitful poesies. Hence grew the common proverb, that al Poets are lyers.

The association of "trueth and historie," the description of poetry as poison mingled with honey, the emphasis upon pleasure derived from poetry as suspect, the reiteration of Plato's contention that passion and vice are replenished by poetry are all familiar, but it must be noted that all other charges are made subordinate to the main thesis of the chapter that poetry is lying. Coignet would, however, except from his condemnation "poesies wherein much trueth and instruction is contained" and also "fables taken out of hystories, whereof, there maye growe some edifying."

Chapter 36 is dedicated to the consideration "Of backbyters, mockers, and evill speakers, and why the Comedians, stage players and Jugglers have been rejected." Coignet contends that plays "infecteth more the spirits, and wrappeth them in passions, then drunkennes it selfe," and the double charge that they are lying and licentious is duly amplified:

And for as much as comedies are compounded of fixions, fables, and lyes, they have of divers beene rejected. As touching Playes, they are full of filthie wordes, which woulde not become verie lacqueys, and courtisanes, and have sundrie inventions which infect the spirite, and replenish it with unchaste, whorishe, cosening, deceitfull, wanton, and mischeevous passions . . . And for that, besides all these inconveniences, Comedians, and stage players, doe often times envie and gnawe at the honor of another, and to please the vulgar people, set before them sundrie lies, and teach much dissolutenes, and deceit, by this meanes turning upside downe all discipline and good manners, many cities wel governed, would never at any time intertaine them.

Henry Crosse in *Vertues Commonwealth*, printed in 1603, again associated lies and lasciviousness as the stock in trade of imaginative literature:

For if a view be had of these editions, the Court of *Venus*, the Pallace of Pleasure, *Guy* of *Warwicke*, *Libbius* and *Arthur*, *Bevis* of *Hampton*, the wise men of *Goatam*, *Scoggins* Jeasts, *Fortunatus*, and those new delights that have succeeded these, . . .: what may we thinke? but that the floud-gates of all impietie are drawne up, . . . for fluant termes, and imbossed words, to varnish theyr lyes and fables to make them glib, and as we use to say, to goe downe without chewing, which as poyson doth by litle and litle, disperse itselfe into every part of the body.[11]

And as to plays, Crosse contended that these modern plays "are altogether made upon lascivious arguments," and that in them "instead of morallitie, fictions, lies, and scurrillous matter is foysted in."[12]

While, then, the characteristic charges against poetry were that it was made up of lies, that it pandered to passion, and that it used pleasure as honey to disguise its poison, the advocates of history as the teacher of morals pleaded its cause in ways which I have already rehearsed. Meanwhile the defenders of poetry were concerned with the matter of imitation, which had become the Platonic word of accusation. Coignet proceeded to prove that this imitation was disguising, counterfeiting, lying. Ascham defined imitation so that it included history, philosophy, and oratory:

IMITATION is a facultie to expresse livelie and perfitlie that example which ye go about to follow. And of it selfe it is large

[11]*Op. cit.*, fols. o1v-o2r.
[12]*Ibid.*, fols. P3v-P4r.

and wide: for all the workes of nature in a maner be examples for arte to folow.[13]

Puttenham claimed that the poet in spite of Plato was first of all a maker or a creator:

Such as (by way of resemblance and reverently) we may say of God; who without any travell to his divine imagination made all the world of nought, nor also by any patterne or mould, as the Platonicks with their Idees do phantastically suppose.

But the poet might also be termed an imitator:

a Poet may in some sort be said a follower or imitator, because he can expresse the true and lively image of every thing is set before him, and which he taketh in hand to describe: and so in that respect is both a maker and a counterfaitor: and Poesie an art not only of making, but also of imitation.[14]

And of all poetry Puttenham thought the historical, next to divine poetry, most admirable, serving the memory as it does and furnishing a basis for determining men's actions:

because it maketh most to a sound judgement and perfect worldly wisedome, examining and comparing the times past with the present, and, by them both considering the time to come, concludeth with a stedfast resolution what is the best course to be taken in all his actions and advices in this world.[15]

Of all the defenders of poetry, however, it was Sidney who penetrated most deeply into the nature of the charges against poetry and into the nature of the rival claims of history and philosophy. For poetry he claimed precedence inasmuch as the first writers were poets. Furthermore philosophy was dependent upon poetry:

even Plato, whosoever well considereth, shall find that in the body of his work, though the inside and strength were Philosophy, the skinne as it were and beautie depended most of Poetrie: . . .[16]

---

[13]Roger Ascham, *The Scholemaster* (1570), reprinted in G. G. Smith, *op. cit.*, I, 5.

[14]George Puttenham, *The Arte of English Poesie* (1589), reprinted *ibid.*, II, 3.

[15]*Ibid.*, II, 40-41.

[16]Sidney in *ibid.*, I, 152.

And as for history:

even Historiographers (although theyr lippes sounde of things doone, and veritie be written in theyr fore-heads) have been glad to borrow both fashion and perchance weight of Poets.[17]

The poet, Sidney affirmed, is indeed a creator, god-like in making as it were a new nature, but he is also an imitator, and poetry an art of imitation, even as Aristotle said, its end being to teach and to delight. Among poets he reckons three kinds: the divine poet, the philosophical, and the true poet. The philosophical poet may be either moral or historical, but whether the philosophical poet is to be properly classed as a poet he refuses to decide, noting only that "he takes not the course of his owne invention," being "wrapped within the folde of the proposed subject."[18]

But Sidney's great contribution is the defense of poetry against the charge of lying by turning defense into counter-attack:

The Historian scarcely giveth leysure to the Moralist to say so much, but that he, loden with old Mouse-eaten records, authorising himselfe (for the most part) upon other histories, whose greatest authorities are built upon the notable foundation of Heare-say, having much a-doe to accord differing Writers and to pick trueth out of partiality, better acquainted with a thousande yeeres a goe then with the present age, and yet better knowing how this world goeth then how his owne wit runneth, curious for antiquities and inquisitive of novelties, a wonder to young folkes and a tyrant in table talke, denieth, in a great chafe, that any man for teaching of vertue, and vertuous actions, is comparable to him. I am *Lux vitae, Temporum magistra, Vita memoriae, Nuncia vetustatis, etc.*[19]

Advancing from these fine satirical descriptions, Sidney argues his case:

The Philosopher therfore and the Historian are they which would win the gole, the one by precept, the other by example. But both

[17]*Ibid.*, I, 152-53.
[18]*Ibid.*, I, 158-59.
[19]*Ibid.*, I, 162.

not having both, doe both halte. For the Philosopher, setting downe with thorny argument the bare rule, is so hard of utterance, and so mistie to bee conceived, that one that hath no other guide but him shall wade in him till hee be olde before he shall finde sufficient cause to bee honest: for his knowledge standeth so upon the abstract and generall, that happie is that man who may understande him, and more happie that can applye what hee dooth understand. On the other side, the Historian, wanting the precept, is so tyed, not to what shoulde bee but to what is, to the particuler truth of things and not to the general reason of things, that hys example draweth no necessary consequence, and therefore a lesse fruitfull doctrine.

Nowe dooth the peerelesse Poet performe both: for whatsoever the Philosopher sayth shoulde be doone, hee giveth a perfect picture of it in some one, by whom hee presupposeth it was doone. So as hee coupleth the generall notion with the particuler example.[20]

Specifically, then, Sidney answers the charge that poets are liars:

I aunswere paradoxically, but, truely, I thinke truely, that of all Writers under the sunne the Poet is the least lier, and, though he would, as a Poet can scarcely be a lyer. The Astronomer, with his cosen the Geometrician, can hardly escape, when they take upon them to measure the height of the starres. How often, thinke you, doe the Phisitians lye, when they aver things good for sicknesses, which afterwards send *Charon* a great nomber of soules drownd in a potion before they come to his Ferry? And no lesse of the rest, which take upon them to affirme. Now, for the Poet, he nothing affirmes, and therefore never lyeth. For, as I take it, to lye is to affirme that to be true which is false. So as the other Artists, and especially the Historian, affirming many things, can, in the cloudy knowledge of mankinde, hardly escape from many lyes. But the Poet (as I sayd before) never affirmeth. The Poet never maketh any circles about your imagination, to conjure you to beleeve for true what he writes. Hee citeth not authorities of other Histories, but even for hys entry calleth the sweete Muses to inspire into him a good invention; in troth, not labouring to tell you what is, or is not, but what should or should not be: and therefore, though he recount things not true, yet because hee telleth them not for true, he lyeth not, . . .[21]

[20]*Ibid.*, I, 164.
[21]*Ibid.*, I, 184-85.

In this regard Sidney is specially concerned with the claims of historiographers:

But now may it be alledged that if this imagining of matters be so fitte for the imagination, then must the Historian needs surpasse, who bringeth you images of true matters, such as indeede were done, and not such as fantastically or falsely may be suggested to have been doone.[22]

But poetry deals with the universal rather than the particular, even as Aristotle pointed out, and furthermore the poet frames his example "to that which is most reasonable," where the Historian in his bare *Was* "hath many times that which wee call fortune to over-rule the best wisedome. Manie times he can yeelde no cause: or, if hee doe, it must be poeticall." Indeed, Sidney says:

the Historian, being captived to the trueth of a foolish world, is many times a terror from well dooing, and an incouragement to unbrideled wickednes.[23]

Sidney also advanced his counter-attack against the attackers by opposing their poison-in-honey charge with the contention that it is through delight that poetry advances beyond mere teaching into that "moving" which is the purpose and the end of teaching. To understand a virtue, to see a virtue exemplified, is not to be moved to virtue. And if virtue is the objective of learning, then,

Poetrie, beeing the most familiar to teach it, and most princelie to move towards it, in the most excellent work is the most excellent workman.[24]

Finally, as to the charge of the opposition that poetry panders to the passions, that it is "a school of abuse," Sidney replies in detail, for each species of poetry, in arguments that are familiar to all students of English literature.

Historical poetry was frequently regarded as poetry of a special

[22]*Ibid.*, I, 167.
[23]*Ibid.*, I, 170.
[24]*Ibid.*, I, 175.

class both by the critics of poetry and by its defenders. On the one hand, Coignet made it an exception to his general charges, while on the other hand, Sidney ranked it as philosophical poetry, outside the ranks of true poetry because in it the poet "takes not the course of his owne invention," being "wrapped within the folde of the proposed subject." The author[25] of the third blast in *A Second and Third Blast of Retrait from Plaies and Theaters* would, however, make no exception, protesting that even the word of God and histories from the Bible were corrupted by those who put them on the stage,

And if they write of histories that are knowen, as the life of *Pompeie;* the martial affaires of *Ceasar,* and other worthies, they give them a newe face, and turne them out like counterfeites to showe themselves on the stage.[26]

In the same vein Stephen Gosson affirmed:

if a true Historie be taken in hand, it is made like our shadows, longest at the rising and falling of the Sunne, shortest all at hie noone. For the Poets drive it most commonly into such pointes as may best showe the majestie of their pen in Tragicall speaches; or set the hearers a gogge with discourses of love; or painte a fewe antickes to fitt their owne humors with scoffes and tauntes; or wring in a shewe to furnish the Stage when it is to bare; when the matter of it selfe comes shorte of this, they followe the practise of the cobler, and set their teeth to the leather to pull it out.[27]

Nevertheless, in spite of Sidney, who would not include historical poems in his true poetry because they were too little poetry, and of men like Stubbes, who would not exclude historical poems from condemnation because they were too much poetry and too little history, most of the defenders of poetry found one of their strongest points in historical poetry, and most of the attackers were inclined to make possible exceptions of

[25]"Anglo-phile Eutheo," thought by E. K. Chambers and others to be Anthony Munday, published in 1580.

[26]*Op. cit.,* p. 105.

[27]*Plays Confuted in Five Actions* (1582?), quoted from E. K. Chambers, *The Elizabethan Stage* (Oxford, 1923), IV, 216.

historical poetry. Webbe in his *Discourse of English Poetrie* claimed that "Poetry is not debarred from any matter, which may be expressed by penne or speeche," and divided it into three kinds, "Comicall, Tragicall, Historicall." Puttenham devoted an entire chapter to "historicall Poesie, by which the famous acts of princes and the vertuous and worthy lives of our forefathers were reported," and his defense of historical poetry is particularly interesting because it is based upon the arguments which we have seen developing in defense of history proper. History corresponds in the soul of man to memory, its functions being to enable man to examine and compare the times past with the present and "by them both considering the time to come," to enable him to decide wisely what he shall do. Furthermore, no oratorical craft is so successful as the use of examples in persuading men what it were good to do, and this use of examples "is but the representation of old memories." Puttenham concluded that "for these regards the Poesie historicall is of all other next the divine most honorable and worthy." Nevertheless he put no strait jacket upon history, for he divided histories into those that are wholly true, those that are wholly false, and those that contain a mixture of true and false, as he explained:

These historical men neverthelesse used not the matter so precisely to wish that al they wrote should be accounted true, for that was not needeful nor expedient to the purpose, namely to be used either for example or for pleasure: considering that many times it is seene a fained matter or altogether fabulous, besides that it maketh more mirth than any other, works no lesse good conclusions for example than the most true and veritable, but often times more, because the Poet hath the handling of them to fashion at his pleasure . . . Againe, as ye know, mo and more excellent examples may be fained in one day by a good wit then many ages through mans frailtie are able to put in ure; . . .[28]

Thomas Nashe admonished all would-be immortals to seek a poet rather than a historian:

Gentles, it is not your lay Chronigraphers, that write of nothing but the Mayors and Sheriefs, and the deere yeere, and the great

[28]Smith, *op. cit.*, II, 42.

Frost, that can endowe your names with never dated glory: for they want the wings of choise words to fly to heaven, which we have: they cannot sweeten a discourse, or wrest admiration from men reading, as we can, reporting the meanest accident.

And he offered himself to any willing "Mecoenas":

I dare presume, that, if any Mecoenas binde me to him by his bounty, . . . I will doo him as much honour as any Poet of my beard-lesse yeeres shall in England. . . On the contrary side, if I bee evill intreated, . . . I will raile on him soundly: . . . in some elaborate, pollished Poem, which I will leave to the world . . . to be a living Image to all ages, of his beggerly parsimony and ignoble illiber-alitie: . . .[29]

This testimony to the power of the poet is all the more interesting because it is echoed by Hamlet as he advises Polonius:

Good my lord, will you see the players well bestowed? Do you hear, let them be well used, for they are the abstracts and brief chronicles of the time; after your death you were better have a bad epitaph than their ill report while you live.[30]

Nashe, indeed, taking his occasion from the book of Cornelius Agrippa, noted a little earlier in these pages, decided to have a bout with the enemies of poetry, and finally arrived at his famous defense of plays, using perforce plays based on history as the foundation of his defense:

Nay, what if I proove Playes to be no extreame; but a rare exercise of vertue? First, for the subject of them (for the most part) it is borrowed out of our English Chronicles, wherein our forefathers valiant actes (that have line long buried in rustie brasse and worme-eaten bookes) are revived, and they themselves raised from the Grave of Oblivion, and brought to pleade their aged Honours in open presence: than which, what can be a sharper reproofe to these degenerate effeminate dayes of ours?

How would it have joyed brave *Talbot* (the terror of the French) to thinke that after he had lyne two hundred yeares in his Tombe, hee should triumphe againe on the Stage, and have his bones newe

[29]Nashe, *op. cit.*, I, 194-95.
[30]Shakespeare, *Hamlet*, II, ii, 555-60.

embalmed with the tears of ten thousand spectators at least (at severall times) . . .

Those to whom all arts are vanity only queried "What do we get by it?" when they saw Henry V leading the French king prisoner and forcing king and dauphin to swear him fealty, and Nashe described bitingly those who saw no good in history as

Respecting neither the right of Fame that is due to true Nobilitie deceased, nor what hopes of eternitie are to be proposed to adventrous mindes, to encourage them forward, but onely their execrable luker, and fillthie unquenchable avarice.

Political ethics were taught in historical plays, furthermore, even as were the triumphs of fame and immortality, said Nashe:

In Playes, all cossenages, all cunning drifts over-guylded with outward holinesse, all stratagems of warre, all the cankerwormes that breede on the rust of peace, are most lively anatomiz'd: they shewe the ill successe of treason, the fall of hastie climbers, the wretched end of usurpers, the miserie of civill dissention, and how just God is evermore in punishing of murther.[31]

Bacon divided humane learning according "to the three partes of Mans understanding, which is the seate of Learning: HISTORY to his MEMORY, POESIE to his IMAGINATION, and PHILOSOPHIE to his REASON:"[32] arguing the case for poetry and history much as did Sidney:

POESIE is . . . nothing else but FAINED HISTORY, which may be as well in Prose as in Verse.

The use of this FAINED HISTORIE, hath beene to give some shadowe of satisfaction to the minde of Man in those points, wherein the Nature of things doth denie it, the world being in proportion inferiour to the soule: by reason whereof there is agreeable to the spirit of Man, a more ample Greatnesse, a more exact Goodnesse; and a more absolute varietie than can bee found in the Nature of things. Therefore, because the Acts or Events of *true Historie*, have not that Magnitude, which satisfieth the minde of Man, Poesie faineth

---

[31]Nashe, *op. cit.*, I, 212-13.

[32]Francis Bacon, *Of the Proficience and Advancement of Learning*, Bk. II, fol. 7.

Acts and Events Greater and more Heroicall; because *true Historie* propoundeth the successes and issues of actions, not so agreeable to the merits of Vertue and Vice, therefore *Poesie* faines them more just in Retribution, and more according to Revealed Providence, because *true Historie* representeth Actions and Events, more ordinarie and lesse interchanged, therefore *Poesie* endueth them with more Rarenesse, and more unexpected, and alternative Variations. So as it appeareth that *Poesie* serveth and conferreth to Magnanimitie, Moralitie, and to Delectation.[33]

The best-known defense of historical poetry as represented in historical plays was, however, that offered by Thomas Heywood:

Thirdly, playes have made the ignorant more apprehensive, taught the unlearned the knowledge of many famous histories, instructed such as cannot reade in the discovery of all our *English* Chronicles: and what man have you now of that weake capacity, that cannot discourse of any notable thing recorded even from *William* the *Conquerour*, nay from the landing of *Brute*, untill this day, beeing possest of their true use, For, or because Playes are writ with this ayme, and carryed with this methode, to teache the subjects obedience to their King, to shew the people the untimely ends of such as have moved tumults, commotions, and insurrections, to present them with the flourishing estate of such as live in obedience, exhorting them to allegeance, dehorting them from all trayterous and fellonious stratagems.

And Heywood extended history beyond domestic history:

If wee present a forreigne History, the subject is so intended, that in the lives of *Romans, Grecians*, or others, either the vertues of our Country-men are extolled, or their vices reproved, . . . either animating men to noble attempts, or attaching the consciences of the spectators, finding themselves toucht in presenting the vices of others.[34]

Heywood's *Apology for Actors* was published in 1612, and three years later, in 1615, John Greene's *Refutation of the Apol-*

[33]*Ibid.*, Bk. II, fols. 17-18.

[34]Thomas Heywood, *An Apology for Actors* (London, 1612), fol. F3.

ogy for Actors answered it, point by point. His argument against Heywood's defense of history plays was the old one of Stubbes and his sympathizers:

Thirdly, he affirmes that Playes have taught the ignorant knowledge of many famous Histories. They have indeed made many to know of those Histories they never did, by reason they would never take the paines to reade them. But these that know the Histories before they see them acted, are ever ashamed, when they have heard what lyes the Players insert amongst them, and how greatly they deprave them. If they be too long for a Play, they make them curtals; if too short, they enlarge them with many Fables, and whither too long or too short, they corrupt them with a Foole and his Bables: whereby they make them like Leaden rules, which men will fit to their worke, and not frame their worke to them. So that the ignorant instead of true History shall beare away nothing but fabulous lyes.

In 1614 there had appeared Richard Brathwait's *Schollers Medley*, described in its subtitle as "an intermixt discourse upon historicall and poeticall relations." The discourse is, indeed, "intermixt," but it must be noticed here. Brathwait's definition of histories as "the true Relators of things done, with a probable collection of things to come, by precedent events," is strictly orthodox, but he proposes also to "entreate of Relations Feigned; yet such as Moralized include an excellent meaning, drained from the uncorrupted Springs of Hellicon," for, he argues,

All Relations feigned are not to be excluded: for many Poeticall Narrations there be which comprehend in them a wonderfull sharpenesse of judgement, pregnancy of Invention, and a great measure of discretion, . . .[35]

Homer is the example chosen to illustrate the possible excellence of such works. And while Brathwait excludes many modern narrations for their ribaldry and their clear defections from truth, he yet accepts as good, certain "Mixt Histories" in which profit and delight are mingled. The seriousness of such subjects as are dealt with in this type of literature attract "a kinde of Maiesty to it," he says, but he lays down three requisites for the perfection of "Histories of this nature":

[35]*Op. cit.*, p. 31.

first, Truth, in sincerely relating, without having any thing (as Tacitus observeth) *haustum ex vano*, foisted in by our owne invention, to smooth the passage of our story.

Secondly, an explanation in discovering, not onely the sequels of things, but also the causes and reasons drawing to the conclusions.

Thirdly, judgement in distinguishing things by approving the best, and disallowing the contrary.

His conclusion in regard to the relative merits of history and "feigned" history is explicit.

To be short, my opinion positively is this: That Historian which can joyne profite with a modest delight together in one body or frame of one united discourse, grounding his story upon an essential truth, deserves the first and principall place: and he who (upon a fained discourse) can proportion it to a likenesse of truth, merits the next.[36]

In 1618 the dispute between history and poetry was dramatized in a moral play called TEXNOΓAMIA; *or, The Marriages of the Arts*, written by Barten Holyday. The play is concerned with the love of Historia for Poeta. Polites undertakes at first to dissuade Historia by the now familiar clichés concerning the unworthiness of her love:

my counsell should be that you would never fancie this *Poeta*, a fellow of that kinde of profession, which all Wise men have ever banish'd out of the commonwealth, as being the Mother of lyes, the Nurse of abuse, and at the Best, but the worst of knowledge; Perhaps you may thinke that *Polites* uses this disswasion because *Poeta's* poore; . . . but I professe I'me chiefly moved at the uncertainty of his courses, which I thinke would not very aptly consort with your sober consistency and stayednesse of life:

to which arguments Ethicus adds his complement of libel:

Thou art a greenehead, *Historia;* I say that *Poeta's* a licentious fellow, a Drinker, a Dicer, a Wencher, a Ballad-maker, a Seducer of young minds, a Scoffer, a Libeller, a Sharker, an Humorist, an

[36]*Ibid.*, p. 67.

Epicure; proud, phantasticall, sullen, slothfull, lewd, irreligious, and in a word an enemy to all the Gods and Vertues.[37]

In spite of the additional warning of Oeconoma that Poeta will never be a good housemate, demanding as he does order in everything about him, Historia persists in her love, arguing that Historias have in former times been loved by the Poetas and instancing Homer, Virgil, and Lucan as proof. The play has a happy ending, however, for Polites finally promises his blessing to Poeta if he will secure Historia as his wife. *The Marriages of the Arts* is a curiosity of literature, but it exemplifies the opposition of the friends of history to poetry, as well as the fundamental ideals motivating their union.

Attacks upon poetry were continually made during the sixteenth and the early seventeenth century by the Puritans, and it is important, I think, to see their focal points.[38] It is well to remember, too, that the Puritan acceptance of history was from the beginning not only positive in its consideration of the contribution of history to wisdom and virtue, but also negative in its defiance of the comparative contributions of poetry. The attempt to compromise the conflict and to achieve the union of history and poetry, thereby attaining the profit and pleasure of both, has produced a goodly portion of our literature.

[37]*Op. cit.*, II, i.

[38]For discussion of the relation of poetry and history during the Renaissance see H. B. Charlton, *Castelvetro's Theory of Poetry* (Manchester, 1913), pp. 48-58; H. T. Swedenberg, *The Theory of the Epic in England 1650-1800* (Berkeley and Los Angeles, 1944), chap. i, especially p. 9.

CHAPTER X

POETICAL MIRRORS OF HISTORY

THE MARRIAGE of history and poetry is of primary concern to us only as it produced the history plays of Shakespeare. But these plays will become more understandable, I believe, if we consider some of the other offspring.

The earliest of the poetical histories to be published during the Elizabethan period was the *Mirror for Magistrates*, suppressed under Mary but "allowed" and printed during the first year of Elizabeth's reign.[1] Undertaken by the printer Wayland as a continuation of Lydgate's *Fall of Princes*, the work was put under the direction of William Baldwin, known as philosopher, poet, printer, and playwright, but also accepted as a historian. John Stow tells how, in 1563, when asked by the printer, Thomas Marshe, to prepare an abridgment of history to supplant that of Grafton, he finally consented "on condicion that some one whiche were bettar learnyd mowght be joyned" with him. Baldwin was thereupon chosen by Marshe (who printed the Elizabethan *Mirror's*) but died before he could perform the task assigned.[2] It is important, I think, to recognize the fact that Baldwin was considered a historian able to supplement the limitations of Stow, probably because of his work on the *Mirror*, for his place in literary history is determined by his success in infusing into historical poetry the current methods and purposes of history. With him history was not mere story, not even moralized story, but a political mirror for those in authority.

---

[1] An account of the history of its publication is included in the Introduction to *The Mirror for Magistrates*, ed. L. B. Campbell (Cambridge, 1938). References to the *Mirror* are to this edition.

[2] John Stow, *A Survey of London*, ed. C. L. Kingsford (Oxford, 1908), I, xlix, ix, x, and notes.

POETICAL MIRRORS OF HISTORY

Anyone who wanders among the Tudor shades is aware of the tremendous popularity of the words *mirror, glass, speculum,* and *image* for titles of literary works. There were mirrors of good manners, of policy, of friendship; mirrors for Martinists, for gamesters, for soldiers. But the mirror of these titles was not merely a looking-glass in which Everyman might grow familiar with his own image. The exact significance of the term is, indeed, nowhere clearly explained, but the Elizabethans seem to have associated it with Plato, and it is probable that the various explanations of his doctrine of ideas and especially that given in the seventh book of the *Republic* accounted for this association. One of the twentieth-century interpreters of Plato has written:

In some way or other, which he never succeeded in explaining, this world of particular things arises by reflection, as it might be, from the supervention of the ideas upon an originally indeterminate or undifferentiated medium, which is to Plato hardly more than a place or locus as it were the visionary depth of a mirror or other feature-less receptacle.[3]

But as I have said, the striking figure of the cave with its chained men beholding the shadows that pass on the screen before them, from the seventh book of the *Republic*, seems to have been dominant in Elizabethan thinking.

Not only titles but literature itself made generous use of the mirror idea. Hamlet said that the object of playing was "to hold, as 'twere, the mirror up to nature, to show virtue her own feature, scorn her own image,"[4] and he proceeded to demonstrate the usefulness of such a mirror by staging *The Murder of Gonzago* to catch the conscience of the king. So well did the players present the image of adultery and fratricide that King Claudius broke off the performance and went to his closet to make his futile attempt at prayer without repentance. Thus Shakespeare himself has given us the perfect example of the way in which the drama was used, not to let John Doe see John Doe

[3]P. H. Frye, *Plato* (University Studies of the University of Nebraska: Lincoln, 1938), p. 42.

[4]*Hamlet*, III, ii, 25-28.

on the stage, but to let him behold there the image or reflection of the idea or type in the Platonic sense of the words. Spenser spoke of the mirror in the same way when he wrote to Queen Elizabeth:

> And thou, O fairest Princesse under Sky,
> In this faire mirrhour maist behold thy face,
> And thine owne realmes in lond of Faery,
> And in this antique Image thy great auncestry.[5]

It is in the descriptions of history, however, that we find the word most frequently used. Paulus Jovius, in dedicating his *Shorte Treatise upon the Turkes Chronicles* explained that when Plato said that a man ought oftentimes to behold himself in a glass, "This glasse that Plato speketh on . . . maye be taken not without a cause (as I thinke) for the bokes of wisdome and manours, whiche the Philosophers and wyse men have lefte to their posteritie in writing, but especially for Chronicles and histories, wherein all thinges mete and necessarie for men of every degree and estate, be most plentyfully and lyvelyst set forthe." As a man may see in a mirror how he changes and grows old, so he can see in histories "the form and figure of all Empires and common welthes" and note their progress and decay.[6] Cooper wrote of Lanquet's chronicle that "a diligent reader may as in a mirrour behold the state and condicion of all realmes at all times."[7] Richard Greenaway, dedicating the *Annals* of Tacitus to the Earl of Essex, offered Tacitus "no otherwise then as a glasse, representing in lively colours of prowesse, magnanimitie and counsell; not onely woorthie personages of ages past and gone, but also your L. owne honorable vertues, whereof the world is both witnes and judge."[8] Baldwin was, therefore, using

---

[5] Edmund Spenser, *The Faerie Queene*, Intro. stanza 4 to Bk. II (Oxford, 1916), p. 69.

[6] *Op. cit.* (London, 1546) in the dedication to Sir Ralph Sadler.

[7] Thomas Lanquet, *An Epitome of Cronicles*, continued by Thomas Cooper and by Robert Crowley (London, 1559) in the dedication by Cooper to the Duke of Somerset; Cooper in the 1560 edition of this work disavowed his connection with the 1559 printing.

[8] *Op. cit.* (London, 1598).

a familiar figure when he put history into a poetic medium and called it the *Mirror for Magistrates*. Addressing the magistrates who act as God's vice-gerents, he explained:

here as in a loking glas, you shall see (if any vice be in you) howe the like hath bene punished in other heretofore, whereby admonished, I trust it will be a good occasion to move you to the sooner amendment. This is the chiefest ende, whye it is set furth, which God graunt it may attayne.[9]

The *Mirror* was thus a work dedicated to the task of expounding the present by reference to the past, using history to teach the political lessons which its authors reckoned most pertinent to the understanding of political events in their own day. It was highly selective, making no attempt to cover all the events of any reign but choosing only those which might be used to mirror contemporary affairs. Halle's chronicle was taken as a basic story source, but Fabyan and More were also consulted. It would take more than one book to present the evidence which goes to the identifying of the contemporary political situations mirrored in its tragedies, but in an earlier paper[10] I tried to demonstrate its method by analyzing the situations reflected in the tragedies of Humphrey, Duke of Gloucester, and Elianor Cobham, his wife, in the time of Henry VI. In the tragedy of Duke Humphrey there was clearly mirrored the contemporary tragedy of Edward, Duke of Somerset, protector during the minority of Edward VI as Duke Humphrey had been protector during the minority of Henry VI. The downfall of the Duke of Somerset was popularly thought to have come about through the enmity between him and his brother Thomas Seymour, and the difficulty between the brothers was laid to the jealousy between their wives, the Duchess of Somerset and Thomas Seymour's wife, who had been queen of England as the last wife of Henry VIII. The downfall of Duke Humphrey is, therefore, presented in the *Mirror* as in part activated by the jealousy between the queen of Henry VI and the wife of the protector, even though the

[9]*Mirror*, p. 64.

[10]"Humphrey Duke of Gloucester and Elianor Cobham His Wife in the *Mirror for Magistrates*," *Huntington Library Bulletin*, V (1934), 119-55.

chronicles tell us that Elianor Cobham had been in exile for some years when Queen Margaret arrived to be the bride of Henry VI. History was simply adjusted to present a more accurate picture of the contemporary situation, and in this case the author of the second part of *Henry VI* (Shakespeare or another) followed the *Mirror* and has received credit by critics ignorant of the *Mirror* for having altered history with dramatic effectiveness. I think it will be found that Shakespeare followed many times the precedent established in the *Mirror* of altering history to fit the contemporary circumstances, and that he is in such cases always praised for his dramatic skill.[11] But what I wish here is to establish the method of the *Mirror*: a particular contemporary situation was chosen to be expounded, and a historic parallel found which set the same political problem.

Moreover, the purpose of the *Mirror* was to teach the lessons which Tudor England thought it was the business of history to teach, the political lessons concerning ruling and being ruled, concerning the duties of judges and counsellors and subjects and kings, which were important to the welfare of state and people. The first tragedy was that of "Robert Tresilian chiefe Justice of Englande, and other his felowes, for misconstruyng the lawes, and expounding them to serve the Princes affections," and it pointed to the lesson intended:

> If sum in latter dayes, had called unto mynde
> The fatall fall of us for wresting of the ryght,
> The statutes of this lande they should not have defynde
> So wylfully and wyttingly agaynst the sentence quyte: ...

The *Mirror* told "Howe kyng Richarde the seconde was for his evyll governaunce deposed from his seat, and miserably murdred in prison," and "How Jacke Cade traiterously rebelling agaynst his Kyng, was for his treasons and cruell doinges wurthely punyshed," and "How Richard Plantaganet duke of Glocester, murdered his brothers children usurping the crowne, and in the third yeare of his raygne was most worthely deprived of life and kingdome in Bosworth playne by Henry Earle of

---

[11]See below, chap. xii, for example.

Richemond after called king Henry the vii." But always the general lesson was explained and its present applicability stressed.

The *Mirror* was an extremely popular work, being published in seven editions between 1559 and 1587. It was, indeed, popular enough to produce two imitation *Mirror's* which, while flattering in their imitation, were ultimately to destroy the reputation of the original work by the addition of much bad poetry written with no clear purpose such as that which distinguished the original work. Probably part of the reason for its popularity was that it furnished a new political guessing game. But it was a work of tremendous importance in the history of English literature, not primarily because of its popularity, but because it used historical poetry for the accepted purposes of history and established literary precedent by its method of mirroring the present in the past.

It is impossible here to record the story of the "literary progeny of the *Mirror for Magistrates*," to use Professor Farnham's phrase,[12] but it is in point to note that the method of the *Mirror* was applied to the drama by one of its writers when Thomas Sackville, together with Thomas Norton, wrote *Gorboduc* to inculcate the lesson of the danger to a kingdom when the succession is not clearly established, a danger which Thomas Norton had been one of a committee of Commons to petition the queen to heed.[13] Professor Schelling says that "Upwards of thirty historical plays exist, the subjects of which are treated in *The Mirour for Magistrates*"[14] and certainly many of them were affected by the purposes and methods of the *Mirror*.

Aside from the poetical tragedies which followed the *Mirror* pattern and aside from the dramas which used history purposively as did *Gorboduc*, there were also long historical narrative poems by which the Elizabethans could learn about the past. It

[12]Willard Farnham, "The Progeny of *A Mirror for Magistrates*," *Modern Philology*, XXIX (1932), pp. 395-410 and chap. viii in *The Medieval Heritage of Elizabethan Tragedy* (Berkeley, 1936).

[13]See H. A. Watt, *Gorboduc: or, Ferrex and Porrex* (Bulletin of the University of Wisconsin: Madison, 1910), for a discussion of the political significance of the play which has been the basis of most later consideration.

[14]Schelling, *The English Chronicle Play*, p. 36.

will be remembered that Hardyng wrote his chronicle in verse, but among those who designed long historical poems the most important for our study are Warner, Daniel, and Drayton. William Warner wrote his *Albions England* with "Historicall Intermixtures, Invention, and Varietie," beginning with "the lives, Actes, and Labors of Saturne, Jupiter, Hercules, and Aeneas,"[15] and in the course of many books bringing the history of events down to his own day. Warner adorned his history with many tales and certainly did not fail to include any interesting story because of its doubtful authenticity. But his work teaches the lessons of history, political lessons generalized for universal application. Thus he expounds the treasons practised against Elizabeth:

> Was never any thryved yet that threatned her amis:
> For of anoynted Princes God sole Judge and Rector is.
> And if Examples might prevaile, then Traytors might perceave,
> They perish in their purpose, or but Spyders webbes do weave.

Listing the dukes punished for treason, he comments:

> Howbeit of the commonwealth none worser did desarve,
> Than such as flattred Princes faults, who faulting, all did swarve.[16]

But of much more significance for the study of Shakespeare is Samuel Daniel, whose *First Fowre Bookes of the Civile Wars between the Two Houses of Lancaster and Yorke*, published in 1595, with the augmentations of later editions, have long been explored for their possible relation to Shakespeare's history plays. Daniel began in epic fashion with an *I sing*, but he did not propose to sing of a hero. Instead he proposed to write of the same period which Halle had written of and for the same purpose, the period which was also to be the subject of most of Shakespeare's histories. He began:

> I Sing the civil warrs, tumultuous broyles,
> And bloudy factions of a mighty land:
> Whose people hauty, proud with forain spoyles
> Upon themselves, turne back their conquering hand:
> Whilst Kin with Kin, brother the brother foyles, . . .

---

[15]From the title page of the 1586 edition.
[16]*Albions England* (1596) Bk. IX, chaps. 44 and 45.

In the 1609 edition of this work Daniel explicitly recorded his original purpose in writing it:

And, whereas this Argument was long since undertaken (in a time which was not so well secur'd of the future, as God be blessed now it is) with a purpose, to shewe the deformities of Civile Dissension, and the miserable events of Rebellions, Conspiracies, and bloudy Revengements, which followed (as in a circle) upon that breach of the due course of Succession, by the Usurpation of Hen. 4; and thereby to make the blessings of Peace, and the happinesse of an established Government (in a direct Line) the better to appeare: I trust I shall doo a gratefull worke to my Countrie, to continue the same, unto the glorious Union of Hen. 7: from whence is descended our present Happinesse.[17]

But he was not content with impressing merely this one particular lesson upon his readers. Throughout the poem the political significance of events is stressed, and political lessons are woven into the texture of the story. For example, when Richard II is dead, and Henry IV stands at last as the sole king of England, his fear buried with Richard, Daniel writes:

> And yet new *Hydraes* lo, new heades appeare
> T'afflict that peace reputed then so sure,
> And gave him much to do, and much to feare,
> And long and daungerous tumults did procure,
> And those even of his chiefest followers were
> Of whom he might presume him most secure,
> Who whether not so grac'd or so preferd
> As they expected, these new factions stird.[18]

Daniel's 1609 dedication gives evidence too of his concern for his work as history, for he asserts that he has followed the truth as it is given in "our common Annalles," since he holds it "an impietie, to violate that publike Testimonie we have, without more evident proofe; or to introduce fictions of our owne imagination, in things of this nature." But he admits that he used "that poeticall licence, of framing speaches to the persons of

[17]From Daniel's dedication to the Countess of Pembroke.
[18]Bk. III, Stanza 86 (1595 ed.)

men according to their occasions; as C. Salustius, and T. Livius (though Writers in Prose, yet in that kinde Poets) have, with divers of other antient and modern Writers, done before me." As for the truth of the "images" which he has drawn, he vouches for it because "Ambition, Faction, and Affections, speake ever one language, weare like colours . . . feed and are fed with the same nutriments." In the early pages of his prose history of England in 1612 he incorporated much of his 1609 dedication and restated certain of his ideas, as when he said:

We shall find still the same correspondencies to hold in the actions of men: Virtues and Vices the same, though rising and falling, according to the worth, or weaknesse of Governors: the causes of the ruines, and mutations of states to be alike: and the trayne of affairs carried by precedent, in a course of Succession under like colours.[19]

Finally, we turn to Michael Drayton, whose life and work have so many probable—and generally unproved—points of contact with Shakespeare's. Drayton's biographer, Professor B. N. Newdigate, says of him:

His reading in old chronicles was immense. They were his principal sources for his Legends, *The Barons Warres*, *The Battaile of Agincourt*, and for large tracts of *Poly-Olbion*. So far from taking his history at second hand from Holinshed, Stow or Camden, he went to the authors from whom Holinshed himself had drawn: Gildas; Bede; Giraldus Cambrensis; Geoffrey of Monmouth; Hoveden; Higden; Nicholas Upton; Hauteville; Froissart; Philip de Commines; Polydore Vergil; Buchanan, and many more. . . . His reading was not confined to printed books. . . . When writing *Peirs Gaveston* he had access to the collections of John Stow; and there is reason to believe that he was able to consult the libraries of Camden, Selden, and Cotton.[20]

The number and variety of his historical poems were outstanding, and many of them concern subjects common to Shakespeare's plays. Several of his *Heroic Epistles* deal with characters familiar to us in Shakespeare. His *Battle of Agincourt*, epic in

[19]*The First Part of the Historie of England* (London, 1612), p. 3.
[20]*Michael Drayton and His Circle* (Oxford, 1941), pp. 23-24.

method and intention, reproduces, with additions, material used in *Henry V*, and according to his latest annotator, *The Miseries of Queene Margarite* made definite use of the three parts of *Henry VI*, as did certain of the *Heroic Epistles*. But in spite of his diligent search of source material and his zealous documentation of his work in footnotes, Drayton's interest in these poems was that of the poet rather than the historian, an interest in character and story and poetic form.

However, Drayton was especially concerned with the period of Edward II and the Barons' Wars, as Daniel had been with the period of Richard II and the succeeding civil wars. His first treatment of the period was in the tragedy of *Peirs Gaveston*, a tragedy written in the *Mirror* tradition and inculcating some of the same political lessons in regard to flatterers about the king that are to be found in Marlowe's *Edward II*. Drayton's first version of his long historical poem on the period was the *Mortimeriados*, published in 1596, but revised into *The Barons Warres* in 1603. Mrs. Tillotson points out the new stress upon political problems in the revised version of the poem and attributes it to the influence of Daniel's *Civil Wars*. She says specifically:

Like Shakespeare and Daniel, Drayton wishes to demonstrate the evils of civil war. Not only does he select his material with this in view; he announces and preaches it directly, and, especially in *The Barons Warres*, is at pains to diagnose and comment on the situation.[21]

Ben Jonson anticipated this judgment when he addressed Drayton:

> I saw, and read, it was thy *Barons Warres!*
> O, how in those, dost thou instruct these times,
> That rebells actions, are but valiant crimes![22]

[21]Michael Drayton, *Works*, ed. J. W. Hebel; Introduction, notes, and variant readings by Kathleen Tillotson and B. N. Newdigate, V (Oxford, 1941), 64-65.

[22]From "The Vision of Ben. Jonson, On the Muses of His Friend M. Drayton," in *The Battaile of Agincourt* (London, 1627). See Newdigate, *op. cit.*, chap. x, for a discussion of the relation of Drayton to Jonson and Shakespeare.

Perhaps it should be noted too that Drayton was concerned with the writing of *Sir John Oldcastle*, a play almost certainly directed to political controversy.

Thus with men like Baldwin and Daniel and Drayton devoting themselves so earnestly to historical studies in preparation for the writing of historical poems, it was inevitable that the purposes and methods of history should infiltrate historical poetry. At the beginning of this book I quoted Professor Schelling as saying that the English chronicle play was closer in its affiliation to the wealth of historic literature in verse and prose which was springing up about it than to other varieties of the drama. This statement goes too far, I should say, but it does serve to emphasize the need for studying the history play as a separate genre from tragedy and comedy. It is still drama, but it cannot be understood by studying alone its dramatic technique. Instead, it must be studied as a form of art which selected and used its subject matter for the purposes universally accepted as appropriate. It is, then, to the consideration of Shakespeare's historical plays as serving the recognized purposes of history that I am directing the second part of this book. What I have written so far is but prologue to this theme.

PART TWO

SHAKESPEARE'S POLITICAL USE OF HISTORY

CHAPTER XI

SHAKESPEARE'S HISTORY PLAYS

THE EDITORS of the first folio edition of Shakespeare's works included ten entries under "Histories." Disregarding the titles of the earlier published quartos and the attribution of genre in these titles, the editors reduced all titles to a formula: "The Life and Death of" King John, Richard II, and Richard III; "The Life of" Henry V and Henry VIII; "The First Part of" Henry IV and Henry VI, etc. The plays were obviously arranged according to the order of their historical events, and their arrangement consequently gives no clue to the order in which they were written or published. Scholars have found a happy hunting-ground in attempting to fix the dates of the plays, but since it is one that I wish to skirt, I am suggesting Chambers' time-table to those who wish to read the discussion of the individual plays with a tentative date of composition in mind. Chambers dates the plays according to the theatrical season rather than the calendar year and arranges them as follows:[1]

> 1590-1 2 and 3 *Henry VI*
> 1591-2 1 *Henry VI*
> 1592-3 *Richard III*
> 1595-6 *Richard II*
> 1596-7 *King John*
> 1597-8 1 and 2 *Henry IV*
> 1598-9 *Henry V*
> 1612-3 *Henry VIII*

The authority of the editors of the First Folio in regard to the Shakespeare canon has been questioned by modern scholarship

[1]E. K. Chambers, *William Shakespeare* (Oxford, 1930), I, 270-71.

with results which Chambers described in *The Disintegration of Shakespeare*.[2] But today it is generally believed that Shakespeare had only a minor part in the writing of *Henry VIII*, while about the authorship as well as the dates of the three parts of *Henry VI*, there can scarcely be said to be a generally accepted opinion. Because the inclusion of these plays in a study of the political import of Shakespeare's histories would, therefore, inevitably rouse discussion of these moot points, I have, as I indicated in the preface, omitted them. But I have included *Richard III*, even though it cannot be said to occupy an assured place in the canon, for the reason that the puzzle as to its dramatic genre has a distinct bearing upon the problems considered in this book regardless of its date or authorship. Obviously the Henry VI plays and *Richard III* were written without the same unified and insistent purposiveness apparent in the later histories, but their evident immaturity cannot decide the question of their authorship, for Shakespeare's purpose and method in writing history matured with the years as did his purpose and method in writing tragedy.

Shakespeare's first editors, however, evidently found some unifying factor which led them to set the ten plays apart from the comedies and tragedies as histories, and it is my purpose to try to establish what it was. But many critics, particularly those of "the nineteenth century and after," have found a closer relation than that of their common dramatic genre existing among the plays. A. W. Schlegel saw in them a great historical poem in dramatic form, to which *King John* served as prologue and *Henry VIII* as epilogue.[3] Marriott discussed the Wars of the Roses plays in terms of the Wagnerian Ring.[4] But by and large, critics have generally chosen to discuss the relationship of the various plays in terms of cycles. Just what they mean by a *cycle* is, however, not always clearly indicated by those who use the term. Professor Dover Wilson, for instance, says in his introduction to *Richard II*:

[2]The annual Shakespeare lecture before the British Academy, 1924.
[3]*Lectures on Dramatic Art*, pp. 419-22.
[4]Marriott, "Shakespeare and Politics," *op. cit.*, p. 685.

Neither did Shakespeare round off his cycle. Perhaps the idea of so doing did not come to the dramatist until his task was well under way. For the cycle, as everyone knows, is in two parts of four plays each, followed by a final play detached from the rest, viz. (a) *Richard II, Henry IV*, parts i and ii, *Henry V*, (b) *Henry VI*, parts i, ii, and iii, *Richard III*, and (c) *Henry VIII*.[5]

A little later he says that Halle in a sense "furnished the frame and stretched the canvas for the whole Shakespearean cycle, *Richard II* to *Richard III*."[6] And still later in the same introduction he refers to the possibility that the author of *The Trouble-some Raigne of John King of England* provided material for the whole cycle, *Richard II* to *Henry V*.[7] Now the word *cycle* used to describe series of plays depicting periods from Richard II through Henry VIII, from Richard II to Richard III, and from Richard II to Henry V lacks definition, and since the lack clouds the significance of the cycles of history as the Elizabethans viewed them, it is necessary to examine certain related concepts which determined that significance.

The word *cycle* inevitably brings to mind a wheel or a circular path, and the *New English Dictionary* provides a definition which may be applied to history: "A recurrent round or course (of successive events, phenomena, etc.); a regular order or succession in which things recur; a round or series which returns upon itself." Machiavelli accounted for the cyclical nature of history by the eternal sameness of men, but Christian historiography added the eternal sameness of God's justice. While there was, of course, talk of Fortune's wheel in this connection, even Fortune was considered subject to divine law and bound to turn her wheel in accordance with the demands of divine justice. The cycles of history were, therefore, mapped out by the Elizabethans in moral terms as recurring patterns of sin and punishment.

For the establishment of this pattern three Biblical texts were most frequently expounded. The first is a text basic to the under-

[5]*Op. cit.* (Cambridge, 1939), p. xxviii.
[6]*Ibid*, p. liv.
[7]*Ibid.*, p. lxxvi.

standing of Shakespeare's histories and tragedies alike: *Venge-ance is mine: I will repaye, saith the Lord.*[8] The conception of a moral universe seemed to the Elizabethan to rest upon this promise of divine retribution for sin. It was, however, understood that God or his duly appointed representative could alone execute punishment, for to the private man vengeance was forbidden. But of special importance in the study of history is the second text, which supplements the first: *The Lord is slow to anger, and of great mercie, and forgiving iniquitie, and sinne, but not making the wicked innocent, and visiting the wicked-nesse of the fathers upon the children, in the third and fourth generacion.*[9] From Hardyng to Raleigh this visiting of the sins of the fathers upon the children's children was the foundation for the interpretation of the cycles of English history, as we shall see. But a third text taken from Christ's own words explained the manner by which God's vengeance was executed by one who sinned in so doing: *it must needes be that offences shall come, but woe be to that man by whome the offence commeth.*[10] These three texts explain the recurrent round of events with which Tudor history and particularly Tudor accounts of the Wars of the Roses were concerned. An usurper seizes the throne; God avenges his sin upon the third heir through the agency of another usurper, whose sin is again avenged upon the third heir.

This was the pattern worked out most strikingly because most briefly by Raleigh, whose purpose in writing this English history was clearly stated:

And that it may no lesse appeare by evident proofe, than by asservation, That ill doing hath alwaies beene attended with ill successe; I will here, by way of preface, runne over some examples, which the work ensuing hath not reached.

To Raleigh the ill-doing of Edward III was paid for by Richard II:

[8]Geneva text (London, 1588), Romans 12:19.

[9]Numbers 14:18.

[10]Matthew 18:7.

This cruelty the secret and unsearchable judgement of God revenged, on the Grand-child of *Edward* the Third: and so it fell out, even to the last of that Line, that in the second or third descent they were all buried under the ruines of those buildings, of which the Mortar had been tempered with innocent bloud. For *Richard* the second, . . . was in the Prime of his youth deposed; and murdered by his Cosen-germane and vassal, *Henry* of *Lancaster*, afterwards *Henry* the fourth.

The ill-doing of Henry IV marked another turn of the wheel which ended with the destruction of his grandson, Henry VI:

This King, whose Title was weake, and his obtaining the Crowne traiterous: . . . he saw (if Soules immortall see and discerne any thinges after the bodies death) his Grand-childe *Henrie* the sixt, and his Sonne the Prince, suddenly, and without mercy, murdered; the possession of the Crowne (for which he had caused so much blood to bee powred out) transferred from his race; and by the Issues of his Enemies worne and enjoyed: . . .

Then came another turn of the wheel with the Yorkist Edward IV gaining the throne which the slaughtered Henry VI had lost, only to have his brother Richard III lose it again:

This cruel King, *Henry* the seaventh cut off; and was therein (no doubt) the immediate instrument of GODS justice. . . How-so-ever, the taking off, of *Stanles* head, who set the Crowne on his, and the death of the young Earle of *Warwick*, sonne to *George* D. of *Clarence*, shews, as the successe also did, that he held somewhat of the errors of his Ancesters, for his possession in the first line ended in his grand children, as that of *Edward* the third and *Henry* the fourth had done.

Raleigh, like many another writer, thus found in the fact that Henry VII's grandchild, Elizabeth, was the last heir in the direct line new proof that history repeats itself in this recurrent cyclical pattern.[11]

But, as I have noted earlier, Hardyng had pointed out the pattern when he wrote of Henry IV, saying that it had long been the common judgment that "Of evill gotten good, The

---

[11]Raleigh, *History of the World*, Preface.

third heyre should not joyse but be uncrouned." And Grafton commented in the same way:

Other there be that ascribe his [Henry the Sixth's] infortunitie, only to the stroke and punishement of God, affirming that the Kingdome, which Henry the fourth his Grandfather wrongfully gat, and unjustly possessed against king Richard the seconde and his heyres, could not by very devine justice, long continue in that injurious stocke: And that therefore God by his divine providence, punished the offence of the Grandfather, in the sonnes sonne.[12]

Apparently referring to this passage in Grafton, Richard Crompton wrote in 1587:

and likewise how H[enry].4. having obteyned the crowne rather by force, then lawfull succession, doubting that he could not bee in saftie thereof so longe as R[ichard].2. dyd lyve, caused the sayd R.2. to bee destroyed in *Pomfret* Castell, whereupon great troubles and sundry insurrectiones, within this Realme did happen unto hym, and though he dyed possessed of the Crowne, yet H.6. his sonnes sonne was put from the same by E.4. as Grafton dooth set it down, whereby the olde saying appeareth to be true, *De rebus male partis vix gaudebit tertius haeres.*[13]

That the other chroniclers to whom Shakespeare was more directly indebted interpreted the Wars of the Roses as exhibiting this long-accepted moral pattern will be apparent in the discussion of the individual plays. And the understanding of the moral significance of this pattern is basic to the understanding of the Shakespeare history sequences.

If we are to talk in terms of cycles, then, we cannot ignore the fact that the completion of a cycle depends upon following a path to the original starting point. If the First Folio editors rightly attributed the ten plays to Shakespeare, he wrote of two cycles of history: from the seizing of the crown by Henry IV to its loss by "the third heir," Henry VI; and from the seizing of the crown from Henry VI by Edward IV to its loss by "the third heir," Richard III. Whether or not Shakespeare

[12]Grafton, *Chronicle at Large*, II, 691.

[13]Richard Crompton, *A Short Declaration of the Ende of Traytors* (London, 1587), D1v.

did write the plays dealing with this second cycle of history, it is clear that in *Richard II, Henry IV*, and *Henry V* he saw the developing pattern of the cycle, from usurpation to usurpation, for he wrote in the epilogue to *Henry V*:

> Henry the Sixth, in infant bands crown'd King
> Of France and England, did this king succeed;
> Whose state so many had the managing,
> That they lost France and made his England bleed:
> Which oft our stage hath shown; and, for their sake,
> In your fair minds let this acceptance take.

But though the sequence of plays is important to the moral patterning of history, each of the Shakespeare histories serves a special purpose in elucidating a political problem of Elizabeth's day and in bringing to bear upon this problem the accepted political philosophy of the Tudors. And as I turn to the study of these individual plays, I wish to stress two points in particular. First, Shakespeare chose for his histories kings who had already been accepted as archetypes and who had been used over and over again to point particular morals. Second, Shakespeare, like all other writers who used history to teach politics to the present, cut his cloth to fit the pattern, and the approach to the study of his purposes in choosing subjects and incidents from history as well as in his altering the historical fact is best made with current political situations in mind. It is on the assumption that history repeats itself that political mirrors of history can be utilized to explain the present. But it does not repeat itself in every detail, and while the larger outlines of historical fact must be preserved to be convincing, the details are often altered to make them more reminiscent of the present. I have, therefore, in the following pages stressed the traditional nature of Shakespeare's interpretations and the effect of contemporary political situations upon the selection and alteration of historical fact in the plays.

CHAPTER XII

THE TROUBLESOME REIGN OF KING JOHN

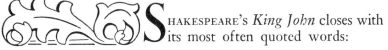S HAKESPEARE's *King John* closes with its most often quoted words:

> This England never did, nor never shall,
> Lie at the proud foot of a conqueror,
> But when it first did help to wound itself.
> Now these her princes are come home again,
> Come the three corners of the world in arms,
> And we shall shock them. Nought shall make us rue,
> If England to itself do rest but true.

Holinshed's chronicle of England records that at the trial of Edward Campion for treason in 1581 it was argued:

This little Iland, God having so bountifullie bestowed his blessings upon it, that except it proove false within it selfe, no treason whatsoever can prevaile against it, and the pope being hereof verie well persuaded, by reason that all his attempts have prooved of no effect: he hath found out a meane, whereby he assureth himselfe to speed of his desire. Secret rebellion must be stirred here at home among our selves, the harts of the people must be obdurated against God and their prince; so that when a foren power shall on a sudden invade this realme, the subjects thus seduced must joine with these in armes, and so shall the pope atteine the sum of his wish.[1]

The theme was one which the Tudors found it necessary to develop again and again, and from the time of Henry VIII it was developed in the story of King John.

It will be remembered that in 1533 Pope Clement VII excommunicated King Henry VIII for his defiance of the church consequent to his troubles over his divorce. In 1535 Clement's

[1]Holinshed (1587 ed.), III, 1323.

126

successor, Paul III, attempted to deprive Henry of his kingdom, sending couriers to all the courts of Europe to ask help in executing the decree. The defection of the English nobles under the influence of the Catholic church came to a climax in the Pilgrimage of Grace, but Henry's reign henceforth was never free from the internal threat of the Catholic clergy and the Catholic nobles, and it was free from foreign intervention in the execution of Paul's bull only because the princes of Europe were otherwise engaged. The Tudor habit of searching history for the mirroring of the present in the past led to finding in the troubles of King John an image of the continuing conflict between church and state, pope and king, which was seen in the troubles of Henry VIII. Politicians studied King John; in 1524 Simon Fish took occasion to offer him for consideration in his *Supplication of Beggars*,[2] and in 1539, during the Christmas season, there was acted before the Archbishop of Canterbury "an enterlude concerning king John" which showed that "King John was as noble a prince as ever was in England, and . . . that he was the begynnyng of the puttyng down of the bishop of Rome." An eighteen-year-old witness of the play affirmed that he thought it "a pity the bp. of Rome should reign any longer, for he would do with our King as he did with King John."[3] John and his troubles with the pope and with Catholic rebels at home could be patterned instructively, and they were.

The play presented before the archbishop in 1539 was undoubtedly the *King Johan* of John Bale, whose theories about history we have already briefly considered,[4] and it offers a

[2]The date of the *Supplication* is disputed, but it was given as 1524 on the title page when it was reprinted in 1546 with *A Supplication of the Poore Commons*. The Preface to the Pickering reprint of 1845 offers evidence supporting the date. The comment on King John was answered by Sir Thomas More in his reply to Fish's work, *The Supplycation of Soules* (entered, 1529).

[3]See *Letters and Papers, Foreign and Domestic, of the Reign of Henry VIII*, XIV, Pt. 1, pp. 22-23, for the full account, part of which is quoted in the Malone Society reprint of *King Johan*, ed. J. H. P. Pafford and W. W. Greg (1931), pp. xvii-xviii.

[4]See above, pp. 62-64. For Bale's comment on Polydore Vergil's ill report of King John, see p. 108 of the Malone Society edition, to which edition I refer throughout this book.

unique opportunity to consider a history play of the reign of Henry VIII fashioned from the same basic material that was used in the two plays of the Elizabethan period, *The Trouble-some Raigne of John King of England* and the Shakespearean *King John*. Unfortunately we do not have Bale's play in its original form, and it is necessary in discussing it to remember the cumulative nature of the text which the editors of the Malone Society reprint have tentatively accounted for as follows:

At some unknown date, between his conversion to protestant views and the autumn of 1536, Bale wrote, among other dramatic experiments, a play in two parts in defense of King John. About 1537, when the violence of his religious opinions led to his expulsion from his living, he formed, under the patronage of Cromwell, a company of actors to perform plays in favour of the reformed religion. Four such pieces of his were 'Compyled' in 1538. The same year he conceived the idea of recasting his two-part play of *King Johan* into a single piece suitable for stage production. In doing so he introduced allusions to contemporary events, and produced the A-version, which was performed at the Archbishop's on 2 Jan. 1539. In 1540 Cromwell fell, and Bale's theatrical propaganda came to an end. Under Edward he seems to have revised the play, but it was probably the original two-part piece on which he worked . . . Then came Mary, and Bale's second exile. On his return, he saw a chance of producing his play before the new sovereign. Elizabeth was to visit Ipswich in Aug. 1561. Bale took up . . . the A-text, and set about revising it. . . .[5]

Though the play dealt with problems recurrent in the reigns of both Henry VIII and Elizabeth, and though it appears to have been revised during Elizabeth's reign, it was directed primarily at mirroring the troubles of Henry VIII with the pope and with the Catholics at home. There were many parallels between John and Henry that could have been noted—the divorce for conscience' sake, for instance—but most of them are ignored because they are irrelevant to the great conflict which centers the interest. Arthur does not appear at all, for Henry VIII had no Arthur problem. What Bale, Reformer and historian, pro-

[5]Pp. xxii-xxiii.

posed as his subject is stated by the Interpreter at the end of the first act:

> In thys present acte, we have to yow declared
> As in a myrrour, the begynnynge of kynge Johan
> . . . .
>
> Thys noble kynge Johan, as a faythfull Moyses
> withstode proude Pharao, for hys poore Israel
> Myndynge to brynge it, out of the lande of Darknesse
> But the Egyptanes, ded agaynst hym so rebell
> That hys poore people, [must] ded styll in the desart dwell
> Tyll that duke Josue, whych was our late kynge Henrye
> Clerely brought us in, to the lande of mylke and honye.[6]

And the political teaching of the play is expounded by Veritas:

> for Gods sake obeye, lyke as doth yow befall
> for in hys owne realme, a kynge is judge over all
> By Gods appoyntment, and none maye hym judge agayne
> But the lorde hymself: In thys the scripture is playne
> He that condempneth a kynge, condempneth God without
>   dought
> He that harmeth a kynge, to harme God goeth abought
> He that a prince resisteth, doth dampne Gods ordynaunce
> And resisteth God, in withdrawynge hys affyaunce
> All subjectes offendynge, are undre the kynges judgement
> A kynge is reserved, to the lorde omnypotent
> He is a mynyster, immediate undre God
> of hys ryghteousnesse, to execute the rod
> I charge you therfor, as God hath charge me
> To gyve to your kynge, hys due supremyte
> And exyle the pope, thys realme for evermore.[7]

But it is the plot which discovers to us the way in which the story is made to reflect the situation under Henry VIII. King Johan, as the play opens, views with pity the poor widow, England, who has come to complain of the wrongs done her by the Catholic church, but Sedition enters, defiantly proclaiming the rights of the pope:

> for his holy cawse, I maytayne traytours and Rebelles

[6] P. 52.
[7] P. 116.

> that no prince can have, his peples obedyence
> except yt doth stand, with the popes prehemynence. . .[8]

Johan warns Clergy, Nobility, and Civil Order against Sedition, coming to the crux of the problem as the Tudor sovereigns saw it:

> but I put the case, that this false thefe sedycyon
> shuld cum to yow thre, and call hymselfe Relygyon
> myght he not under, the pretence of holynes
> cawse yow to consent, to myche ungodlynes?[9]

Sedition, sent away temporarily while Clergy remains to argue with Nobility, is soon back again threatening the pope's bull, but the king is reported indifferent to papal action. Dissimulation then brings in Private Wealth, Private Wealth brings in Usurped Power, and Usurped Power brings back Sedition again. As they consult what to do with Johan, Sedition offers a plan:

> suspend him. and curse hym, both with yowr word and wrytyng
> yf that wyll not holpe, than Interdyght his land
> with extrem cruellnes, and yf that wyll not stand
> cause other prynces, to revenge the churchys wronge,

adding that

> for clene remyssyon, one kyng wyll subdew another
> yea the chyld sumtyme, wyll sle both father and mother.[10]

Sedition, clothed in the habit of Religion, is successful in securing the submission of the nobles to the church by promising remission of their sins, and he then releases them from obedience to their king. The clergy aid by preaching the danger of hell incurred by all the people through the interdicting of their land on the king's account, urging them to depose the king and to make sure that succeeding kings will not depart from the church. Johan, meanwhile, continues to defy the pope, contending that the power of princes is God-given, and that the office of the clergy is to give Christian counsel, not to bear the sword.

But the clergy, the lawyers, and the nobility are all traitors

[8]P. 12.
[9]P. 26.
[10]P. 48.

to their king, and Johan is unable to promise restitution to England and her poor blind son, Commonalty. Cardinal Pandulphus is, therefore, able to make the commons (Commonalty) also submit to the church. Threatened by the cardinal with the armies of the Scots on the north, the French on the south, the Spanish on the west, and the Danes and Norwegians on the east, the helpless king, in spite of the exhortations of England, submits in order to avoid the horrors of war and yields his crown. Five days later, after acceding to all the demands of the church, he receives his crown again from the cardinal. The play moves on to the death of Johan by poisoning and to the final admonitions by Veritas, Nobility, Civil Order, Clergy, and Imperial Majesty, all of which repeat the central lesson set forth by Veritas in the passage which I have already quoted.

Thus Bale's play, while presenting King Johan as the forerunner of Henry VIII in freeing England from the dominion of the church, yet mirrors the central problem of the reign of Johan as being that which beset the Tudor reigns: the disaffection of Englishmen, particularly the clergy and the nobles, under the influence of the Catholic church, with sedition clothed in the garments of religion. The claim of the pope to act as God's agent in giving and withholding earthly crowns was also set forth at length. The use made of historical material was that which historians had agreed upon as the proper use of history. The plot was political. The personifications were political: 1) political units—England, Nobility, Clergy, Commonalty, etc.—and 2) political virtues and vices—Sedition, Treason, Private Wealth, Usurped Power, Civil Order, etc. The historical characters, though much more like the universalized characters of the moraiities, such as Everyman and Kindred, than like their historical counterparts, performed their accepted function in a historical play by acting as a mirror which could teach and warn those of the latter time.

Because he fails to take into consideration the purpose of history as the Tudors saw it, Professor Dover Wilson is startled to discover that Bale was not alone in his treatment of King John as the Moses of the Reformation:

Nor is the point of view peculiar to Bale. We are not surprised to find it running as an undercurrent through the chapters on John in Foxe's *Acts and Monuments*. But it is rather remarkable that Holinshed, the greatest of Elizabethan historiographers, with the medieval chronicles before him and concerned to write history and not a Protestant homily, should go further out of his way to defend the 'Moses' of the Reformation than the martyrologist himself.[11]

As a matter of fact, Grafton had incorporated in his *Chronicle* practically intact the account of King John given by Foxe in the 1563 edition of his work. Holinshed, however, seems to have made a new study of the reign, reviewing the older chronicles and passing judgment upon them as well as upon John. But the point of view in regard to the Catholic church is the same.

It was apparently from Holinshed's chronicle that the anonymous author of *The Troublesome Raigne of John King of England*[12] selected the episodes which he rearranged and combined into a new chain of cause and effect. The play was in two parts, perhaps because *Tamburlaine* was in two parts, and the address "To the Gentlemen Readers" set forth the continuing conception of John as a Christian martyr:

> You that with friendly grace of smoothed brow
> Have entertained the *Scythian Tamburlaine*,
> And given applause unto an Infidel:
> Vouchsafe to welcome (with like curtesie)
> A warlike Christian and your Countryman.
> For Christs true faith indur'd he many a storme,
> And set himselfe against the Man of Rome,
> Untill base treason (by a damned wight)
> Did all his former triumphs put to flight.

There is no evidence to show that Shakespeare knew Bale's *King Johan*, but it is generally agreed that he derived his play of *King John*, scene by scene, from *The Troublesome Raigne*, though he made it into a one-part play. *King John* is, indeed, so like *The Troublesome Raigne* that for our purpose it seems unnecessary to discuss the plays separately. Shakespeare omitted

[11]*King John* (Cambridge, 1936), Introduction, pp. xiii-xiv.
[12]Published in 1591.

the scene in which Faulconbridge ransacks the monastery and convent, with its indecorous and irreverent comedy; he omitted the actual poisoning of King John; and he made minor charges in other episodes which have been listed by editors,[13] but which do not change fundamentally the plot or the political significance of the play.

In order to understand, however, the way in which these Elizabethan plays retold the story of King John to make it a useful mirror, it is necessary to survey the story of that unhappy king as it was told by the Elizabethan chroniclers and particularly by Holinshed, who remains the accepted ultimate source. The Boswell-Stone arrangement of source material in *Shakespeare's Holinshed*, however useful, shows only the relation of individual episodes in the plays to their historical sources and befogs for those students of Shakespeare who do not go independently to the chronicles the importance of the changes in chronology and in the interrelation of events which were made by the dramatist. The story of King John was subjected to unusual distortion as it passed from chronicle to play, and I propose to rehearse, therefore, in their chronological order as given by Holinshed[14] the most important of the events culled by the author of *The Troublesome Raigne* and adopted by Shakespeare. But I omit the events irrelevant to the story as told by the Elizabethan dramatists.

In the beginning of John's reign there was trouble over Arthur. At the time of Richard Coeur de Lion's death the matter of the succession was in dispute. Richard had willed the throne to his brother John, and Eleanor, the queen mother, supported John's claim against that of her grandson Arthur, the son of John's deceased elder brother, Geoffrey, and his wife Constance, a woman whom Eleanor much misliked. Constance entrusted Arthur to the protection of Philip, the French king.

[13]Ivor B. John, the editor of the English Arden edition (London, 1907 and 1925), has given a carefully compiled list in his Introduction.

[14]I have used the 1587 edition of Holinshed as the one generally accepted as Shakespeare's source in writing his histories. It is also the edition presumably used by the author of *The Troublesome Raigne*.

War between Philip and John during the year 1199, the first year of the reign, was concluded by the marriage of the dauphin to Blanche, niece to John, who resigned his claim to all the towns taken by the French except Angiers and was given some other territory. But by 1202 Philip was making demands in the name of Arthur which John refused, the peace was ended, and in the ensuing struggle Arthur was taken prisoner. Holinshed records:

It is said that king John caused his nephue Arthur to be brought before him at Falais, and there went about to persuade him all that he could to forsake his freendship and aliance with the French king, and to leane and sticke to him being his naturall uncle. But Arthur like one that wanted good counsell, and abounding too much in his own wilfull opinion, made a presumptuous answer, not onelie denieng so to doo, but also commanding king John to restore unto him the realme of England, with all those other lands and posses- sions which king Richard had in his hand at the houre of his death. For sith the same apperteined to him by right of inheritance, he assured him, except restitution were made the sooner, he should not long continue quiet. King John being sore mooved with such words thus uttered by his nephue, appointed . . . that he should be straitlie kept in prison, as first in Falais, and after at Roan within the new castell there.[15]

John caused himself to be again crowned king at this time, just as demands were being made for Arthur's release. Holinshed takes account of the various rumors as to Arthur's final disap- pearance, noting in particular the rumor that John had ordered Arthur's eyes to be put out, but that Hubert de Burgh, his cus- todian, had ventured to disobey, thinking that the king had issued the order in angry fury and would repent it. The false news of Arthur's death, according to this rumor, brought such a tempest of disapproval from the "Britains" that John was later glad to announce that he was alive. But after his removal to Rouen in 1203 Arthur disappeared, and it was only rumor that made John either accessory to or active as the agent of his death. Constance had taken a new husband, who claimed in her name Arthur's dukedom of Brittany, and later joined with John against the French king to fight for his right.

[15]Holinshed, III, 165.

THE TROUBLESOME REIGN OF KING JOHN

John's troubles concerning Arthur were thus over in 1203, but in 1205 began his great conflict with the pope, for in that year he entered into a dispute with the monks of Canterbury over the election of a new archbishop. The matter was finally taken to the pope, who put aside the opposing candidates and demanded the election of a third person, Stephen Langton. The resulting quarrel led ultimately to the pope's excommunicating King John and interdicting his realm. Philip of France was called upon to execute the pope's bull. After a period of defiance and disaffection among his subjects John was forced in 1213 to yield his crown to the pope, and receiving it again at the hands of the papal legate, was forced to promise tribute for himself and his heirs. Peter the hermit had prophesied in January that at the feast of the Ascension John should be cast out of his kingdom, but the king had had the prophet cruelly executed. Now many saw his prophecy fulfilled.

But a third problem, that of internal conflict, arose for King John, newly reconciled to the church. In difficulty with his barons, he was aided by the pope, who proceeded to excommunicate those in rebellion against their king, his vassal. The barons appealed to the French king. Philip, having gladly prepared to execute the pope's bull against John, was equally ready to go to the aid of the rebelling barons. The dauphin, defying excommunication, set out for England, and the last year of John's reign saw the French invading England. The dying Frenchman, Melun, warned the disloyal nobles of the dauphin's intention to conquer England; but when John died, he left to his son a kingdom in which the French were still battling to an undetermined end. The peace was not made until 1218, after the battle of Lincoln and after the destruction of a French fleet which had been sent to the aid of the dauphin.

John's untimely death was variously explained, as Holinshed records, but according to the story which accounted for his death by poison administered by a monk, the monk was motivated (say Foxe, Grafton, and Holinshed) by his resentment at John's indifference to the welfare of his poor subjects.

The historical John thus had his troubles one at a time: first

Arthur supported by France, then the pope supported by France, then the rebel barons of England aided by France. But while he met the rebellion of his barons, John was supported by the pope, and the great battles of his closing years were fought against the excommunicated nobles and the excommunicated dauphin who was to be their chosen king. The end of the conflict did not come until the second year after John's death, and it came in a tripartite reconciliation among England and France and the church.

But this is not the way in which Shakespeare, basing his play upon *The Troublesome Raigne*, tells the story. The Arden editor has listed the changes, noting

above all, the close weaving together of the Papal interference, the death of Arthur, the baronial revolt as if brought about by Arthur's supposed murder, and the French invasion . . .

He comments, however, that "all these are felt to be dramatic gains."[16] Perhaps the changes do make for dramatic gains, but if Shakespeare's play is considered as a history play, mirroring the great political problem of Elizabeth's reign, it is to the pattern of events in Elizabeth's reign rather than to dramatic genius that we must look for the explanation. It is then easy to see why we find, if I may paraphrase the summary,

above all, the close weaving together of the Papal interference, the imprisonment and death of Mary, the revolt of the nobles as if brought about by Mary's imprisonment and death, and the Spanish attempt at invasion,

for this was the actual pattern of events in the long conflict between Elizabeth and the Catholic church.

Elizabeth had been deprived, of course, as soon as she was born. Cardinal Allen, who hoped to be another Pandulphus, in his *Admonition to the Nobility and People of England and Ireland* wrote in 1588:

And first of all it is notorious to the whole worlde, that Henrie the supposed father to this pretensed Queene, besides the infinite

[16]Ivor B. John, p. xxvii.

quantety and enormeous qualety, of his most execrable wickednes,
. . . was in fine, for his horrible sacriledges, murtheringe of Saintes,
and rebellion against Gods Churche, lawfully excommunicated and
deprived by Paulus tertius in the yeare 1535. and therewithall by
name and in particuler all the issue that should procede of his incest-
uous copulation with Anne Bullen, was moste justly declared illegitimate and uncapable of succession to the croune of England: and
that aswell by the sentence of the said Paule, and of his predecessor
Clement the VII. in the yeare of our lorde 1533. (bothe which stande
in their full force still) as by sundry actes of parliament made by
Henry him self and never repealed legitimating her sister and declaring her to be base, she must nedes be adjudged by lawe and nature
unable to inherite the croune.[17]

Henry VIII had, however, been empowered by Parliament, as
Pollard says, "to entail his kingdom like a fee," and he had
named Elizabeth as the third heir, passing over the right of the
Scotch line to succeed, if her heirs failed, in favor of the line
of his younger sister.[18] By reason of an unrepealed act of Parliament Elizabeth was still illegitimate when she succeeded, but
Parliament acted swiftly to declare her "to bee, both by the
Divine and Civill Law, and the Statutes of this Realme, . . . the
lawfull, undoubted, and direct Queene of *England*, rightly and
lawfully descending from the Royall Blood, according to the
order of succession."[19] Camden tells of the uncertainties of the
time and notes:

there were some that drew against her Majestie most dangerous in-
vectives and conclusions, in such manner as if she had not bin the
lawfull Queene, although the Lawes of *England* many yeeres ago
determined, . . . That the Crowne once possessed, cleareth and purifies all manner of defaults or imperfections.[20]

Though Elizabeth's right to the crown was disputed in
many quarters, the focus of the hopes of the Catholics both at

[17]*Op. cit.,* pp. viii-ix.
[18]On the whole matter of the will of Henry VIII see A. F. Pollard, *England
under Protector Somerset* (London, 1900), pp. 2-7.
[19]William Camden, *Annales* (London, 1625), Bk. I, p. 14.
[20]*Ibid.*

home and abroad became more and more definitely Mary of Scotland, granddaughter of Henry's oldest sister and wife of the dauphin of France, who became king in 1559. Mary Tudor had played her Spanish husband's game and had involved England in a war with France which lost Calais, the last English continental stronghold. Elizabeth was firm in her determination to regain Calais, but the French king met this determination implacably. Philip of Spain was bound to stand with the English, whose city had been lost in his wars, and as long as he hoped to marry Elizabeth and continue his influence in England, he did so. But when Elizabeth made it clear that his hopes were groundless, he ceased to be firm with France. The result was that the treaty of Cateau-Cambrésis, concluded on April 2 and 3, 1559, left Calais in the possession of the French for a period of eight years, when it should revert to the English and a large sum be paid them.[21] But Philip decided to marry Elizabeth, the daughter of the French king, in lieu of Elizabeth of England, good faith yielded to commodity, and the English were deprived of Calais forever. Professor Neale says of Mary Stuart and the English demand for Calais during these transactions:

Mary's claim had been mooted as a debating point during the peace negotiations. If we surrender Calais, the French said to the Spaniards, to whom shall we surrender it, for the Dauphin's wife is the rightful Queen of England?[22]

And he adds that after the peace, "Mary openly quartered the arms of England on her coat of arms, and English ambassadors were invited to feast off plate that flaunted her claim."

In 1560, however, the Treaty of Edinburgh was concluded, which recognized Elizabeth's right to the throne and bound the king and queen of France to abstain from her arms and title. But Mary found ways of procrastinating, her signature was not affixed, and she continued her claims. There followed the death of the French king, Mary's return to Scotland, and the series

[21] The modern standard account is Alphonse de Ruble, *Le Traité de Cateau-Cambrésis* (Paris, 1889). Among earlier sources Camden is particularly helpful (*Annales*, I, 18-25).

[22] J. E. Neale, *Queen Elizabeth* (New York, 1936), p. 84.

of swift-moving events in Scotland which ultimately led to her seeking refuge from her own people in England and to her spending the rest of her life as a prisoner in the country where she claimed the right to rule. The great test of her power in England came in the Northern Rebellion of 1569 and its aftermath.[23]

The putting down of the Northern Rebellion did not settle the conflict for the Catholics of England, however, and in February, 1570, Pope Pius V issued a bull of excommunication against Elizabeth which deprived her of her "pretended" title to her kingdom, released her subjects from their allegiance, and interdicted obedience to her laws and commands.[24] The bull was not "published" in England until May, and the pope did not succeed in securing the expected continental military support in executing it. The English Catholics were, therefore, placed in a difficult position. Pope Pius' successor, Gregory XIII, did, however, send two expeditions to Ireland to be launched against England, one in 1578 and the other in 1579. Both were unsuccessful, though reinforcements, organized in Spain, were sent in 1580. In 1580 also a new kind of mission was sent to England from the pope, bent ostensibly on saving English souls by the missionary efforts of Jesuit priests, with the famous Robert Parsons and Edward Campion as their leaders. Neale summarizes the significance of these attempts:

The efforts of the Papacy to bring about the "Enterprise of England," of which at this very time there was a pitiful manifestation in the Irish expedition, were unceasing. Those efforts always contemplated and relied upon support from a Catholic rising in England itself. Hence, the missionaries were in effect engaged in facilitating the destruction of Elizabeth.[25]

By 1582, says Professor Meyer in his study of *England and the Catholic Church under Queen Elizabeth*, Parsons advised Pope Gregory that the time for action had come and urged him

[23]See the chapter on *Henry IV* for a discussion of the Northern Rebellion as reflected in that play.

[24]The bull was translated in Camden, *Annales*, II, 245-48.

[25]Neale, p. 249.

to support the Duke of Guise's plan of invading England by renewing the excommunication. A new bull was drawn up bearing the date of September 24, 1583, and was to have been taken by William Allen when he should go with the invading army. But in 1583 a more dangerous Catholic plot, the Throckmorton plot, revolving about Mary as its center, revealed to Walsingham's spies the intrigues of the Spanish with many English gentlemen in collusion with the pope in what was known as "the Enterprise of England."[26] The progress of the Catholic plotting and of Walsingham's spying on the plotters is too complicated for recital here even if such a recital were desirable. It is only necessary to recall that the end was the inevitable elimination in 1587 of the central figure, Mary of Scotland, to Elizabeth's great grief (pretended or real).

In 1587, however, the execution of the pope's bull had finally been arranged for in an agreement between the pope and Spain, the terms of which provided:

The pope is willing to aid the king of Spain in his pious undertaking against England. If this is carried out in 1587 the pope will give one million gold ducats. The money will at once be placed in readiness. Payment of 500,000 ducats to be made as soon as the Spaniards have landed in England; the remainder in payments every two months. If England is conquered, the Spaniards to set up a good catholic sovereign, of whom the Holy See may approve, and who shall receive investiture from the pope.[27]

The defeat of the Armada in 1588 made an end to this attempt to execute the pope's bull against Elizabeth, though there were later abortive Spanish undertakings for its accomplishment.

Meanwhile the papal blessing implicitly offered to anyone who should rid the world of the "pretensed" queen, Elizabeth, had not gone unheeded. There were many attempts on her life, but those which seem most to have roused the public were the plots of Dr. Parry in 1584; the Babington plot of 1586-87, which

[26]A. O. Meyer, *England and the Catholic Church under Queen Elizabeth*, trans. J. R. McKee (London, 1916), pp. 285-86.

[27]*Ibid*., p. 520 (Appendix, Document XX). See also p. 323 for a discussion of the so-called bull issued by Sixtus V.

was the direct cause of Mary's execution; and the plot of the Jewish physician, Dr. Lopez, in 1594. The Babington plot planned the death of Elizabeth as the opening move in "the English Enterprise." Dr. Lopez was proved to be in the service of Philip of Spain, but whether his deed was part of a larger plan is still dark. In the case of Dr. Lopez, the *Calendar of State Papers* gives an abstract of the evidence laid before the jury which may serve as a summary of events hitherto recounted:

As an induction, it was showed that the grounds of all the traitorous plots against Her Majesty and the realm was not for any offence or cause on her part, but for her constant defence of Christ's cause and His Holy Word against the Pope, etc., and for protecting her dominions against the ambition of the King of Spain. That hereupon the Pope and King of Spain conspired against her, the King, by his power and greatness, propping up the Pope's falling, rotten, chair, and the Pope, under pretext of religion, preparing the way for the King's ambition. This was the original motive of the cursed bull of Pius V. From this root sprung all the rebellions, treasons, and devilish practices since attempted.

This course continued until the year 1588 . . . then their invincible navy, as they called it, in the height of their pride, was sent to root out true religion, and destroy by fire and sword all true professors of it, and to make a bloody conquest of England; but it was defeated by God and Her Majesty's princely care and providence, and by the valiantness of her nobles and true subjects. The King and his priests, despairing of prevailing by valour, turn to cowardly treachery, and what they could not do by the cannon, they attempt by crowns. To achieve this, they put in practice three devilish attempts,—to burn the navy and ships with poisoned fireworks; to seduce some of the chief of the nobility to rebellion; and to take the blood of a virgin Queen, as whilst she lives they are hopeless; they have therefore plotted to murder her violently or by secret poison.[28]

It is apparent that Elizabeth's troubles with the Catholic church were for long centered about the person of Mary of

[28]*Calendar of State Papers, Domestic, 1591-1594,* pp. 445-46. The Catholic explanation of these events is well presented by J. H. Pollen, "The Politics of English Catholics during the Reign of Queen Elizabeth," *Month,* LXXXXIX (1902), 43-60.

Scotland. While Arthur, therefore, did not figure in Bale's play of *King Johan*, he was an essential figure in any mirroring of the problems of Elizabeth's reign in that of King John. And, as I have said, it is easy from this point of view to see why Shakespeare wove together with complete disregard for historical accuracy "the Papal interference, the death of Arthur, the baronial revolt as if brought about by Arthur's supposed murder, and the French invasion." For Mary was the focusing point of the opposition of the Catholic church, of France and then of Spain, and of the English rebels. Likewise it will be understood that the omission of Magna Carta from Shakespeare's play of *King John* has nothing to do with Shakespeare's opinion of that venerable document, for there was no Magna Carta to bother Elizabeth, just as there had been no Arthur to add to the troubles of Henry VIII.

Long before Shakespeare's play, however, both Catholics and Protestants were arguing the conflicts of Elizabeth and the Catholic church in terms of the conflicts of John's reign. It was no less a person than John Leslie, Bishop of Ross and Mary's most persistent supporter, who, in 1569, argued Mary's right to succeed in terms of Arthur. His argument, ostensibly directed to urging that she be allowed to succeed rather than to supplant Elizabeth, considered at length the rejection of the Scotch line from the succession and proved from Arthur's case that it is weak ground "to make the place, of the nativitie of an inheritour to a kingdom a sufficient barre against the right of his bloude." He contended that since Richard I had named Arthur—born in Brittany and not son of a king—heir apparent, John was considered an usurper for excluding him and a murderer for imprisoning and making away with him. He added:

For the whiche facte the Frenche kinge seased upon all the goodlie contries in France belonginge to the kinge of Englande, as forfeited to him being the chiefe lorde. By this owtragious deede of kinge John we lost Normandie with all, and our possibilities to the inheritaunce of all Britanie . . .[29]

[29]John Leslie, *A Defence of the Right Highe, Mightye and Noble Princesse Marie Queene of Scotland and Dowager of France* (London, 1569), fols. 77-79.

Furthermore, he pointed out that the English nobles rebelling against John gave allegiance to the French king, Philip, in the right of his wife Blanche (who had been born in Spain and hence outside England), and to their son Lewis. In 1584 Leslie included Mary's son James in arguing for her right and her son's right to succeed, and he still used Arthur as a basis for his long exposition of the issues at stake.[30]

But King John was also made a case in point in 1571 when, after the Northern Rebellion, there was published the famous *Homilie against Disobedience and Wylfull Rebellion*, appointed to be read in all the churches, and thus made familiar to all Englishmen. The argument concerning John is very long, and I shall quote only a part, but it is important as representing the official acceptance of John as a proper mirror for Elizabethan England:

And to use one example of our owne countrey: The Byshop of Rome dyd pyke a quarell to kyng John of Englande, about the election of Steven Langton to the bishoprike of Canterburie, wherein the kyng had aunciént ryght, . . . the Byshop of Rome having no right, but had begun then to usurpe upon the kynges of Englande, and all other Christian kinges, as they had before done against their soveraigne lords the Emperours: proceedyng even by the same wayes and meanes, and likewise cursing kyng John, and discharging his subjects of their othe of fidelitie unto their soveraigne lorde. Nowe had Englishmen at that tyme knowen their dutie to their prince set foorth in Gods worde, woulde a great meanie of the nobles, and other Englishmen, naturall subjectes, for this soveraigne and unnatural usurper his curse of the kyng, and for his fayned discharging of them of their othe of fidelitie to their naturall lorde, . . . have rebelled against their soveraigne lord the kyng? Woulde Englishe subjects have taken part against the kyng of Englande, and against Englishmen, with the Frenche king and Frenchmen, being incensed against this Realme by the byshop of Rome? . . . would they have driven their naturall Soveraigne Lorde the king of Eng-

---

[30]In *A Treatise Towching the Right, Title, and Interest of the Most Excellent Princesse Marie, Queene of Scotland, and of the Most Noble King James, Her Graces Sonne, to the Succession of the Crowne of England.* See especially fols. 34-36.

lande to such extremitie, that he was inforced to submit him selfe unto that forraine false usurper, the byshop of Rome . . . ?

The homily joins "unto the reportes of histories, matters of later memorie," chiefly the current matter of the Bishop of Rome's connection with the Northern Rebellion.[31] King James later, in 1615, in his *Defence of the Rights of Kings* chose to go back to John in offering a lengthy exposition of the rights of kings in relation to the church.[32]

But even in the matter of rebellion the Catholics too were willing to argue the case of John, as is seen in Cardinal Allen's *Defence of Sir William Stanley's Surrender*, for he wrote:

what disgrace, or shame was it, for al the chiefe Lordes of our countrie, to revolt from King John, in his dayes? and absolutely to denie him ayde, and assistance, even in his lawfull warres, until he returned againe to the obedience of the Sea Apostolike, and were absolved from the censures of the same, which he had justly incurred?[33]

It is no wonder, then, that Shakespeare, like the author of *The Troublesome Raigne*, should have chosen to mirror the conflict of England and the Catholic church in the troubles of John. The major political problems of concern whenever "the things that be Caesar's" are to be determined in relation to "the things that be God's" will best be considered separately. But in order to demonstrate how Shakespeare (following *The Troublesome Raigne*) used the story of John to reflect the particular aspects of the general problem as they presented themselves in his own time, it is necessary to note some of the departures from history and some particular adaptations of history which appear when the plot of *King John* is reviewed against the background of

[31]Alfred Hart, *Shakespeare and the Homilies*, writes of the book of homilies as "A New Shakespearean Source-Book," but he does not mention the passage on King John.

[32]*The Political Works of James I*, ed. C. H. McIlwain (Cambridge, Mass., 1918), pp. 259-62.

[33]*Op. cit.*, ed. Thomas Heywood (Chetham Society Publication XXV; 1851), p. 26. The original title was *The Copie of a Letter . . . Concerninge the Yeelding up, of the Citie of Daventrie . . . by Sir William Stanley, Knight.*

the historical account of the reign of that much troubled king.

The opening scene of Shakespeare's play reveals Chatillon, newly arrived to present the French king's support of Arthur's claims in defiance of John's "borrowed majesty," sent back to his master with angry words from the English king. Turning to his mother as she bewails the necessity for war, John declaims,

> Our strong possession and our right for us.

To which Elinor answers:

> Your strong possession much more than your right,
> Or else it must go wrong with you and me: . . .

Boswell-Stone notes that "There is no historical authority for Chatillon's embassage; nor did Philip demand that England and Ireland should be yielded to Arthur,"[34] but he might have added that for Mary of Scotland, the wife of the dauphin, such demands were made and were supported by the French. To these demands Elizabeth offered her strong possession much more than her right, and previous commentators have noted that these words, amplified from a passage in *The Troublesome Raigne*, and having no historical authority, were, in fact, put there to echo the situation of Elizabeth rather than John.[35]

The second act begins with Austria and his forces, Philip of France and the dauphin, Arthur and his mother, and the French forces gathering before Angiers. Chatillon enters, returning from England, and almost at the same time King John and his mother, Faulconbridge, and the English forces appear. The kings of France and England exchange accusations and offer counterclaims. Elinor asserts

> I can produce
> A will that bars the title of thy son.

And Constance replies:

> Ay, who doubts that? a will! a wicked will;

which exchange, though possible between the mothers of John

---

[34]W. G. Boswell-Stone, *Shakspere's Holinshed* (New York, 1896), p. 47.
[35]See Richard Simpson, "The Politics of Shakespere's Historical Plays" in *New Shakespere Society Transactions*, I (1874), 399.

and Arthur, would certainly ring familiarly in the ears of the generation which had heard the long debate over the much-disputed will of Henry VIII, with its passing over of the rights of the Scotch line.[36]

King Philip proposes to let the men of Angiers decide the title by choosing to whom they will submit; but the men of Angiers refuse to open their gates to either force, not being able to decide who is the real king of England, even though John again advances his chief argument,

> Doth not the crown of England prove the king?

There is no such uncertainty expressed by the men of Angiers in the chronicles, but it will be remembered that in the negotiations preceding the 1559 treaty of Cateau-Cambrésis the citizens of Calais were said to have quibbled in exactly this fashion.[37] The reconciliation effected in the play between the kings of France and England through a marriage between the Dauphin Lewis and Blanche, niece of King John and daughter of the King of Castile, ignores the claims of Arthur, for whom Philip had gone to war. It is upon this occasion that Faulconbridge makes his great speech upon commodity, concluding,

> Since kings break faith upon commodity,
> Gain, be my lord, for I will worship thee.

It is a perfect comment on the treaty of Cateau-Cambrésis and on Philip of Spain's perfidy in regard to Calais, but there is nothing in Holinshed to justify such an interpretation of the French Philip's treatment of Arthur.

As Constance bewails to Arthur the woes resulting from this match-making treaty, Cardinal Pandulph as agent of the pope arrives to chide John for his attitude toward the appointment of Stephen Langton as archbishop of Canterbury. John as king defies the pope, and as an Englishman defies the foreign priest. His message goes further:

[36]Noted by Simpson, p. 400.

[37]Noted by Simpson, pp. 400-401.

> But as we, under heaven, are supreme head,
> So under Him that great supremacy,
> Where we do reign, we will alone uphold,
> Without the assistance of a mortal hand:
> So tell the pope, all reverence set apart
> To him and his usurp'd authority.

Of course, the historic John never claimed the title of *supreme head*, and it is a definite anachronism appearing at any time previous to the reign of Henry VIII. I shall have more to say on this point later, but it should be noted here in passing. Upon this challenge Pandulph excommunicates John in the name of the pope and blesses his murderer. Then releasing King Philip from his newly-sworn oath of amity to the English king, he urges him to become the champion of the church in executing the pope's bull, as King Philip of Spain was asked to become the champion of the church in executing the papal bull against Elizabeth.

Since there is no account in Shakespeare's play of the intervening wars and of the capture of Arthur, as there is in *The Troublesome Raigne*, it is something of a surprise to find, after alarums and excursions, that Arthur is now in the power of King John, who entrusts him to Hubert de Burgh with ominous muttered commands of "Death," and "A grave," even as he quite casually authorizes Faulconbridge to ransack the monasteries.

In the midst of the mad grief of Constance for her son and the discouraged sorrowing of King Philip and the dauphin for the French armado wrecked by a tempest, Pandulph appears to counsel patience and offer hope. He assures Lewis that John will surely not suffer Arthur to live for long, and that as the husband of Blanche, the dauphin will be recognized as the next heir and acclaimed by the people when they hear of Arthur's death. Critics have seen in this advice of Pandulph a reference to similar advice given to Philip of Spain when he was counseled to await the death of Mary Stuart in the expectation of papal support for his cause. Very recently it has come to light that Robert Parsons was, apparently without the knowledge of the pope, making such suggestions to the Spanish king just before

Mary's death.[38] At any rate, it is a scene impossible historically, for Arthur had vanished three years before John's troubles with the church, as has already been pointed out.

Hubert is now shown, about to carry out the royal command to put out Arthur's eyes but relenting at the crucial moment, while a younger, wiser, and humbler Arthur than is shown in the chronicles interprets John's position, "He is afraid of me and I of him." It is an interpretation which explains perfectly the relation between Elizabeth and Mary through the long years of Mary's confinement in England.

King John, demanding and receiving a second coronation with the nobles renewing their oaths of fealty, promises them a boon, and they demand Arthur's freedom as the promised boon. Hubert makes an untimely entrance to announce the death of Arthur, and the angry nobles leave the presence of the king, while he sorrows for his sins:

> They burn in indignation. I repent:
> There is no sure foundation set on blood,
> No certain life achieved by others' death.

John's sorrows press upon him. A messenger reports his mother's death, just three days after the death of Arthur's mother.[39] There is news of the hermit's prophecy that John will yield his throne before Ascension Day. When word is also brought that the French have arrived, and that the nobles have gone to seek the grave of Arthur, the much-troubled king implores,

[38]Tentatively suggested by Simpson, p. 401. Under date of March 18, 1587, Parsons wrote the reasons that made it inadvisable to make known to the pope the interest that Philip of Spain had in "the Enterprise." He thought that when the whole of Elizabeth's kingdom and the neighboring islands were in the King of Spain's hands the time would be more propitious "for then the Queen of Scotland will be either dead or alive: if she is dead—and it is probable that the heretics having her in their power and being under the impression that the expedition is being made in support of her cause, will put her to death—there will be no other Catholic prince alive who can compete with His Majesty." If she were still alive, he said, the claims of Lancastrian descent could be urged. *Letters and Memorials of Father Robert Parsons, S.J.*, ed. L. Hicks, S.J. (Catholic Record Society Publications, XXXIX: London, 1942), I, 292-94.

[39]Not historically correct. Constance died in 1201, Elinor in 1204.

> O, let me have no subject enemies,
> When adverse foreigners affright my towns
> With dreadful pomp of stout invasion!

But the omen of five moons seen in the sky makes the people murmur, and John chides the faithful Hubert for having obeyed his command for Arthur's death. Hubert's admission that Arthur still breathes brings short-lived joy, for Arthur, despairing, has killed himself while trying to escape, and the nobles, finding his body, are determined to seek revenge for what they deem his murder.

Now there is in the Elizabethan chronicles no indication that John mourned the death of Arthur, for there is no record of his ever having admitted that Arthur was dead. But there is ample evidence of Elizabeth's grief over the death of Mary and of her blaming her counsellors for having executed her command. And the whole history of the almost twenty years of Mary's stay in England tells the tale of the support given her by the Catholic nobles and of their constant threat of rebellion on her behalf. But of all this more will be said a little later.

John in desperation yields his crown to Pandulph and receives it from him again as from the pope. Thereafter the pope supports the king, but the nobles, angered by Arthur's death, plot with the dauphin, who refuses to drop his claims at the cardinal's command, protesting,

> What penny hath Rome borne,
> What men provided, what munition sent,

as Spain might well have protested after having undertaken the English Enterprise with the promised financial support of the Catholic church.

The great armado of the French is wrecked as was the Spanish Armada in 1588. The play hurries to its end. John appears, stricken with illness. The dying Melun betrays the real French design on England,[40] the nobles become again loyal Englishmen,

---

[40]Simpson suggested (p. 402) a parallel with Medina Sidonia. The authority is William Watson, *Important Considerations* (1601), p. 25. Watson's book is interesting because it sets forth the position of the English Catholics who are loyal to Elizabeth and opposed to the foreign-inspired activities of the pope, Spain, and the Jesuits.

and the dauphin is forced to leave England. John is poisoned by a monk, and Prince Henry is recognized as his successor when peace is restored between France and England. The theme of the play is sounded as a finale:

> This England never did, nor never shall,
> Lie at the proud foot of a conqueror,
> But when it first did help to wound itself.

The concluding words[41] which I have quoted from the summary of the evidence placed before the jury when Dr. Lopez, in the pay of Spain, had tried to poison Elizabeth are here in point, for after the defeat of the Armada, Spain had indeed tried by golden crowns "to seduce some of the chief nobility to rebellion," and to murder Elizabeth "violently or by secret poison." Nor was it forgotten in Elizabethan England that in 1589 Henry III of France had been poisoned by a monk.

But such indications of the ways in which the historical narrative were altered in order to make the mirroring of the contemporary situation more effective fail to suggest the full significance of the history play as a political play. In order to grasp that significance we must see also the use that is made of dialogue and situation to set forth the great political problems involved. Of these there were four, it seems to me: 1) the right of Elizabeth to the throne; 2) the right of the pope to deprive a ruler of his crown; 3) the right of subjects to rebel; and 4) the right of a king to be answerable for his sins to God alone. All four of these problems are discussed in *King John*, and all four were stated explicitly in the sentence upon Elizabeth pronounced in the papal bull of 1570.

As to the first of these problems, the papal bull refers to Elizabeth as "the pretended Queene of England," and I have already pointed out that she had been deprived as soon as she was born. It was upon the will of Henry VIII and the ratification by Parliament of the succession there ordered that Elizabeth depended for her claim to the throne. In case of the failure of Elizabeth's heirs, the will passed over the Scotch line descending

[41]See p. 141.

from Henry's elder sister Margaret in favor of the heirs of his younger sister Mary. I have earlier quoted Camden's statement that the laws of England had long since determined "That the Crown once possessed, cleareth and purifies all manner of defaults or imperfections," and it was upon this point of law that Elizabeth stood, even as John was represented as standing. The episodes in which the matter is discussed in the play have already been enumerated and need not be reviewed here.

The second problem, the alleged right of the pope to deprive a king, was, of course, of tremendous concern during the reigns of Henry VIII and Elizabeth. The bull explained the grounds of the papal authority:

Hee that rules in the Heavens above, and to whom all power is given both in Heaven and Earth, gave unto one onely upon Earth, viz. to *Peter*, . . . and to the *Pope* of Rome, *Peters* Successor, a holy, Catholique and Apostolique Church, . . . to governe it in the fulnesse of power. And this he ordayned as chiefe above all Nations and Kingdomes, to pull downe, destroy, dissever, cast off, plant, and erect: . . .[42]

William Allen as "Cardinal of England," coming to act as papal legate and to restore the English church to Rome as Pandulph had done earlier, wrote that among the reasons why Elizabeth could not be considered queen, the one above all, was

that she never had consente nor any approbation of the See Apostolike, without which, she nor any other can be lawfull Kinge or Quene of Englande, by reason of the auncyent Acorde, made betwene Alexander the .III. the yere 1171. and Henry the II. . . . This accorde afterwardes beinge renewed, aboute the yere 1210. by Kinge John, who confirmed the same by othe to Pandulphus the Pope his legate . . .[43]

Foxe and after him Grafton had given a full account of the Council of the Lateran in which Pope Innocent III

---

[42]Camden, *Annales*, II, 245.

[43]*An Admonition to the Nobility and People of England and Ireland concerninge the Warres Made for the Execution of His Holines Sentence, by the highe and mightie King Catholike of Spaine. By the Cardinal of Englande* (1588), pp. 9-10.

made this Act, and established it by publique decree, that the Pope shoulde have from thence foorth the correction of all Christian Princes, and that no Emperour should be admitted, except he were sworne before, and were also crowned of him.[44]

Even when James came to the throne in 1603, succeeding Elizabeth, this was the main difficulty, for as Godfrey Davies says,

If the Pope would relinquish his claim to the power of deposition and would not insist on his precedence over monarchs, James seems to have believed that reconciliation with Rome was possible.[45]

James indeed pleaded for tolerance in religious matters, but decried the Catholic priests:

Their point of doctrine is that arrogant and ambitious Supremacie of their Head the Pope, whereby he not onely claimes to bee Spirituall head of all Christians, but also to have an Imperiall civill power over all Kings and Emperors, dethroning and decrowning Princes with his foot as pleaseth him, and dispensing and disposing of all Kingdomes and Empires at his appetite. The other point which they observe in continuall practise, is the assassinates and murthers of Kings, thinking it no sinne, but rather a matter of salvation, to doe all actions of rebellion and hostilitie against their naturall Soveraigne Lord, if he be once cursed, his subjects discharged of their fidelitie, and his Kingdome given a prey by that three crowned Monarch, or rather Monster their Head.[46]

Since papal bulls had attempted to deprive two of the Tudors of their crowns and had interdicted their land, to both Elizabeth and James the question of the pope's supremacy over kings was of even more importance than was the king's supremacy over a national church. But it was the latter problem that brought the clash between the pope and King Henry VIII as well as

[44]Grafton, *Chronicle*, Pt. II, p. 110. The account is taken from John Foxe, *Actes and Monumentes* (London, 1563), p. 66.

[45]Godfrey Davies, "The Character of James VI and I," *Huntington Library Quarterly*, V (1941), 51.

[46]In a speech delivered in 1603. McIlwain, *op. cit.*, p. 275. For Elizabethan attacks on this papal pretense to authority see Thomas Bilson, *The True Difference betweene Christian Subjection and Unchristian Rebellion* (Oxford, 1585), p. 529; and William Cecil, *The Execution of Justice in England* (London, 1583), fol. A3.

between the pope and King John. Nor does the papal bull directed against Elizabeth neglect this aspect of the problem:

It is She, who after shee had possessed the Kingdome, usurping (monster-like) the place of the chiefe Soveraigne of the Church in England, and the principall jurisdiction and authoritie thereof, hath throwne into miserable ruine the whole Kingdome, . . .

and it lists among her sins the fact that she has

displaced the Bishops, Rectors, and Catholique Priests from their Churches and Benefices, and disposed of them to Heretiques, and is bold to take upon her to judge and determine Ecclesiasticall affaires; . . . inforced divers to . . . acknowledge her the onely Soveraigne over temporall and spirituall things . . .[47]

It was the pope's refusal to accept John's candidate for archbishop of Canterbury and the king's refusal to accept the pope's nomination that ultimately brought about the excommunication of the king and his deprivation. Though to Elizabeth and to her successor the matter of pre-eminent importance was the pope's right to give and take away kingly crowns, yet the right of the king to be supreme head of the church was the concave of the convex of the problem. Elizabeth declared by proclamation, says Camden,

That she attributed no more unto her selfe, then what did of long time belong to the Crowne of England; which was, that next under God, she had supreme Soveraignetie and power over all the States of *England*, whether Ecclesiasticall or Laye, and that no other Forraigne Power, had, or could have any Jurisdiction or authority over them.[48]

In the growing nationalism of Elizabethan England the matter of national versus foreign supremacy over the national church was also, it should be noted, a potent factor in forming opinion.[49]

---

[47]Camden, *Annales*, II, 246-47.

[48]*Op. cit.*, I, 34. "Supreme soveraignetie" was not an appeasing phrase.

[49]The act (Jan. 1 of the first parliament in the first year) is "An acte restoringe to the crowne the ancient jurisdiction over the state ecclesiastical and spirytuall, and abolyshynge all forrayne power repugnant to the same." It mentions repeatedly "usurped and forrayne power."

It is against this background of conflict between pope and queen that we must then listen to Shakespeare's Pandulph challenging John in the name of the pope:

> Why thou against the church, our holy mother,
> So wilfully dost spurn; and force perforce
> Keep Stephen Langton, chosen archbishop
> Of Canterbury, from that holy see: . . .

And we must hear John, in the voice of Elizabeth, reply:

> What earthy name to interrogatories
> Can task the free breath of a sacred king?
>
> . . . .
>
> Tell him this tale; and from the mouth of England
> Add thus much more, that no Italian priest
> Shall tithe or toll in our dominions;
> But as we, under heaven, are supreme head,
> So under Him that great supremacy,
> Where we do reign, we will alone uphold,
> Without the assistance of a mortal hand:
> So tell the pope, all reverence set apart
> To him and his usurp'd authority.[50]

There has been some tendency on the part of Catholic writers to quibble about the meaning of *supreme head* in John's speech,[51] inasmuch as Elizabeth did not use her father's title but that of *supreme governour*, but the pope's bull makes it clear that he did not quibble over it, and Cardinal Allen said that "we speak no untrewth . . . nor abuse not the world when we say she is called and taken for the Supreme head of the Church of England."[52] The anachronism in making John appropriate the title so much in dispute can hardly have been accidental.

[50]III, i, 141-60.

[51]See, for instance, G. M. Greenewald, *Shakespeare's Attitude Towards the Catholic Church in "King John"* (Washington, D.C., 1938), p. 67.

[52]The words in the bull were *supremi Ecclesiae capitis locum.* Cf. William Allen, *A True, Sincere, and Modest Defence of English Catholiques* [Ingolstadt, 1584], p. 9. Allen's *Admonition to the Nobility* (p. 11) said "She usurpeth by Luciferian pride, the title of supreme ecclesiasticall government."

154

With nice irony Shakespeare portrays Lewis as also defying the pope's supreme power to make and unmake kings when, after John's submission to Rome, Cardinal Pandulph orders the dauphin to wind up his "threatening colours," and put away his threats of war against England:

> Am I Rome's slave? What penny hath Rome borne,
> What men provided, what munition sent,
> To underprop this action? . . . . . .
> Have I not heard these islanders shout out
> "Vive le roi!" as I have bank'd their towns?
> Have I not here the best cards for the game,
> To win this easy match play'd for a crown?
> And shall I now give o'er the yielded seat?
> No, no, on my soul, it never shall be said.[53]

The third of the problems was of much broader scope than the phase which is presented in connection with the Catholic conflict, for in both Protestant and Catholic circles there was a bitter fight as to the right of a subject to rebel. The basis of the Catholic rebellions throughout the reign of Elizabeth was constantly affirmed to be, as I have already indicated, the papal bull which decreed:

Being then supported by His Authoritie, who hath placed Us upon this Soveraigne Throne of Justice, . . . doe pronounce and declare the said ELIZABETH an Heretique, and favourer of Heretiques, and those who adhere unto her in the foresaid things, have incurred the Sentence of Anathema, and are cut off from the unitie of the bodie of Christ. That shee is deprived of the righte which shee pretends to the foresaid Kingdome, and of all and every Seigniorie, Royaltie, and privilege thereof: and the Peeres, Subjects, and People of the sayde Kingdome, and all others upon what terms soever sworne unto her, freed from their Oath, and from all manner of dutie, fidelitie, and obedience: As Wee doe free them by the authoritie of these Presents, and exclude the said ELIZABETH from the right which she pretendeth to the said Kingdome, and the rest before mentioned. Commanding moreover, and enjoyning all, and every the Nobles, as Subjects, people, and others whatsoever, that they shall not once

---

[53] V, ii, 97-108.

dare to obey her, or any her directions, Lawes, or Commandements, binding under the same Curse, those who doe any thing to the contrary.[54]

The official pronouncement of the Tudors "against disobedience and wylfull rebellion" was made in the homilies of 1547 and 1571, the latter of which, I have already pointed out, discusses at length the case of King John. The king, according to the doctrine here enunciated, is vice-gerent to God, a god under God, accountable only to God. A subject may not judge his king, however evil, but must leave his punishment to God. Rebellion against a king is rebellion against the King of kings, the God of gods, and will surely call forth God's vengeance. But during the troubled years when the ideas of the Reformers were in ferment, and when both Catholics and Reformers were forced to rationalize their desires, there were many questions raised corollary to the fundamental and generally accepted position. In the first place, there arose the question already discussed, whether the natural heir or the *de facto* ruler should be regarded as God's vice-gerent. Second, there was the burning question of whether the subject should obey man rather than God if the ruler was in opposition to God; and whether resistance, if offered, should be merely passive, or might be active as rebellion. Finally, there was the question of whether a king once crowned might be deposed and his subjects released from their oaths of allegiance.

The Tudors upheld the principle that "the Crown once possessed, cleareth and purifies all manner of defaults or imperfections." They had to. They also insisted that under no circumstances was a subject permitted to judge his king or to undertake to execute judgment upon him by rebelling. But Cardinal Allen was arguing with much support from facts when he wrote in his *Defence of English Catholiques*:

that to resist the Magistrat, defend themselves in cases of conscience, and to fight against the superiour for religion, is a cleere and ruled

[54]Camden, *Annales*, II, 247-48.

case; and no treasonable opinion at al against the Prince, if we wil be judged by Protestants: . . . The question therefore is not . . . of the Princes lauful creation or consecration: but whether a Prince laufullie invested and annointed, may be for anie cause, namelie for matter of Religion, resisted by his subjects? We say the Protestants of al sectes doe both holde and practize it, England it selfe speciallie allowing of the same . . . But it is sufficient for us, that with these men (if we may beleeve either their words or deeds) it is no treason to resist the Soveraigne, for defence of Religion; nor no treasonable assertion to hould that a lauful Prince may be deposed in case of revolt from God. And so say also on the other side al Catholique men and schooles in the Christian world concerning this point.[55]

Allen distinguished Catholic rebels from Protestant rebels in that they did not make individual decisions in regard to their duty to their king, but submitted to the decision of the Christian church in the matter. And he listed examples of heretics excommunicated and deprived, not forgetting John:

For great injuries also done to holie Church, and for persecution of Bishops and religious, was *John* one of our kinges of England with his whole land interdicted, and brought (after long strugling against God and the Sea Apostolique) to yeeld his Croune to the courtesie of the Popes Legate, and to make both his realmes of England and Ireland, tributaries. The authentical instrument whereof *John Bodin* saith he hath seen.[56]

Yet Shakespeare does not make his English rebels so much obedient to the church as determined to revenge Arthur's wrongs. Of Arthur as warring against John before he was captured, Shakespeare says nothing. It is Arthur as prisoner who is presented, for it was Mary as prisoner who received the support of the English nobles. Holinshed makes no mention of John's nobles taking any interest in the captive, but the Catholic nobles under Elizabeth instigated the Northern Rebellion and the struggles of the next years, the Duke of Norfolk was executed

[55]Allen's *Defence of English Catholiques* (pp. 80, 81, 84) answers *The Execution of Justice.*

[56]*Ibid.,* p. 111.

for his efforts in Mary's behalf and his alleged plan to marry her, and there was no time during her stay in England when certain of the nobility were not interested in securing her freedom. It is, therefore, fitting that the pleas so often heard by Elizabeth should be offered to John on behalf of the nobles by the Earl of Pembroke as they

> heartily request
> The enfranchisement of Arthur; whose restraint
> Doth move the murmuring lips of discontent
> To break into this dangerous argument,—
> If what in rest you have in right you hold,
> Why then your fears, which as they say, attend
> The steps of wrong, should move you to mew up
> Your tender kinsman, and to choke his days
> With barbarous ignorance, and deny his youth
> The rich advantage of good exercise.[57]

Discovering the body of Arthur, and believing him to have been murdered by Hubert at the king's command, the nobles forswear obedience to the king and vow revenge.

But rebellion in John's England was, as in Elizabeth's England, linked with foreign intervention, for the nobles turn to an alien leader in their struggle against the king. Faulconbridge sums up the result:

> Now powers from home and discontents at home
> Meet in one line; and vast confusion waits, . . .[58]

The state in 1581 argued against Campion, as I have said earlier:

Secret rebellion must be stirred here at home among ourselves, the harts of the people must be obdurated against God and their prince; so that when a foren power shall on a sudden invade this realme, the subjects thus seduced must joine with these in armes, and so shall the pope atteine the sum of his wish.[59]

Historically Pandulph and the pope did not participate in John's quarrel with Arthur, but telescoping the various troubles

---

[57]IV, ii, 51-60.
[58]IV, iii, 151-52.
[59]See the opening of this chapter.

of John as he does, Shakespeare makes the Pandulph in his play plot to use the murder of Arthur as a means to rebellion even before it happens:

> John hath seized Arthur; and it cannot be
> That, whiles warm life plays in that infant's veins,
> The misplaced John should entertain an hour,
> One minute, nay, one quiet breath of rest.
> A sceptre snatch'd with an unruly hand
> Must be as boisterously maintain'd as gain'd;
> And he that stands upon a slippery place
> Makes nice of no vile hold to stay him up:
> That John may stand, then Arthur needs must fall; . . .[60]

Then, he says,

> This act so evilly born shall cool the hearts
> Of all his people and freeze up their zeal, . . .[61]

That will be the opportune moment for Lewis and the French invasion, for

>   the hearts
> Of all his people shall revolt from him,
> And kiss the lips of unacquainted change,
> And pick strong matter of revolt and wrath
> Out of the bloody fingers' ends of John.
> . . . . 'tis wonderful
> What may be wrought out of their discontent,
> Now that their souls are topful of offence.[62]

Even so did the Pandulph of Elizabethan England plot with Philip of Spain before and after the death of Mary.[63]

The nobles in *King John*, moved to revolt by their desire for vengeance on the murderer of Arthur, are yet grieved that re-

[60]III, iv, 131-36.
[61]III, iv, 149-50.
[62]III, iv, 164-80.
[63]Martin Haile, *An Elizabethan Cardinal* (London, 1914), gives a full account of Cardinal Allen's relations with King Philip and notes the delay of the king in making war on England until after Mary's death. See especially pp. 300-301.

bellion is their lot and sad at heart as they advance the fortunes of the dauphin. Salisbury speaks for them:

> But such is the infection of the time,
> That, for the health and physic of our right,
> We cannot deal but with the very hand
> Of stern injustice and confused wrong.
> And is't not pity, O my grieved friends,
> That we, the sons and children of this isle,
> Were born to see so sad an hour as this;
> Wherein we step after a stranger, march
> Upon her gentle bosom, and fill up
> Her enemies' ranks,—I must withdraw and weep
> Upon the spot of this enforced cause,—[64]

And when the dying Frenchman, Melun, warns them that Lewis will be unfaithful to his promises to them and urges them to "Unthread the rude eye of rebellion," Salisbury is again the spokesman, joyous now, who promises,

> We will untread the steps of damned flight, . . .[65]

It is the great wonder of Elizabeth's reign that in the year after Mary's execution, in the great year of the Armada, Englishmen answered the prayer which Shakespeare gives to John:

> O, let me have no subject enemies,
> When adverse foreigners affright my towns
> With dreadful pomp of stout invasion![66]

Associated with this problem of rebellion is the fourth of the Elizabethan problems I have listed, the divine right of a king to be judged by God alone. All the Tudors had to deal with "disobedience and wylfull rebellion," and all agreed that a subject may not judge his king. But Elizabeth had a harder problem to decide, whether a king may judge another king. Certainly there is no indication in the chronicles that John was ever

[64]V, ii, 20-30.
[65]V, iv, 52.
[66]IV, ii, 171-73.

troubled over his right to do as he would and could with Arthur, but in the treatment of Arthur's death Shakespeare clearly mirrors Elizabeth's dilemma in regard to the Scottish queen. Holinshed allows the reader to decide for himself which of the rumors concerning Arthur's death he will believe. Shakespeare chose to represent John as having commanded the execution of Arthur,[67] but his actual death he represented as accident. Since John never seems to have admitted that Arthur was dead, it does not need saying that he gave no evidence of sorrow over having killed him. But Shakespeare portrays John's sore repentance and his furious reproaching of Hubert when he believes him to have executed the royal command.[68]

Elizabeth's dilemma was real. Parliament and the privy council had long demanded that she accede to their desire to rid England of the menace to the throne and the nation which they felt Mary to be. On the other hand, Elizabeth did not want to kill a king. Deep in her heart she always understood the truth incorporated in the Latin epitaph set up near Mary's tomb soon after her death but quickly removed, according to Camden, from the English translation of whose work I quote part of the closing sentences:

by one and the same wicked sentence is both Mary Queene of Scots doomed to a naturall death, and all surviving Kings, being made as common people, are subjected to a civill death. A new and unexampled kinde of tombe is heere extant, wherein the living are included with the dead: for know, that with the sacred herse of Saint Mary here lieth violate and prostrate the majestie of all Kings and Princes: . . .[69]

[67]The apparent confusion between the command to murder Arthur in III, iii, and the frustrated attempt to blind rather than murder him in IV, i, is explained by Dover Wilson as due to Shakespeare's misunderstanding of *The Troublesome Raigne* (Intro. to *King John*, xxii-xxiii).

[68]Simpson, *op. cit.*, p. 400, briefly noted the resemblance to the situation between Elizabeth and Secretary Davison. Evelyn M. Albright revived the comparison in her paper on "Shakespeare's *Richard II* and the Essex Conspiracy," *PMLA*, XLII (1927), 686.

[69]The Latin version is retained in the 1625 translation (Bk. III, p. 208) but is put into English in the 1635 edition, Bk. III, p. 344.

When Elizabeth did finally consent to a trial, and when Mary was convicted and sentence given, Elizabeth was still loath to sign the death warrant. Neale says:

In signing the death warrant Elizabeth had gone as far as she was prepared to go. She expected someone else to take the responsibility and the blame for dispatching it; and the wretched Davison, perceiving that it might fall to him to be made the scapegoat, spread the responsibility to Burghley and other councillors. They quietly sent the warrant off.[70]

Henry III of France and James VI of Scotland, as friend and son of Mary, had to acknowledge the popular clamor in their countries over Mary's death by protesting it. But the English were apparently almost hysterical with joy. However, says Neale,

Elizabeth in contrast was grief-stricken. She could neither eat nor sleep. . . . Her position was not unlike that of Catherine de Medici after the Massacre of St. Bartholomew: she had to resort to miserable subterfuges to turn the infamy of the deed from her—or turn it sufficiently to maintain her alliances with other sovereigns. "I never saw a thing more hated by little, great, old, young and of all religions," the English ambassador in France wrote, "than the Queen of Scot's death, and especially the manner of it. I would to God it had not been in this time." In Scotland the people were terribly incensed, and many cried for war. Libels were set up in the streets against James and his Anglophil ministers, and odious epigrams on "Jezebel, that English whore." . . . Elizabeth had probably foreseen this and prepared for it by leaving the dispatch of the death warrant to others. She now declared that she had never meant to send it, that Davison had acted improperly in showing it to other councillors, and they in dispatching it.[71]

There had to be a scapegoat, and the victim was Secretary Davison, who was fined and sentenced to imprisonment during

[70]Neale, *op, cit.*, p. 277.

[71]*Ibid.*, p. 279. See also Camden, *Annales* (1625), Bk. III, pp. 209-19, Nicholas Nicolas, *Life of William Davison* (London, 1823), pp. 77-200, and A. F. Pollard, *History of England, 1547-1603*, p. 396.

the queen's pleasure, his release coming just after the defeat of the Spanish Armada.

What Shakespeare records as a dialogue between King John and Hubert, totally out of character and inconsistent with the story of King John as told in the chronicle, is a dialogue that in essence did take place between Queen Elizabeth and Secretary Davison:

> *K. John.* Why seek'st thou to possess me with these fears!
> Why urgest thou so oft young Arthur's death?
> Thy hand hath murder'd him: I had a mighty cause
> To wish him dead, but thou hadst none to kill him.
>
> *Hub.* No had, my lord! why, did you not provoke me?
>
> *K. John.* It is the curse of kings to be attended
> By slaves that take their humours for a warrant
> To break within the bloody house of life,
> And on the winking of authority
> To understand a law, to know the meaning
> Of dangerous majesty, when perchance it frowns
> More upon humour than advised respect.
>
> *Hub.* Here is your hand and seal for what I did.
>
> *K. John.* O, when the last account 'twixt heaven and earth
> Is to be made, then shall this hand and seal
> Witness against us to damnation!
> How oft the sight of means to do ill deeds
> Make deeds ill done! Hadst not thou been by,
> A fellow by the hand of nature mark'd,
> Quoted and sign'd to do a deed of shame,
> This murder had not come into my mind:
> . . . .
> And thou, to be endeared to a king,
> Make it no conscience to destroy a prince.
>
> *Hub.* My lord,—
>
> *K. John.* Hadst thou but shook thy head or made a pause
> When I spake darkly what I purposed,
> Or turn'd an eye of doubt upon my face,

As bid me tell my tale in express words,
Deep shame had struck me dumb, made me break off,
And those thy fears might have wrought fears in me:
But thou didst understand me by my signs
And didst in signs again parley with sin:
Yea, without stop, didst let thy heart consent,
And consequently thy rude hand to act
The deed, which both our tongues held vile to name.
Out of my sight, and never see me more!
My nobles leave me; and my state is braved,
Even at my gates, with ranks of foreign powers:
Nay, in the body of this fleshly land,
This kingdom, this confine of blood and breath,
Hostility and civil tumult reigns
Between my conscience and my cousin's death.[72]

The Bastard, too, might well have been speaking of Elizabethan England when he spoke his elegiac lines over Arthur:

From forth this morsel of dead royalty,
The life, the right and truth of all this realm
Is fled to heaven; and England now is left
To tug and scamble and to part by the teeth
The unowed interest of proud-swelling state.[73]

It is easy to see that the aspect of the problem of regicide which interested Shakespeare in *King John* was the aspect presented by the problem of the refugee queen, Mary of Scotland. He gave little time and attention to the murder of King John at the end of the play, the poisoning being merely reported instead of shown as in *The Troublesome Raigne*. Indeed, there are few tears shed for John on the stage, and the play hurries to its end with no time wasted in damning the monk or even explaining his motive. Yet Shakespeare had represented the anathema pronounced upon John as not only excommunicating him

[72]IV, ii, 203-48. It must be noted that this conversation takes place just before Hubert tells the king Arthur is still alive. There is no account of John's reception of the news of Arthur's actual death.

[73]IV, iii, 143-47.

and commanding his subjects to cease their obedience to him, but also as sanctioning and promising to reward his secret murder:

> Then, by the lawful power that I have,
> Thou shalt stand cursed and excommunicate:
> And blessed shall be he that doth revolt
> From his allegiance to an heretic;
> And meritorious shall that hand be call'd,
> Canonised and worshipp'd as a saint,
> That takes away by any secret course
> Thy hateful life.[74]

The bull against Elizabeth had not been explicit in regard to her murder, but that the sanction of the deed was implicit in it is proved by the famous letter of the Cardinal of Como, dated December 12, 1580, which says in part:

> Since that guilty woman of England rules over two such noble kingdoms of Christendom and is the cause of so much injury to the Catholic faith, and loss of so many million souls, there is no doubt that whosoever sends her out of the world with the pious intention of doing God service, not only does not sin but gains merit, especially having regard to the sentence pronounced against her by Pius V of holy memory. And so, if those English nobles decide actually to undertake so glorious a work, your Lordship can assure them that they do not commit any sin.[75]

Though the attempts of the Catholic partisans of Mary and of Spain to merit the promised papal blessing were well known, and though the attempt by Dr. Lopez was a popular scandal at the time when the play was probably written, yet Shakespeare makes nothing of the poisoning of the King. The play is concerned, not with mirroring the whole conflict of Elizabeth and the Catholic church, but with reflecting that part of the conflict which centered about Mary. Therefore, Shakespeare weaves together the troubles of King John with Arthur and his troubles with the church and his troubles with the rebel nobles in support

[74]III, i, 171-78.

[75]A. O. Meyer, *op. cit.*, pp. 269-71, 490-91; Greenewald, *op. cit.*, pp. 98-99.

of a foreign power in the pattern familiar to his contemporaries, slighting other aspects of the long contest.

Events crowd the stage in the last scenes to hurry the play to its end. The armado intended to supply the French is wrecked, even as was the Spanish Armada, the nobles are returned to their allegiance by the warning of Melun, rule passes to Prince Henry as John dies, poisoned. Peace is once more in sight as Faulconbridge utters the famous words quoted at the beginning of this chapter as the theme of the play:

> This England never did, nor never shall,
> Lie at the proud foot of a conqueror,
> But when it first did help to wound itself.
> Now these her princes are come home again,
> Come the three corners of the world in arms,
> And we shall shock them. Nought shall make us rue,
> If England to itself do rest but true.

It is fitting that Faulconbridge should thus sum up the significance of the play, for it is he who acts as chorus to the play. Many students, bothered by the unheroic hero, have, like Professor Dover Wilson, tried to set up Faulconbridge as hero. With admirable consistency some of the same critics would make Falstaff the hero of the Henry IV plays. It is true that Faulconbridge is, like Falstaff, generally considered the most interesting character of the play, and that, unlike Falstaff, he is certainly the most heroic. But *King John* with Faulconbridge as hero is a play without form and void, signifying nothing. He is outside the structure of the play as he is outside it historically. He avenges his father's death. He acts as a foil to the king in his more unkingly moments. He loots the monasteries—off stage. But he is remembered chiefly because, as chorus, he says some of the most admirable things in the play. It should be noted, however, that his comments are in the nature of political comments. Our familiar quotations from the play are from his words of political wisdom on the nature of political opportunism and treachery, on the political significance of Arthur's death, on the true secret of England's weakness and strength. In the plot he is only important as was the vice in the old moralities, in pricking others on to action.

The truth of the matter is that the history play was not often privileged to reflect a hero in its mirror, for that was not the mission of the history play. That Shakespeare was able to depict King John in his conflict with the church as speaking his eloquent defiance of the pope and the foreign priest without making him the great Christian warrior reflects the greatness of Shakespeare and of his understanding of the genre in which he was writing.

CHAPTER XIII

AN INTRODUCTION INTO THE DIVISION BETWEEN
LANCASTER AND YORK*

WHEN HALLE wrote his chronicle of the long struggle that preceded *The Union of the Two Noble and Illustre Famelies of Lancastre and Yorke*, he opened it with a section which he entered as "An introduccion into the devision of the two houses of Lancastre and Yorke." The section began with the quarrel between Mowbray and Bolingbroke in the presence of Richard II, which to Halle seemed the inception of the struggle that later devastated England as the Wars of the Roses. Late in Elizabeth's reign, Sir John Hayward wrote a book about *The First Part of the Life and Raigne of King Henrie the IIII.* in which he devoted one hundred and thirty-six pages out of a total of one hundred and forty-nine to Richard II. He later justified his extensive treatment of the deposition and murder of Richard II in a supposed life of Henry IV by explaining that he had to write of Richard II in so far as his follies were "either causes or furtherances of the fortunes of the other," and claimed that he followed Halle in commencing his story where he did.[1] Shakespeare's play of *Richard II* will be better understood if we remember that he began the action of his play exactly where Halle began his "introduccion," with the quarrel between Mowbray and Bolingbroke before the king. And like Hayward he wrote of Richard II's follies in so far as they were "either causes or furtherances" of the fortunes of Henry IV—but no further.

*Much of the first twenty pages of this chapter is taken, sometimes word for word, from my article, "The Use of Historical Patterns in the Reign of Elizabeth," *Huntington Library Quarterly*, I (Jan. 1938), 135-69.

[1]Published 1599. Cf. *Calendar of State Papers, Domestic, 1598-1601*, pp. 539-40. Hayward's examination, Jan. 22, 1600, records: "Selected out this single history as Hall begins there, and Ascham, in his *Schoolmaster*, commends that before any other."

THE DIVISION BETWEEN LANCASTER AND YORK

The main concern of Shakespeare's play is with the deposition of Richard II and his subsequent murder. The long-continued follies of Richard are discussed in the dialogue—his favoritism, his alienation of his subjects by heavy financial burdens imposed upon them, his farming out of crown lands, his connection with his uncle's murder—but they are not presented on the stage. The play which we know as *Richard II: or Thomas of Woodstock* made them part of the action, but Shakespeare in his play about Richard II merely summed them up in the accusations against Richard as contributing causes to his downfall. If we consider *Richard II*, then, as one of a cycle of plays teaching the lessons of political crime and political punishment, from the unlawful seizing of the crown to its loss by the third heir, we shall do well to think of it as the introduction to the cycle which is concerned with the rise and fall of the house of Lancaster. But each play in the cycle must also be considered as an individual and distinct unit, and thus *Richard II* comes to be also a play dealing with the problem of the deposition of a king.

It should be said at the outset that Shakespeare's play about Richard II has none of the extreme departures from historical fact and none of the false orientation of fact which marked his play about King John, and which furnished clues to his intention. As the editor of the English Arden text says: "In no other historical play does Shakespeare keep so closely to the Chronicle."[2] Only in telescoping times and places, in changing occasionally the order of events, and in altering minor details does he depart from the accounts of the historical Richard. Yet the latest editor of the play, Professor Dover Wilson, acknowledges that "the traditional notion of Shakespeare's dependence upon Holinshed seems to be evaporating," and adds further evidence to strengthen the earlier claims of various scholars for the influence of works other than Holinshed.[3] Both of these editors, however,

---

[2]*The Tragedy of King Richard II*, ed. Ivor B. John (London, 1925), p. xiii.

[3]*King Richard II*, ed. John Dover Wilson (Cambridge, 1939), Introduction, pp. xxxviii-lxxvi. See also R. M. Smith, *Froissart and the English Chronicle Play* (New York, 1915).

favor the idea of a play behind the play of *Richard II*, as *The Troublesome Raigne* was behind *King John*. I have no intention of trying to navigate the troubled waters of source and ur-play discussion in this book, as I have said before, but if another author wrote a play from which Shakespeare derived his *Richard II*, the evidence of the traditional treatment would only be strengthened.

It was continually remembered in Elizabethan England that three English kings had been deposed: Edward II, Richard II, and Henry VI. But the conditions of Henry VI's twice yielding his crown were complex and his rightful claim confused, so that it was regularly Edward II and Richard II who became the accepted mirrors in which one could see reflected the problems that were connected with the deposing of a king. Indeed, the way in which Richard II has become the permanent pattern of the deposed king was shown in 1936 and 1937, when his picture and his life appeared in the pages of newspapers and magazines, and when Shakespeare's play was revived on the stage and quoted everywhere.

For many years of Elizabeth's reign there was certainly talk of the lessons to be learned from the time of Richard II. Perhaps it will be well to consider the genesis of that talk before considering the main problem of the play. John Stow went back to Gower for a basic account of Richard:

> When this King first began to raigne, the Lawes neglected were,
> Wherefore good fortune him forsooke, and th'earth did quake
> for feare,
> The people also whom he pollde, against him did rebell.
> The time doth yet bewaile the woes, that Chronicles doe tell.
> The foolish counsell of the lewde, and yong he did receive,
> And grave advise of aged heads, he did reject and leave.
> And then for greedy thirst of Coyne, some subjects he accused,
> To gaine their goods into his hands, thus he the realme abused.[4]

Halle recorded that

unprofitable counsailers wer his confusion and finall perdicion. Suche

---

[4]John Stow, *The Annales of England* (London, 1605), p. 439.

another ruler was kyng Edwarde the seconde, whiche two before named kynges fell from the high glory of fortunes whele into extreme misery and miserable calamitee.[5]

The *Mirror for Magistrates* has Richard explain to the interlocutor of the ghosts, William Baldwin:

> I am a Kyng that ruled all by lust,
> That forced not of vertue, ryght, or lawe,
> But alway put false Flatterers most in trust,
> Ensuing such as could my vices claw:
> By faythful counsayle passing not a strawe. . . .
>
> For mayntenaunce whereof, my realme I polde
> Through Subsidies, sore fines, loanes, many a prest,
> Blanke charters, othes, and shiftes not knowen of olde,
> For whych my Subjectes did me sore detest.[6]

Holinshed at the conclusion of the chronicle of the events of his reign comments:

Thus was king Richard deprived of all kinglie honour and princelie dignitie, by reason he was so given to follow evill counsell, and used such inconvenient waies and meanes, through insolent misgovernance, and youthfull outrage, though otherwise a right noble and woorthie prince.

Holinshed moralizes that "it is an heavie case when God thundereth out his reall arguments either upon prince or people," but he adds that it is his own opinion that Richard was the "most unthankfullie used of his subjects, of any one of whom ye shall lightlie read."[7]

Such was the commonly accepted account of Richard's follies as they contributed to the rise of Henry IV. Now, early in her reign Elizabeth commenced to be accused of the same follies. Indeed, almost as soon as she came to the throne, gossip began to circulate concerning the role which Robert Dudley (the son of the Duke of Northumberland executed five years earlier for his part in the plot to put Lady Jane Grey on the throne) was play-

[5]Halle, *op. cit.* (London, 1548), fol. xxxiii.
[6]*Op. cit.*, pp. 113-14.
[7]Holinshed, *Chronicle*, III, 507-8.

ing in her affairs. On April 18, 1559, the Count de Feria wrote to King Philip of Spain:

During the last few days Lord Robert has come so much into favour that he does whatever he likes with affairs and it is even said that her Majesty visits him in his chamber day and night. People talk of this so freely that they go so far as to say that his wife has a malady in one of her breasts and the Queen is only waiting for her to die to marry Lord Robert.[8]

By July we find the Bishop of Aquila[9] reporting to the Spanish king that the Bishop of Ely, being deprived, "had words with Bacon and told him that if the Queen continued as she had begun to be ruled by those about her, both she and her kingdom would be ruined."[10]

In September, 1560, the Spanish ambassador wrote to the Duchess of Parma that Cecil had confided in him his thought of retiring, since "he clearly foresaw the ruin of the realm through Robert's intimacy with the Queen, who surrendered all affairs to him and meant to marry him." Cecil, according to this writer, earnestly wished Leicester in Paradise, but "ended by saying that Robert was thinking of killing his wife, who was publicly announced to be ill, although she was quite well . . ." Bishop Quadra thereupon related that the very next day he met the queen, who told him that Leicester's wife was dead or nearly so, and the good bishop added that, whatever happened, nothing could be worse from his point of view than to have Cecil at the head of affairs, "but the outcome of it all might be the imprisonment of the Queen and the proclamation of the earl of Huntingdon as King."[11] In January, 1561, the same ambassador reported that Henry Sidney had seen him concerning the possible use of King Philip's good offices in urging the marriage of Leicester to the queen, in which case he promised that Robert would become vassal to the king of Spain, and he commented on the state of public opinion concerning the death of Robert's wife, noting that even preachers in

[8]*Calendar of State Papers, Spanish, 1558-1567*, pp. 57-58.
[9]Alvaro de la Quadra, Bishop of Aquila.
[10]*Cal. S. P., Span., 1558-1567*, p. 85.
[11]*Ibid.*, p. 175.

their pulpits were preaching about it in a way that was prejudicial to the honor of the queen.[12]

In January, 1578, Sir Francis Knollys, Elizabeth's kinsman, was applying the lessons of Richard's reign, prophesying that Elizabeth would be utterly overthrown if she did not suppress and subject her will and affections to good counsel, for "who woll not rather shrynkingly ... play the partes of King Richard the Second's men then to enter into the odious office of crossing of her Majestie's wylle?" He lists the problems that need settlement and warns of the dangers inherent in the uncertain state of affairs, "And then King Richard the Second's men woll flock into courte apace, and woll show themselves in theyr colors."[13]

So violent had the scandalous rumors concerning the queen become by 1580-81 that Parliament was moved to enact new and stricter statutes, with graduated penalties of extreme severity for those who spoke ill of her. Finally, in 1584, the scandal-mongering concerning the queen and Leicester came to a head in *The Copie of a Leter, wryten by a Master of Arte of Cambridge to his friend in London concerning some talke past of late between two worshipful and grave men about the present state, and some procedings of the Erle of Leycester and his friends in England*. The work, attributed to the Jesuit Parsons, was apparently published on the Continent but was eagerly read on both sides of the channel. Manuscript copies in numbers seem to have been passed about everywhere, and in 1585 a French translation with additions was causing the British ambassador uneasiness.[14] The *Leter* (often referred to as *Greencoat* because of its appearance, and in its seventeenth-century edition entitled *Leicester's Commonwealth*) summed up the dissatisfactions and contentious arguments of all the malcontents of the time and is worth studying. The charge that Elizabeth was dominated by her favorites

[12]*Ibid.*, pp. 178-82.

[13]Thomas Wright, *Queen Elizabeth and Her Times* (London, 1838), II, Pt. 1, pp. 75-76.

[14]*Cal. S. P., For., 1584-1585*, p. 387. For a full discussion of the gossip about Leicester and an account of the major accusations made by the *Leter* see chap. xvi dealing with *Richard III*.

rather than guided by her trusty advisers was a focal point of the attack. Kings and princes have often been shipwrecked upon the rock of "their too much affection towards some unworthy particular persons," the *Leter* said, and it pointed to history and particularly English history:

For wheras, since the conquest, we number principalie, thre just and lawful kinges, to have come to confusion, by alienation of their subjectes: that is, Edward the second, Richard the second, and Henry the sixt, this onlie point of to much favour towardes wicked persons, was the chiefest cause of destruction, in al thre. As in the first, the excessive favour towardes Peter Gavesten and two of the Spencers. In the second, the like extraordinarie, and indiscrete affection towardes Robert Vere Earle of Oxeford, and Marques of Dubline, and Thomas Mowbray, two moste turbulent and wicked men, that set the kinge against his owne uncles and the nobilitie.[15]

Any grudge, or grief, or misliking, or repining, or complaint, or murmur against Elizabeth's government on the part of those who wished amendment of affairs and not the overthrow of all, the author contends, is due to "this man." And he adds that Leicester afflicts the people "as never did before him, either Gaveston, or Spencer, or Vere, or Mowbray, or anie other mischievous Tyraunt, that abused moste his Princes favour within our Realm of England."[16]

Sir Philip Sidney answered the attack by arguing that those who do not consider the time ripe for showing their hate against the prince "vomit it out against his counsellors." And as for Gaveston and Vere and "Delapool," he asks pointedly whether those who destroyed these favorites were content, and whether they did not rather pass on to destroy also the kings themselves, Edward II, Richard II, and Henry VI.[17]

In 1585, as Adlard pointed out, "letters signed by Burghley and the rest of the Council were sent to the justices of the peace

[15]Pp. 187-88.

[16]Pp. 188-89.

[17]*The Miscellaneous Works of Sir Philip Sidney*, ed. William Gray (Boston, 1860), p. 308.

for the suppression of the libels in circulation against Leicester, and a letter with the Queen's sign manual was sent to the Lord Mayor, Sheriffs, and Alderman of London to the same effect."[18] This letter offers ample proof of the popularity and dangerous efficacy of the attacks upon Leicester, particularly that of the book under consideration.

But the charge that the queen was ruled by favorites and gave them undue power over her kingdom was repeated in regard to almost everyone about her. Sir Christopher Hatton, for instance, was said to have won the queen's favor when, aged twenty-one, he appeared before her in a masque presented by one of the inns of court. He was first made a gentleman-pensioner, then advanced to power and riches, finally being appointed to the office of lord chamberlain, though he was not a lawyer. Gossip inevitably resulted.[19]

In 1592 Parsons published *A Declaration of the True Causes of the Great Troubles, Presupposed to be Intended against the Realme of England*, attacking Walsingham and Cecil as well as the then deceased Leicester. Lord Burghley, whose charms at this distance appear to have been something less than seductive, was accused of being "farr more noysome and pernitious to the realme, than ever were the Spencers, Peeter of Gaverstone, or any other that ever abused either Prince or people."[20]

Sir Robert Naunton's *Fragmenta Regalia* bore the significant subtitle of "Observations on the late queen Elizabeth, her times and favorites." But he defended the queen, contending that her ministers and instruments of state "were onely Favorites, not Minions; such as acted more by her own Princely rules and judgements, then by their own wills and appetites," and he added specifically that "we find no Gaveston, Vere, or Spencer, to have swayed alone, during forty four years." He also registered his

[18]George Adlard, *Amye Robsart and the Earl of Leycester* (London, 1870), pp. 56-58.

[19]Sir Harris Nicolas, *Memoirs of the Life and Times of Sir Christopher Hatton* (London, 1847), pp. 462-69, gives an interesting account of the dislike with which this appointment was received.

[20]*Op. cit.*, p. 68.

disagreement with the commonly accepted opinion "that my Lord of Leicester, was absolute and above all in her Grace."[21]

However, Richard II was not reserved as a mirror for Elizabeth alone. In 1592 Robert Bowes wrote to Burghley about King James of Scotland:

The Council and ministers are persuaded that something will be attempted against some favourites about the King, and fear that this may open the way to the practices intended by the Papists and Spain, . . . By a libel lately set upon the door of the King's outer chamber the King was warned to beware that he be not used as King Richard the second was in England.[22]

While there were other lessons which Richard was used to mirror, it was as a king who was dominated by favorites and who allowed favorites to rule and ruin his kingdom that he was generally thought of during the first thirty years or so of Elizabeth's reign. Of course, the fact that his follies had led to his deposition gave point to the warnings. But as Elizabeth grew older and the matter of succession was still undecided, Richard was used to mirror new problems as well as old, and the most favored favorite of the aging queen was deeply involved in the discussions.

In 1594 Robert Parsons (under the pseudonym of Doleman) dedicated to the Earl of Essex *A Conference about the Next Succession to the Crowne of Ingland*, in which the author seemed to advance the title of the Infanta of Spain. The dedication to Essex was made conspicuous by being announced on the title page, and the terms of the author's address to the earl made the recipient suspect, for Parsons claimed to be personally indebted to the earl and to his forbears. Even more incriminating was his statement:

But for the second pointe of publique utilitie, I thought no man more fit then your honour to dedicate these two books unto, which treat of the succession to the crowne of Ingland, for that no man is in more high and eminent place or dignitie at this day in our realme, then your selfe, whether we respect your nobilitie, or call-

---

[21]*Op. cit.* (London, 1641), pp. 5-6.
[22]*Cal. Scot. Papers, 1589-1593*, p. 700.

ing, or favour with your prince, or high liking of the people, and consequently no man like to have a greater part or sway in deciding of this great affaire (when tyme shall come for that determination) then your honour, and those that will assist you and are likest to follow your fame and fortune.

This was bad enough, but Parsons added fuel to the flames when he said that he had decided to publish the work, "for that it is not convenient for your honour to be unskillful in a matter which concerneth your person and the whole realme."

The book represented a meeting of certain persons as taking place in Antwerp during April and May, 1593, at which time the question of the English succession was discussed. When it was reported to the group that Parliament had not acted in the matter, and that one or two "had bin checked or committed for speaking in the same," two lawyers (one of the common law and the other of the civil law) proceeded to justify the queen, because it was not good for her, nor for the realm, nor yet for the successor that her successor should be declared during her lifetime. Then ensued the conference concerning the succession, during the first session of which three main points were considered:

1. That succession by blood is not determined either by the law of nature or by divine law but by specific and particular laws of each commonwealth, and that such laws are subject to alteration.

2. That monarchy is probably the best of the three forms of government, but that in England the authority of the king is limited by counsellors (as in an aristocracy) and by the voice of the commons (as in a democracy). It should always be remembered that the people must *accept* their king.

3. That princes may for good cause be deposed.

This last point was emphasized by the argument that "lawful Princes have oftentymes by their common wealthes bin lawfully deposed, for misgovernment, and that God hath allowed and assisted the same, with good success to the weale publique." The examples of English history were again reviewed: the evil John was followed by the good Henry III; the evil Edward II by the good Edward III; the evil Richard II by the good Henry IV; the weak Henry VI by the not bad Edward IV; and the notorious Richard III by Henry VII.[23]

The second part of the conference was devoted to a discussion of the respective claims of the various would-be successors to the English throne. Inevitably the author retold the difficulties between the houses of Lancaster and York and repeated the history of the inception of the trouble between Richard II and Henry IV. The problem was restated:

the question is first, whether Richard the second were justly deposed or no, and secondly whether after his deposition the house of Yorke or house of Lancaster should have entred, and thirdly if the house of Lancaster did commit any wronge or injustice at their first entrance to the crowne, yet whether the continuance of so many years in possession, with so many approbations and confirmations thereof by the commonwealth were not sufficient to legitimate their right.[24]

Now, both reason and authority testify to the right of the commonwealth to deliver itself from the government of "a tyrant, a Tigar, a fearse Lion, a ravening wolfe, a publique enimy, and a bloody murtherer,"[25] Parsons said, and he quoted as authority the civil lawyer:

By examples in like manner of al realmes christian he declared, how that often-tymes they have deposed their princes for just causes, and that God hath concurred and assisted wonderfully the-same, sending them commonly very good kings after those that were deprived, and in no country more than in Ingland it selfe, yea in the very lyne and familye of this king Richard, whose noble grandfather king Edward the third was exalted to the crowne by a most solemne deposition of his predecessor king Edward the second, wherfore in this point their can be little controversie . . .[26]

As to the manner of Richard's deposition, Parsons asserted that adherents of the House of Lancaster affirmed that it could not have been better done:

[23]Cf. Pt. I, pp. 56-63.
[24]Pt. II, p. 60.
[25]Pt. II, p. 61.
[26]Pt. II, p. 62.

First for that it was done by the choise and invitation of al the realme or greater and better parte therof as hath bin said. Secondly for that it was done without slaughter, and thirdly for that the king was deposed by act of parlament, and himselfe convinced of his unworthy goverment, and brought to confesse that he was worthely deprived, and that he willingly and freely resigned the same: nether can their be any more circumstances required (saye these men) for any lawful deposition of a Prince.[27]

It is not surprising that Essex should be out of favor at court for being in favor with the author of this most disquieting treatise, and evidence is not lacking that the disfavor with which he was regarded was very marked. A letter from Robert Beale to Sir Robert Sidney, dated September 25, 1595, asked Sidney to procure him one of the books:

I heare that of late a verye vile Booke hathe ben printed in *Englishe*, in *Antwerp*, touching the Succession of this Crowne, diffaminge her Majestie, and dishablinge all the Tytles of suche, that herafter maye pretende anye Interest therunto, and derivinge a strange Pretence from *John of Gaunt*, Duke of *Lancaster*, uppon the Kinge of *Spaine*, which he mindethe shortlye to challenge: I trust the Lorde will never suffer him to prevayle in so wicked and unjust a Cause. . . . I heare also, that it is dedicated to the Erle of *Essex*, of an Intent surlie to bringe him in Jalousye and Disgrace here.[28]

On November 5, 1595, Rowland Whyte also reported to Sir Robert Sidney:

UPON *Monday* last, 1500 [Queen Eliz.] shewed 1000 [Earl of *Essex*] a printed Booke of t—t, Title to a—a: In yt their is, as I here, daungerous Praises of 1000 of his Valour and Worthines, which doth hym harme here. At his comming from Court he was observed to looke wan and pale, being exceedinglie troubled at this great Piece of Villanie donne unto hym: he is Sick, and continewes very ill . . .

To this letter the writer appended a postscript which identified the mischievous book:

[27]Pt. II, p. 67.

[28]Arthur Collins, *Letters and Memorials of State* (London, 1746), I, 350.

The Book I spake of is dedicated to my Lord *Essex*, and printed beyond Sea, and tis thought to be Treason to have it. To wryte of these Things are dangerous in so perillous a Tyme; but I hope yt wilbe no Offence to impart unto you Thactions of this Place.[29]

A week later Whyte reported to Sidney that the earl had now put off "the Melancholy he fell into, by a printed Booke delivered to the Queen," and the harm had been averted.[30] On November 22 Essex presented to the queen a device which symbolized his persevering loyalty.[31]

The book on the succession was, however, not easily forgotten. Among the State Papers are "Notes [by Lord Burghley] out of a seditious book, touching the succession to the Crown of England; showing that the author justifies alteration in the succession of Kings, and argues against the King of Scots, and in favour of an Infanta of Spain, or the King of Spain and his son."[32]

And it is interesting to note that, also from 1595, Burghley left a six-page manuscript of notes upon the reign of Edward II, marking those who were friends or enemies of the king.[33]

Camden wrote that when the Catholics grew hopeless of James's religion and could find no English Catholic of proper antecedents for the crown,

they cast their eyes upon the Earle of *Essex*, (who never approved the putting of men to death in the cause of Religion,) feigning a Title from *Thomas of Woodstock*, King *Edward* the third's sonne, from whom hee derived his Pedigree.

Camden also seems to have accepted Essex's innocence, for he added:

But the Fugitives favoured the *Infanta of Spaine*, although they feared lest the Queene and the Estates would by Act of Parliament prevent it by offering an oath to every one, and they held it sufficient

[29]*Ibid.*, pp. 357-58.
[30]*Ibid.*, p. 360.
[31]*Ibid.*, p. 362. The device is printed in full in John Nichols, *The Progresses and Public Processions of Queen Elizabeth* (London, 1788), II, 627-34.
[32]*Cal. S. P., Dom., 1595-1597*, p. 157.
[33]*Ibid.*, p. 158.

if they could set the King and the Earle of *Essex* at enmity. And indeed to this purpose there was a booke set forth and dedicated to *Essex*, under the counterfeit name of *Dolman*, not without the remarkeable malice of *Parsons* the *Jesuit* against *Dolman* a Priest of a quiet spirit, (if we may give credite to the Priests,) for the Authors of the booke were *Parsons* a most deadly adversary of *Dolmans*, Cardinall *Allen*, and Sir *Francis Inglefield*.[34]

The answers to Parsons were numerous. Peter Wentworth wrote *A Pithie Exhortation to Her Majestie for Establishing Her Successor to the Crowne*, which was not published until 1598, after the author's death, but which was evidently well known before its publication. For this study the significant part of his argument in favor of establishing the succession is the contention that princes have not generally been deposed and murdered by their declared successors. Inevitably he reviewed the cases of Edward II, Richard II, and Henry VI. Of Richard he said:

And king Richard the sec. was deposed, not by one whome he had made his knowne successor, but by Henry the fourth: no successor to him by right, but an usurper, and that for his great misgovernment, as it doth appeare in the storie by 28. articles objected against him at his deposing: wherein his nobility and commons shewed, that they liked rather to have an usurper to raigne over them, that would preserve the crowne and them, then a rightfull king, that would perill the crowne and state also.[35]

Sir John Harington (Elizabeth's godson) wrote in defense of King James's right to succeed a *Tract on the Succession to the Crown*, answering the work of Parsons from *Greencoat* to the *Conference*. He made it quite plain that he regarded the historical parallels collected by Parsons as eminently dangerous and thereby acknowledged their truth. He accused Parsons of harping on

a seditious string of deposing of Princes for disabilitie and weakenes, and that in such a tyme, when malecontentes so abound in citie and

[34]Camden, *The Historie of the . . . Princesse Elizabeth* (London, 1630), Bk. 4, p. 57.

[35]Pp. 79-80. With this tract was published also *A Treatise containing M. Wentworth's Judgement concerning the Person of the True and Lawfull Successor*.

countrye, when in the Court the common phrase of old servantes is that their is no commiseracion of any man's distressed estate, that a few favourites gett all, that the nobilitie is depressed, the Clergy pilled and contemned, forraine invasions expected, the treasure at home exhausted, the coyne in Ireland imbased, the gold of England transported, exactions doubled and trebled, and all honest heartes so troubled that save the immovable resolucion of justice and fidelity in that worthy King of Scotts is so knowen, that no man dare make such a motion to him: It were more doubte by the reading of your booke, that the Nobility should call him in before his tyme then exclude him after his tyme, . . .[36]

In 1599, before the Earl of Essex sailed on his Irish expedition, a new book came forth to call attention to the story of the deposing of Richard II and the accession of Henry IV. This book was *The First Part of the Life and Raigne of King Henrie the IIII.* and was dedicated by its author, Sir John Hayward, to the Earl of Essex, the dedication reading in part:

Magnus si quidem es, et presenti judicio, et futuri temporis expectatione: in quo, veluti recuperasse nunc oculos, caeca prius fortuna videri potest; Dum cumulare honoribus eum gestit, qui omnibus virtutibus est insignitus. Hunc igitur si laeta fronte excipere digneris, sub nominis tui umbra (tanquam sub *Ajacis* clipio *Teucer* ille *Homericus*) tutissime latebit.

This was dangerous praise, but a preface to the reader (by "A.P."), in making the usual apology for history, whether of governments or of men, explained that

by describing the order and passages of these two, and what events hath followed what counsailes, they have set foorth unto us, not onely precepts, but lively patterns, both for private directions and for affayres of state: . . .

Here was a book of 149 pages, supposedly dealing with the first part of the reign of Henry IV: yet, as I have said, the first 136 pages of the 149 were devoted to reciting the history of

---

[36]*A Tract on the Succession to the Crown*, printed from a MS in the chapter library at York and ed. by Clements R. Markham (London, 1880), pp. 76-77. The tract is dated December 18, 1602.

Richard II and the reasons which led to his deposition by Henry IV, "so farre forth as the follies of the one, were either causes or furtherances of the fortunes of the other."

At the very beginning of Richard's reign, Hayward reported, "flatterie brake in, and private respects did pass under publike pretences,"[37] and he adorned the tale with a moral, noting that "it is oftentimes as daungerous to a Prince, to have evil and odious adherents, as to be evill and odious himselfe." Accordingly, after Scrope had been deposed from the chancellorship, Richard named Michael de la Pole Chancellor of England and Robert Vere Marquess of Dublin, and Michael de la Pole "made open sale of his princes honour."[38] The Duke of Hereford in conversation with Thomas Mowbray, Duke of Norfolk, charged that the king had no regard for the princes and peers but cared only for new-found favorites, and that as a result (1) the honor of the king's person was blemished, (2) the safety of the state was endangered, and (3) the dignity of the realm was impaired.[39]

The king, Hayward recorded, let out his revenues to farm, extracted great sums from his people, made new impositions, and borrowed from everyone, so that affairs were in sad contrast with affairs at the death of Henry II, who through good management had left £900,000, besides jewels and plate, at his death. And as for Ireland:

If any thing were happily atchieved by some of the nobility, it was by the Kings base hearted parasites, to whom millitary vertue was altogether unpleasant, so extinuated, or depraved, or envied, that it was seldome rewarded, so much as with countenance and thankes: yea sometimes it procured suspicion and danger; . . .

Those about the king told him

it was a perillous poynt, to have the name of a man of private estate, famous for the same in every mans mouth. Hereupon, few sought to rise by vertue and valure, the readier way was, to please the pleas-

---

[37]*Op. cit.*, p. 5.
[38]*Ibid.*, pp. 6-10.
[39]*Ibid.*, pp. 42-43.

ant humour of the Prince. Likewise matters of peace, were managed by men of weakest sufficiency, by whose counsell either ignorant or corrupt, the destruction of the best harted nobility, was many times attempted, and at the last wrought.[40]

The people inevitably turned for help to someone, and they sought Henry, Duke of Herford,

not at his own motion or desire, but because he was generally esteemed meet: as being of the royall bloud, and next by descent from males to the succession of the crowne: one that had made honourable proofe of his vertues and valure: the onely man of note that remained alive, of those that before had stood in armes against the King, for the behoofe of the Common-wealth: . . .[41]

The messengers sent to the exiled duke included the Archbishop of Canterbury, then also in exile in France, and he it was who most eloquently pleaded the example of foreign and English precedents to convince the duke of the righteousness as well as the necessity of deposing the king. It was promised that no bodily harm should come to the king, but that the rebels would proceed only against his counsellors. The duke accepted the plea of necessity, and went about his affairs, Hayward records. When the duke returned to London, the people met him with great acclaim, casting slurs upon King Richard. Hayward adds:

Againe, the Duke for his part was not negligent to uncover the head to bowe the body, to stretch forth the hand to every meane person, and to use all other complements of popular behaviour wherewith the mindes of the common multitude are much delighted and drawen; taking that to bee courtesie, which the severer sort accompt abasement.[42]

When Richard tardily returned from Ireland on hearing the news of this threat to his throne, he landed at Milford Haven in Wales but, uncertain and unresolved, found himself exposed to various counsels. Among the arguments advanced that he should

[40]*Ibid.*, pp. 54-55.
[41]*Ibid.*, p. 61.
[42]*Ibid.*, p. 71.

yield his crown without a struggle certain ones stand out: he had no children and hence would not by yielding his throne disinherit the rightful heir; a private life would be sweeter to him than that of a ruler, since the "crown and sceptar are things most weighty to weld," and indeed, when he lost "the credit and the countenance of a King," he would also lose its cares and sorrows, as philosophers and kings before him had perceived. The king might even gain fame for having relinquished his crown when it was best for his people that he do so, and no infamy could come to him when he relinquished it willingly. This was the line of argument to which Richard responded, deciding finally to yield his crown to his cousin. Thirty-one articles reciting the king's crimes are recorded by Hayward. The assent of the people being received, the deposition was formally voted by both houses of Parliament, and the resigning of the crown took place with the symbolically meaningful ceremony here recorded.

The Bishop of Carlisle alone dared to voice his opposition, and Hayward gives an entirely disproportionate account of his speech (nine pages of text). If it is remembered that Parsons in his *Conference* asked

first, whether Richard the second were justly deposed or no, and secondly whether after his deposition the house of Yorke or house of Lancaster should have entred,

it will be understood why Hayward makes Carlisle pose the questions,

First, whether King *Richard* be sufficiently deposed or no:
Secondly, whether King *Henrie* be with good judgment, or justice chosen in his place.

Hayward is answering Parsons also, it would seem, when Carlisle states that he is not speaking of a popular or of a consular state but of a state like the ancient empires or modern kingdoms, such as England, where the king is the source of whatever authority nobles and people may have, and is not elected by them (Parsons had said *accepted*). In answer to the first question he states what Hayward's readers must have recognized as the orthodox Tudor position, that even though the king do evil, God will not permit the people to rebel. If subjects may judge their prince, there will be cries of oppression every time taxes are levied; it will be called cruelty when any are put to death for traitorous attempts at regicide; anything against the lust and liking of the people will be called tyranny.

In answer to the second question, he said that if Henry sought the crown as heir, then he must wait for the death of the present king. If he claimed it by conquest, whoever heard of an insurrection by a subject called conquest by war? Nor can the king legally give away his throne, since he cannot legally give away even his jewels. History shows, the bishop continued, what terrible woes follow upon such wrongs as are proposed, for God surely punishes them. But the bishop was seized and imprisoned for his speech. Hayward proceeds with the story of the end of Richard II and the first troubled year of the reign of Henry IV with the authority of the chronicles.

Before I touch upon the fate of this book, it must be noted that in 1603 Hayward published *An Answer to the First Part of a Certaine Conference, Concerning Succession, published not long since under the name of R. Dolman*, and that in his dedication to King James he says:

I here present unto your Majestie this defence, both of the present authoritie of Princes, and of succession according to the proximitie of bloud: wherein is maintained, that the people have no lawfull power, to remove the one, or repell the other: In which two points I have heretofore also declared my opinion, by publishing the tragicall events which ensued the deposition of King *Richard*, and usurpation of King *Henrie* the fourth. Both these labours were undertaken with particular respect, to your Majesties just title of succession in this realme: . . .

In this defense of his earlier interest it would seem that Hayward was associating his account of the fall of Richard II and the rise of Henry IV with his somewhat belated answer to Parsons (or Doleman). In the prefatory address to Parsons in the later book he pours contempt on him for having in his *Confer-ence* fed the humors of "such discontented persons, as wante or disgrace hath kept lower than they had set their swelling thoughts," but acknowledges that he has kept silence partly be-cause of "the nimble eare which lately was borne to the touche of this string." Whether or not Hayward—or even Essex—in reality stood for the succession of King James by right of blood is not here in point, though I believe a good defense of this view can be made. And whether Hayward intended, through Henry IV, to teach the dangers of rebellion to Essex as he here implies, or to teach the reasons for rebellion to an erring queen, it is equally true that he used the recognized pattern in dealing with the problem of the deposition of a king.

Parsons' dedication of the *Conference* to the Earl of Essex had brought that unhappy young man temporary alienation from the queen, but Hayward's dedication of his book on Henry IV was to have much more serious consequences. It will be remem-bered that when Essex made his tempestuous return from Ire-land, against the queen's orders, in September of 1599, he was suspected and remitted to custody. On November 29, censure was pronounced on him in Star Chamber. In March he was al-lowed to return to his own house in charge of Sir Richard Berke-ley. In June of 1600 he was tried before special commissioners, censured, and ordered to remain a prisoner in his house and not to execute any of his offices. Great stress was laid on Hayward's book during these proceedings as evidence of Essex's ambitions and intentions, and in July Hayward was summoned to court and examined. Two days later he was sent to the Tower of Lon-don. The printer Wolfe was also questioned and revealed that three weeks after the first printing of Hayward's book, the Archbishop of Canterbury had ordered the dedicatory epistle to Essex cut out. All later editions were burnt in the Bishop of London's house—to the financial grief of the printer, he com-plained. Hayward was again examined.

On August 26, Essex was released from custody at the queen's desire. He commenced to woo her favor once more, but when she found that his ultimate purpose in the wooing was to have restored to him the farm of sweet wines upon which his wealth depended, she seems to have been bitterly disillusioned. Essex's debts were large and pressing, and the renewal of the grant could save him, but Elizabeth gave her final refusal in October. It is pertinent to recall the advice which Bacon said he gave the queen when she was expressing her dissatisfaction with Essex's conduct in Ireland: "to discontent him as you do, and yet to put armes and power into his hands, may be a kind of temptation to make him prove cumbersome and unruly."[43] But Elizabeth continued to discontent him even while she gave him liberty to get into mischief. And he was a desperate man.

On Febuary 3, 1601, the leaders among the Essex malcontents met and planned an uprising. On February 6 several of those most involved, among them Sir Charles Percy and Sir Gilly Merrick, went to the Globe to arrange with Augustine Phillips for the Lord Chamberlain's company—Shakespeare's company—"to play the deposing and killing of Richard II." The actors protested that this play was "so old and long out of use" that it would attract but a small audience, but the young lords insisted, and the play was presented on the afternoon of December 7, with the Essex faction in attendance. On February 8, Essex plunged into the rebellion for which he and his arch supporter, the Earl of Southampton, were brought to trial together on February 19. On February 25 Essex was executed. Only Mary of Scotland had played so theatrically a tragic role.

Ironically Essex, the favored of favorites, insisted that his purpose had been to get the ear of the queen and save her from the unworthy advisers who surrounded her—Cecil, Raleigh, Cobham, Howard, and Gray especially. He even accused Cecil of favoring the Spanish succession, though he later acknowledged his error, and Cecil swore his comment on the matter had been relative to Parsons' *Conference*. To the last Essex insisted that he would not have shed the queen's blood.

The facts that Hayward's account of the deposing of Richard

---

[43]Sir Francis Bacon, *His Apologie, in Certaine Imputations Concerning the Late Earle of Essex* (London, 1605), p. 25.

II and the usurpation of Henry IV was made a matter of prime consideration in determining Essex's fate, and that a play "of King Henry the Fourth, and of the killing of Richard the Second" was used by Essex's friends as a curtain-raiser to his rebellion have provided us with a clearly authenticated account of the Elizabethan recognition of history as a political mirror potentially dangerous. In the State Papers are to be found two and a half pages of notes and interrogatories by Attorney General Coke, dating from the time when Hayward was first questioned

in proof that the Doctor selected a story 200 years old, and published it last year, intending the application of it to this time, the plot being that of a King who is taxed for misgovernment, and his council for corrupt and covetous dealings for private ends; the King is censured for conferring benefits on hated favorites, the nobles become discontented, and the commons groan under continual taxation, whereupon the King is deposed, and in the end murdered.[44]

Bacon said that Queen Elizabeth was "mightily incensed" with the book, "thinking it a seditious prelude to put into the peoples heades boldnesse and faction."[45]

Hayward was questioned on specific statements. To the query as to why he wrote in the preface that history affords "not onely precepts, but lively patternes, both for private directions and for affayres of state," he replied that he was speaking of histories in general and not his book in particular. As to why he inserted the comment that Henry II left £900,000 in the treasury, he said a historiographer could insert any history of former times. The speech saying that the subject was bound to the state rather than the person of the king, he found in Bodius and inserted as spoken by the Earl of Derby and the Duke of Hereford, for "it is a liberty used by all good writers of history to invent reasons and speeches," but he added that Bodius admitted that in a monarchy the subject was bound to the king.[46] Oftentimes Hayward claimed older authority for suspected statements, but he admitted that he had never heard of benevolences in the time of Rich-

[44]*Cal. S. P., Dom., 1598-1601*, p. 449.
[45]Bacon, *op. cit.*, p. 34.
[46]Bodius is identified as Boethius in the State Papers.

ard II, that the archbishop's oration with its eight instances proving that "deposers of kings and princes have had good success," was without authority, though he insisted the introduction of such a speech was the prerogative of a historian. And besides, he added, the Bishop of Carlisle answered it. As to his description of the duke as "not negligent to uncover the head, bow the body," etc., he was within his rights as historian in particularizing a general statement for which he had authority. His examination is interesting because the questions reveal the points that were barbed, and Hayward's answers show a canny defensive use of the accepted theory of historiography.[47]

In the 1601 trial of Essex these matters were again threshed out. Cecil accused the earl of having for five or six years plotted to become king and affirmed that the proof of his intentions was in "the book written on Henry IV., making this time like that of Richard II., to be reframed by him as by Henry IV." The trial also elicited evidence concerning the playing of the play about Richard II on the eve of the rebellion. In this connection, it should be noted that there is one curious and unexplained reference in the testimony offered in the 1600 trial to Essex's having been often present "at the playing of" Hayward's book, and "with great applause giving countenance to it." The relation of Hayward's book and "the playing thereof," to Shakespeare's *Richard II* is not settled, but Chambers, like Miss Albright and others, would identify the play chosen by Essex's followers as Shakespeare's. At any rate, members of the Chamberlain's company were arraigned and questioned, though Shakespeare was apparently not involved and none of the actors was punished.[48]

---

[47]*Cal. S. P., Dom., 1598-1601* (examination of Hayward, Jan. 22, 1601), pp. 539-40. For Hayward's examination July 11, 1600, see p. 449.

[48]Accounts of the Essex trial are here summarized from the records in the *Calendar of State Papers, Domestic, 1598-1601;* J. E. Neale, *Queen Elizabeth,* chap. xix; G. B. Harrison, *Robert Devereux Earl of Essex* (New York, 1937), pp. 248-325. See Evelyn M. Albright, "Shakespeare's *Richard II* and the Essex Conspiracy," *PMLA,* XLII, 686-720; Ray Heffner, "Shakespeare, Hayward, and Essex," XLV, 754-80; a reply by Miss Albright, XLVI, 694-719; replies to replies, XLVII, 898-901; also Margaret Dowling, "Sir John Hayward's Troubles over his Life of Henry IV," *The Library,* 4th ser., XI, 212-24.

There are several glancing references to Richard II and Henry IV in the records of the time to show that both before and after the Essex incident the history of that time was made to furnish allusions for the gentlemen of Elizabeth's court, but the crowning recognition of the historical parallel came from Elizabeth herself. On August 4, 1601, William Lambarde "presented her Majestie with his Pandecta of all her rolls, bundells, membranes, and parcells that be reposed in her Majestie's Tower at London," so goes the story, and as she turned over the pages, "her Majestie fell upon the reign of King Richard II, saying, 'I am Richard II, know ye not that?'" And when Lambarde replied with a reference to Essex, the queen added, "He that will forget God, will also forget his benefactors; this tragedy was played 40 times in open streets and houses."[49]

It is surely not necessary to go on proving that through the greater part of Elizabeth's reign she was being compared to Richard II, that malcontents were using the reign of Richard to point the moral, and that the problem of the deposition of a king was regularly discussed in terms of Richard II. The queen's own statement, the controversial literature of the period, and the interrogatories and depositions at the Essex trials make these conclusions unimpeachable. But there were also several dramas dealing with the times of Richard II concerning the significance of which we have only the internal evidence offered in their texts.

Three of these plays have survived. The first is *The Life and Death of Jacke Straw*, first published in 1593, which deals with the problem of rebellion. The second is a play, called by its Malone Society editors *Richard II: Or Thomas of Woodstock*,[50] which has come down to us only in Egerton MS 1994, where the title page is missing. It is generally assigned to a year between 1590 and 1595. It is a witty play in spite of its tragic close, portraying the struggle for power between Richard II's giddy favorites and his three good uncles, the dukes of York, Lancaster, and Gloucester—Richard's true counsellors. The favorites win,

---

[49]Hist. MSS Comm., *Fourth Report* (London, 1874), col. 300.
[50]Ed. by W. P. Frijlinck (1929) in Malone Society Reprints, general ed. W. W. Greg.

and the king leases them the lands and revenues of his kingdom, so that he becomes landlord rather than king of England. Fearing that the commons in their resentment will appeal to Thomas of Woodstock, Duke of Gloucester, the favorites plot his capture and death. The king even goes with them when as maskers they seize the duke. They take him to Calais, and too late the king tries to revoke the order for his death. At the urging of the Duchess of Gloucester his brothers seek revenge. Of the favorites Greene is killed, Bagot is forced to flee, and Bushy, Scrope, and Lapoole are taken prisoners with the king.[51] The third of the surviving plays is Shakespeare's *Richard II*.

Besides these plays there is a play to be inferred from the reference to Essex's having been present at the playing of Hayward's book. There is the play presented on the eve of the Essex uprising. There is the play which Queen Elizabeth said had been "played 40 times in open streets and houses." And Dr. Simon Forman recorded one at the Globe April 30, 1611. Any or all of these may have been Shakespeare's, but opinion on the subject can be only arbitrary.

Now three quartos of Shakespeare's *Richard II* appeared in 1597 (1) and 1598 (2) without the scene in which Richard yields his sceptre and his crown to Bolingbroke. In 1608 the scene was restored to the play, and in some of the surviving copies there is a cancel title page which points out this fact, for it reads:

The Tragedie of King Richard the Second: With new additions of the Parliament Sceane, and the deposing of King Richard, As it hath been lately acted by the Kinges Majesties servantes, at the Globe.

Chambers and others have argued conclusively that this scene must have been cut out of the original play, rather than added in the 1608 edition, because the Abbot's subsequent comment, "A woeful Pageant have we here beheld," is without meaning when the scene and its woeful pageant are deleted. Miss Albright listed many likenesses between Hayward's book and Shakespeare's play and between the character and actions of Henry IV

[51]On the interrelation of the plays about Richard II, see F. S. Boas, *Shakespeare and the Universities* (Oxford, 1923), chap. vii.

in the play and the Earl of Essex in real life. Even Chambers, as great a skeptic as scholar, suggested that

the interest taken by Essex in the play led to some popular application of the theme to current politics, and this in turn to the intervention of the censor, perhaps at the theatre, but more probably when the play came to be printed.[52]

But, as I have shown, "popular application of the theme to current politics" was far from depending on Essex's interest in the play; it had been habitual for many years.

One thing seems to me certain, that a play about Richard II published in 1597 and probably, according to Chambers, written in 1595 or earlier, could not have been written apropos of Essex's actions between 1599 and 1601. Even though the earl was plotting to become king as early as was asserted at the time of the trial, it is hard to see how Shakespeare could have anticipated his claims, his arguments, and his actions in detail. Furthermore, just as Elizabeth was not the only ruler who was warned about favoritism by reference to Richard II, Essex was not the only aspirant for the English throne who might be taught the dangers of usurpation. He was not the outstanding claimant at all; that was James of Scotland. Moreover, James at intervals was laying claim to the English lands of the Earl and Countess of Lennox, his father's parents. No alien could inherit English land; if James could possess himself of this inheritance, it might help in claiming the crown. His insistence on gaining his inheritance might well have been compared to the demand of Bolingbroke. Also he seems to have wanted, and after the death of his mother to have been offered the title of Duke of Lancaster, Bolingbroke's title. Finally, his desire to be declared heir and his willingness to anticipate his inheritance are amply documented. Miss Stafford has published the arguments he drew up in 1592 for and against invading England.[53] Until Elizabeth's death he never stopped

[52]E. K. Chambers, *William Shakespeare*, I, 355.

[53]The best general account of James's activities as hopeful heir is found in Helen G. Stafford, *James VI of Scotland and the Throne of England*, published for the American Historical Association, New York, 1940. See in the following chapter a discussion of his haste to wear the crown.

demanding recognition and playing with the idea of using force. There was certainly some sort of connection between Essex and James, and James was invited to co-operate after Essex's first trial. He had a strong force on the border when Essex was planning his rebellion. As Neale says, "possibly an accident, possibly not." Essex pretended to be loyal to James. Perhaps he was. It is possible that he planned to be, like Northumberland, the ladder whereby James should mount the throne. It is a matter that is not likely to be decided. But that James's waiting was impatient no one has cared to deny. If, therefore, Shakespeare was writing about any single individual, which I do not think he was, it might better have been James than Essex, James who was not Elizabeth's heir but only her father's sister's grandson—to misquote Richard II.

However, Shakespeare's intentions can only be discussed after consideration of his play, which, as I have said earlier, opens exactly where Halle began his introduction into the troubles of the houses of Lancaster and York, with the quarrel between Bolingbroke and Mowbray. It is a proper scene to introduce a play of kingship, for, to the sixteenth century, above all else a king was an administrator of justice, acting as God's deputy. And it is as God's justicer that Richard first appears. Shakespeare has given us the measuring rod of Richard's own conception of his office by which to judge how far short he falls of his ideals. The charges and counter-charges which are hurled between the two dukes are very like those heard more than once at Elizabeth's court, but they derived from Holinshed. And Richard has opportunity to proclaim his justice as he assures Mowbray of his right to defend himself against the slanders of the king's cousin:

> Mowbray, impartial are our eyes and ears:
> Were he my brother, nay, my kingdom's heir,
> As he is but my father's brother's son,
> Now, by my sceptre's awe, I make a vow,
> Such neighbour nearness to our sacred blood
> Should nothing privilege him, nor partialize
> The unstooping firmness of my upright soul:

> He is our subject, Mowbray; so art thou:
> Free speech and fearless I to thee allow.

When each has thrown down his gage and taken up that of the other, Richard, unable to reconcile them, speaks to them both:

> We were not born to sue, but to command;
> . . . .
> Since we can not atone you, we shall see
> Justice design the victor's chivalry.

But before justice speaks again, a scene intervenes which poses the problem fundamental in the deposing of a king: May a subject give sentence on his king? Must he suffer under an unjust king without recourse? The second scene of the play intrudes this question with the pleading of the Duchess of Gloucester to John of Gaunt to seek vengeance for the death of her husband and his brother. To her Gaunt lays down the accepted Tudor philosophy of kingship, which his son is later to deny in becoming Henry IV:

> But since correction lieth in those hands
> Which made the fault that we cannot correct,
> Put we our quarrel to the will of heaven;
> Who, when they see the hours ripe on earth,
> Will rain hot vengeance on offenders' heads.

The duchess pleads the shedding of the sacred royal blood, taunts him with cowardice and despair, warns him of the threat to his own life, but Gaunt persists:

> God's is the quarrel; for God's substitute,
> His deputy anointed in His sight,
> Hath caused his death: the which if wrongfully,
> Let heaven revenge; for I may never lift
> An angry arm against His minister.

To the duchess's impassioned query, "Where then, alas, may I complain myself?" he replies again, "To God, the widow's champion and defence."

Yet in the first scene of the second act Gaunt does not fail to chide the king for having spilled the royal blood:

> That blood already, like the pelican,
> Hast thou tapp'd out and drunkenly caroused:
> My brother Gloucester, plain, well-meaning soul,
> Whom fair befal in heaven 'mongst happy souls!
> May be a precedent and witness good
> That thou respect'st not spilling Edward's blood: . . .

Thus in spite of his hatred for Richard's sin, Gaunt refuses to yield to the pleas of the duchess. That "God's is the quarrel" when God's deputy sins, and that to him alone belongs vengeance was the orthodox Tudor position, but it was not that taken by the historical Gaunt. Holinshed says only that after various proposals for revenging their brother's death the dukes of York and Lancaster "(after their displeasure was somewhat asswaged) determined to cover the stings of their griefs for a time, and, if the king would amend his maners, to forget also the injuries past." The other play of *Richard II: Or Thomas of Woodstock* presented the uncles of the king actually taking their vengeance. This interpretation is a Shakespeare addition.

In the minds of many Elizabethans the blood of Mary Stuart cried from the ground against Elizabeth as did that of Thomas of Woodstock against Richard II, and Samuel Daniel took occasion to moralize in general terms upon Gloucester's death:

> And this is sure though his offence be such,
> Yet doth calamitie attract commorse,
> And men repine at Princes bloudshed much
> How just-soever judging tis by force:
> I know not how their death gives such a tuch
> In those that reach not to a true discourse:
> That so shall you observing formall right
> Be still thought as unjust and win more spight.[54]

But to any who would avenge the royal blood spilled by the king, Shakespeare has Gaunt give the answer that every loyal

[54]Daniel, *The First Fowre Books of the Civile Wars* (London, 1595), Bk. I, stanza 51.

subject of Elizabeth gave to those who would avenge the death of Mary, "God's is the quarrel."

After this scene, which does not further the action, and which can have been introduced only to restate the Tudor theory of kingship, we return to Richard as the agent of justice in the quarrel between Bolingbroke and Mowbray. After the pageantry is over and each combatant has proclaimed himself and his cause, just as the marshal commands the trumpets to sound and the combat to begin, Richard throws his warder down and orders the dukes to their chairs. Then he pronounces sentence of banishment on both, lest their quarrel

> Might from our quiet confines fright fair peace,
> And make us wade even in our kindred's blood; . . .

Mowbray's exile is unlimited, but even the ten years' term fixed for Bolingbroke is abated to six for his father's sake. And when that father, nearing death, is not grateful, Richard returns to his role of defender of justice as he addresses him:

> Thy son is banish'd upon good advice,
> Whereto thy tongue a party-verdict gave:
> Why at our justice seem'st thou then to lour?

But however well he has played his role in meting out justice and mercy, Richard soon demonstrates that he cannot play it long, for the fourth scene shows him gloating in most injudicious fashion as, surrounded by his parasites, he confides to his cousin Aumerle:

> He is our cousin, cousin; but 'tis doubt,
> When time shall call him home from banishment,
> Whether our kinsman come to see his friends.

And then he reveals his hidden reason for Bolingbroke's banishment:

> Ourself and Bushy, Bagot here and Green
> Observed his courtship to the common people;
> How he did seem to dive into their hearts

> With humble and familiar courtesy,
>
> .   .   .   .
>
> Off goes his bonnet to an oyster-wench;
> A brace of draymen bid God speed him well
>
> .   .   .   .
>
> As were our England in reversion his,
> And he our subjects' next degree in hope.

It is a passage even more imaginatively detailed than that which elicited special questioning in Hayward's book, and as Miss Albright has shown, it is a description that might well have applied to the Earl of Essex, famous for his courtesy and in love with the power which popularity brought. There is no one whom it seems to fit so well, and it would have fitted the earl in the earlier nineties as well as in the later years. But whatever the current application of the description, in Richard's mouth it reveals jealousy masking as justice, and trickery as mercy.

Before he goes to his Irish wars Richard must finance them, and he does so by planning to "farm our royal realm," to issue blank charters for the rich, and finally to seize the possessions of old Gaunt, who is reported as dying opportunely.

In a remarkable theatrical victory over time Bolingbroke seems to have gone to France, arranged a marriage, been thwarted through the intervention of Richard, and gathered forces to return to England to demand his rights during the brief period in which Richard goes to Ely House to visit his uncle. From his death-bed there we hear Gaunt make his great poetical oration upon "This blessed plot, this earth, this realm, this England," which he now sees leased out and shamed:

> That England, that was wont to conquer others,
> Hath made a shameful conquest of itself.

It is the most eloquent of the patriotic speeches in the history plays and familiar now to many who know nothing else in them, but Richard does not hear it. When he enters Gaunt's presence, he is met with a punning speech on Gaunt's name and then with a bitter denunciation of his sins. He has let flattery rule, he has spilled the royal blood, he has leased out his land, and he is deposing himself:

> A thousand flatterers sit within thy crown,
>
> . . . .
>
> O had thy grandsire with a prophet's eye
> Seen how his son's son should destroy his sons,
> From forth thy reach he would have laid thy shame,
> Deposing thee before thou wert possess'd,
> Which art possess'd now to depose thyself.
>
> . . . .
>
> It were a shame to let this land by lease;
>
> . . . .
>
> Landlord of England art thou now, not King: . . .

These are the sins that, throughout the play, are balanced against Richard's right as king to be accountable only to God.

Peter Wentworth in his famous speech of 1576, which he was not allowed to conclude to the House of Commons, and which brought him to residence in the Tower of London, offered a prayer on Elizabeth's behalf which is in point here:

And I beseech the same God to endue her majesty with his wisdom, whereby she may discern faithful advice from traitorous sugared speeches, and to send her majesty a melting, yielding heart unto sound counsel, that will may not stand for a reason: and then her majesty will stand when her enemies are fallen, for no estate can stand where the prince will not be governed by advice.[55]

From the beginning of her reign the charge most often brought against Elizabeth, as we have seen, was that she was swayed by favorites. But like Gaunt and York and Gloucester, "plain, well-meaning soul," who thought themselves true advisers and branded any whom the king preferred as favorites, all those to whom Elizabeth would not listen denounced those to whom they thought she was listening too much. Leicester, the accused of all accusers, thought himself in danger from the false reports that

---

[55]Quoted from the reprint in W. H. Dunham and S. Pargellis, *Complaint and Reform in England, 1436-1714* (New York, 1938), p. 265.

were whispered in the queen's ear by those whom she unjustly favored. Essex, the most spoiled young man at court, directed his rebellion, he said, only to rescuing the queen from such men as Raleigh and Cobham whom she was favoring.

As to the second charge, Elizabeth too was censured for spilling the royal blood in permitting Mary Stuart to die, and there were many who thought she pointed the way to her own destruction thereby, as I have shown in the discussion of *King John*. Daniel had dared to make the application of the lesson to be learned from Gloucester's death general and pointed.

The third charge as well was made against Elizabeth, that she leased out her kingdom. Such favorites as Leicester and Essex became rich through her grants of lands and special privileges, the farm of sweet wines to Essex, for instance. Aiding the French and the Dutch, fighting in Ireland, arming against the Spaniards cost Elizabeth much treasure. Neale says:

In the four years from 1589-93 she spent about £300,000 in aid of Henry IV. Adding the cost of her forces in the Netherlands for the same time, this meant an expenditure on warfare of at least £800,000, apart from the Irish wars and naval expenditures. In a single one of these years she was compelled to sell crown lands to the value of over £120,000.[56]

It will be remembered that Coke's summing up of charges directed at Elizabeth's reign by Hayward when he was concerned with that of Richard II, noted:

the King is censured for conferring benefits on hated favourites, the nobles become discontented, and the commons groan under continual taxation whereupon the King is deposed, and in the end murdered.

These are the three sins which represent the antecedent action of the play of *Richard II*; they are the sins which posed the question repeatedly asked, whether Richard II were justly deposed or no. But they are also the sins which were brought up time after time when the fate of Richard II was pointed out to Elizabeth as a warning. The question as to whether Richard II de-

[56]Neale, *op. cit.*, p. 323.

served to be deposed might have remained an academic question, however, had he not in his folly committed a new sin, which brought about his destruction. Gaunt's admonitions stilled by death, the brash young king thinks of his Irish wars:

> And for these great affairs do ask some charge,
> Towards our assistance we do seize to us
> The plate, coin, revenues and moveables,
> Whereof our uncle Gaunt did stand possess'd.

The action precipitates the wrath of the mild Duke of York, and he prophesies:

> If you do wrongfully seize Hereford's rights,
> . . . .
> You pluck a thousand dangers on your head,
> You lose a thousand well-disposed hearts,
> And prick my tender patience to those thoughts
> Which honour and allegiance cannot think.

Ironically Richard creates York lord governor while he is at the wars but disdains his advice.

Then we see the gathering of the forces who are to oppose the king, Northumberland first among them. And we hear the charges reiterated. From Northumberland:

> The king is not himself, but basely led
> By flatterers; . . .

From Ross:

> The commons hath he pill'd with grievous taxes,
> And quite lost their hearts; the nobles hath he fined
> For ancient quarrels, and quite lost their hearts.

From Willoughby:

> And daily new exactions are devised,
> As blanks, benevolences, and I wot not what: . . .

So speaking, Willoughby introduces the word *benevolences*, which in the trial of Essex was taken to indicate that the times of Elizabeth rather than those of Richard II were in question.

But all these charges have been called forth anew by word that Bolingbroke has been "Bereft and gelded of his patrimony." In his fate they see the fate of all. Then Northumberland has news, news of the approach of the banished duke "with eight tall ships, three thousand men of war," and many supporters. Thus we hear the first word of the rebellion, which, as always, seems undertaken for righteousness' sake:

> If then we shall shake off our slavish yoke,
> Imp out our drooping country's broken wing,
> Redeem from broking pawn the blemish'd crown,
> Wipe off the dust that hides our sceptre's gilt,
> And make high majesty look like itself,
> Away with me in post to Ravenspurgh; . . .

The news of the rebellion is brought to the queen and Bushy; York enters with word that the nobles have fled, and that the commons are cold and may revolt to Bolingbroke; a servant reports the death of the Duchess of Gloucester: "a tide of woes" York says. Then he faces his problem:

> Both are my kinsmen:
> Th' one is my sovereign, whom both my oath
> And duty bids defend; th' other again
> Is my kinsman, whom the king hath wrong'd,
> Whom conscience and my kindred bids to right.

But it is a problem which he never solves except by scolding his recalcitrant nephew in the next scene as he comes to the assembly of Bolingbroke's supporters, who are greeting him as he lands. His nephew pleads:

> I am a subject,
> And I challenge law: attorneys are denied me;
> And therefore personally I lay my claim
> To my inheritance of free descent.

And York replies with sound doctrine:

> To find out right with wrong, it may not be;
> And you that do abet him in this kind
> Cherish rebellion and are rebels all.

Against the defiance of all those gathered about the new Duke of Lancaster, he cannot or will not fight, and he offers them refuge for the night. To Bolingbroke's invitation to go to settle matters with Richard's favorites, "The caterpillars of the commonwealth," he makes uncertain reply, for

> Things past redress are now with me past care.

Act III of the play depicts the progress of the rebellion to victory over the king. It begins with Bolingbroke's passing sentence of death upon Bushy and Green because they have "misled a prince, a royal king," separating him from his queen, making him misinterpret his cousin, and taking as their own the possessions of the banished man. It should be noted that Henry is already in this scene assuming the role of God's deputy in administering justice.

Henry's strong determination in executing his judgments is, however, made the background for the appearance of Richard as he greets his kingdom once more, saluting its soil with his royal hand, sure that the very earth will repel rebellion. The *French Academie* said of a king:

For as God hath placed the Sun in the heavens as an image of his divine nature, which lightneth, heateth, quickneth, and nourisheth al things created for mans use, either in heaven or earth: so the soveraign magistrate is the like representation and light in a city or kingdom, especially so long as the feare of God, and observation of justice are imprinted in his heart.[57]

This is the image which Richard sees as he describes the rebellion of Bolingbroke while he was away at the Irish wars:

> So when this thief, this traitor, Bolingbroke,
> Who all this while hath revell'd in the night,
> Whilst we were wandering with the antipodes,
> Shall see us rising in our throne, the east,
> His treasons will sit blushing in his face,
> Not able to endure the sight of day,
> But self-affrighted tremble at his sin.

[57]Peter de la Primaudaye, *The French Academie*, trans. T. B. (London, 1586), p. 607.

He continues to the most important pronouncement of the divine right of kingship:

> Not all the water in the rough rude sea
> Can wash the balm off from an anointed king;
> The breath of worldly men cannot depose
> The deputy elected by the Lord: . . .

But he fails to heed the admonition of the Bishop of Carlisle:

> Fear not, my lord: that Power that made you king
> Hath power to keep you king in spite of all.
> The means that heaven yields must be embraced,
> And not neglected; else, if heaven would,
> And we will not, heaven's offer we refuse,
> The proffer'd means of succour and redress.

At times he rouses himself to remind himself that a king goes forth like a lion, strong in his right and in his might:

> I had forgot myself: am I not king?
> Awake, thou coward majesty! thou sleepest.
> Is not the king's name twenty thousand names?

York sorrows over him:

> Yet looks he like a king: behold, his eye,
> As bright as is the eagle's, lightens forth
> Controlling majesty; alack, alack, for woe,
> That any harm should stain so fair a show!

It is Richard, however, who first mentions deposition, seeming to wish to taste to the full his cup of woe:

> What must the king do now? must he submit?
> The king shall do it: must he be deposed?
> The king shall be contented: must he lose
> The name of king? a' God's name, let it go:

and later, as Henry protests he comes but for his own, it is Richard who says:

> What you will have, I'll give, and willing too;
> For do we must what force will have us do.

The short fourth act portrays the deposition of Richard. Briefly we glimpse Bolingbroke enacting the part of God's deputy
again as he adjudicates the quarrel between his cousin Aumerle
and Bagot over responsibility for the death of Thomas of Woodstock in a scene clearly intended to act as a foil to the first scene
of the play, in which Richard presides over the quarrel between
Bolingbroke and Mowbray. Henry too serves justice by permitting Bagot to speak freely in accusing the king's cousin, Aumerle,
but he determines to postpone his decision

> Till Norfolk he repeal'd: repeal'd he shall be,
> And, though mine enemy, restored again
> To all his lands and signories: . . .

The news of Norfolk's death makes such a test of his justice unnecessary, but he has made the gesture which sets him in contrast
with Richard.

The deposition scene which follows recalls all the arguments
which have been recited in the preceding pages. At the outset of
the play Richard gave Mowbray liberty to speak of Bolingbroke

> Were he my brother, nay, my kingdom's heir,
> As he is but my father's brother's son,

but now York reports to Bolingbroke that Richard

> Adopts thee heir, and his high sceptre yields
> To the possession of thy royal hand: . . .

Hayward has the Bishop of Carlisle argue that an heir must wait
for the death of his predecessor before he can assume the crown,
and also that the king cannot legally give away his crown.[58]
Shakespeare omits the first of these arguments, seeming to assume that Bolingbroke has become Henry IV by conquest,
though as I have said, Bolingbroke nowhere in the play has demanded the crown or refused to bow the knee to his king. But
now before the king has been deposed he cries,

> In God's name, I'll ascend the regal throne,

[58]*Op. cit.*, pp. 106-7.

only to be roughly told by the Bishop of Carlisle that if he ascends the regal throne it cannot be in God's name. Then "Stirr'd up by God," the bishop speaks on the old questions: first, whether Richard was justly deposed, and second, whether Henry should have succeeded him. To the first question Carlisle answers

> What subject can give sentence on his king?
> And who sits here that is not Richard's subject?
> Thieves are not judged but they are by to hear,
> . . . .
> And shall the figure of God's majesty,
> His captain, steward, deputy elect,
> Anointed, crowned, planted many years,
> Be judged by subject and inferior breath,
> And he himself not present?

It is the answer which was first enunciated by Gaunt:

> God's is the quarrel; . . . .
> . . . . for I may never lift
> An angry arm against His minister.

It is the answer implicit in Richard's exclamation:

> Revolt our subjects? that we cannot mend;
> They break their faith to God as well as us:

it is the answer best given by Richard in the statement already quoted:

> Not all the water in the rough rude sea
> Can wash the balm off from an anointed king;
> The breath of worldly men cannot depose
> The deputy elected by the Lord: . . .

In Holinshed, Carlisle is reported as concerned only with the injustice of passing judgment on a king in his absence. Shakespeare adds the all-important question as it was shaped in Tudor times:

> What subject can give sentence on his king?

And it is answered repeatedly in his play in passages which are not authorized in the chronicle.

THE DIVISION BETWEEN LANCASTER AND YORK

The answer to the second question, as to whether Henry should succeed the deposed Richard, follows inevitably, and Carlisle says:

> My Lord of Hereford here, whom you call king,
> Is a foul traitor to proud Hereford's king:

he then proceeds to pronounce the warning which is to find its fulfillment in the long years ahead, until the wheel has come full circle and Henry's son's son meets the fate his grandfather imposed upon Richard. It is to the rebels chiefly that Carlisle speaks:

> And if you crown him, let me prophesy;
> The blood of English shall manure the ground,
> And future ages groan for this foul act;
> Peace shall go sleep with Turks and infidels,
> And in this seat of peace tumultuous wars
> Shall kin with kin and kind with kind confound;
> . . . .
> O, if you raise this house against this house,
> It will the woefullest division prove
> That ever fell upon this cursed earth.
> Prevent it, resist it, let it not be so,
> Lest child, child's children, cry against you "Woe!"

But again Carlisle was repeating what Richard had already proclaimed:

> For well we know, no hand of blood and bone
> Can gripe the sacred handle of our sceptre,
> Unless he do profane, steal, or usurp.

And he too had prophesied:

> Yet know, my master, God omnipotent,
> Is mustering in his clouds on our behalf
> Armies of pestilence: and they shall strike
> Your children yet unborn and unbegot,
> That lift your vassal hands against my head,
> And threat the glory of my precious crown.
> Tell Bolingbroke—for yond methinks he stands—
> That every stride he makes upon my land

> Is dangerous treason: he is come to open
> The purple testament of bleeding war;
> But ere the crown he looks for live in peace,
> Ten thousand bloody crowns of mothers' sons
> Shall ill become the flower of England's face,
> Change the complexion of her maid-pale peace
> To scarlet indignation, and bedew
> Her pastures' grass with faithful English blood.

Yet at the crucial moment Richard yields his crown, his sceptre, his possessions, the allegiance of his subjects, and hails his successor:

> Long mayst thou live in Richard's seat to sit,
> And soon lie Richard in an earthy pit!
> God save King Harry, unking'd Richard says,
> And send him many years of sunshine days.

It is only after the deposition that Shakespeare has Northumberland demand that Richard read a confession of his sins that will justify that deposition. (Holinshed had him acknowledge his sins and resign his throne before Henry proclaimed himself and was crowned.) When that demand is made, Richard turns upon the earl, suggesting that were the lord to read over his own sins, he would find the deposing of a king "Mark'd with a blot, damn'd in the book of heaven." And to all the Pilates standing by washing their hands of him he warns that water cannot wash away their sin. But he sees himself a traitor with the rest, untrue to the king. Even the king cannot unmake an anointed king, he seems to say.

With Richard calling for a looking-glass, he repeats the theme of his disillusion:

> O flattering glass,
> Like to my followers in prosperity,
> Thou dost beguile me!

At the close of Act IV what Halle calls "the unquiet time of Henry IV" has commenced. The introduction is over, and the wheel is beginning to turn.

Act V portrays the end of Richard's tragedy with his murder,

but it also shows us the inception of all the ills that are to beset
Henry IV and make his time the pattern of an unquiet reign. We
first see Richard saying farewell to his queen. So dispirited is he
that she chides him:

> hath Bolingbroke deposed
> Thine intellect? hath he been in thy heart?
> The lion dying thrusteth forth his paw,
> And wounds the earth, if nothing else, with rage
> To be o'erpowr'd; . . .

But as Northumberland comes to take him to Pomfret and to
order the queen to France, Richard turns upon him:

> Northumberland, thou ladder wherewithal
> The mounting Bolingbroke ascends my throne,
> . . . . thou shalt think,
> Though he divide the realm, and give thee half,
> It is too little, helping him to all;
> And he shall think that thou, which know'st the way
> To plant unrightful kings, wilt know again,
> Being ne'er so little urged, another way
> To pluck him headlong from the usurped throne.

What Richard here prophesies is, of course, the subject of Shakespeare's *Henry IV*, and is the first foreshadowing of the punishment that God will bestow upon the usurper.

We find that the unquietness of the reign has already begun
as Aumerle is revealed a participant in the plot of the maskers
against the new king. Henry's way with the rest of the dissent-
ers is extremely short, but he here seizes his chance to show
mercy to his cousin for the mother's sake. Next we hear of his
worry over his "unthrifty son," the "young wanton and effeminate boy," whose precocious sins foretell the second of Henry's
troubles to come. Finally we discover that the kingdom of his
mind is as unquiet as is the kingdom about him. Richard alive is
the threat that gnaws his mind with fear. "Have I no friend will
rid me of this living fear?" he asks and is answered by Sir Pierce
of Exton, a friend like those who served Richard, a flattering

friend who desires to please the king rather than to advise him unacceptably.

As Shakespeare presents the murder of Richard, we are reminded of the words of his queen,

> The lion dying thrusteth forth his paw,
> And wounds the earth, if nothing else, with rage
> To be o'erpowr'd; . . .

Kingly in his last desperate struggle, he compels his murderer to admiration and to swift regret. Exton is at once aware of his mortal sin:

> As full of valour as of royal blood:
> Both have I spill'd; O would the deed were good!
> For now the devil, that told me I did well,
> Says that this deed is chronicled in hell.

In the midst of another session of justice, when the king is receiving news of the executions of rebels and evil doers which he has commanded, and is mingling mercy with justice in his sentence upon Carlisle, Exton enters with bearers carrying the coffin of the murdered Richard. What follows his offering of his buried fear to Henry IV is a repetition of the scene between King John and Hubert after the supposed death of Arthur. Exton's reward is the harsh speech of the king:

> They love not poison that do poison need,
> Nor do I thee: though I did wish him dead,
> I hate the murderer, love him murdered.
> The guilt of conscience take thou for thy labour,
> But neither my good word nor princely favour:
> With Cain go wander thorough shades of night,
> And never show thy head by day nor light.
> Lords, I protest, my soul is full of woe,
> That blood should sprinkle me to make me grow:

and then:

> I'll make a voyage to the Holy Land
> To wash this blood off from my guilty hand: . . .

Beset by rebellion, worried over the deeds of his son and heir, conscience-stricken so that he must needs expiate his sin, Henry IV may rule with justice and mercy, but he is unable to exult in the throne he has usurped. He has taken upon himself the quarrel that was God's, as his father would not do. Neither he nor his heirs is ever able to wash away the blood of Richard that sprinkled him to make him grow.

In his play of *Richard II* Shakespeare thus offered the follies of Richard II only as a background for the presentation of the problem that was so often discussed during Elizabeth's reign, the problem of the deposition of a king. That problem received its most disturbing treatment in Parsons' *Conference about the Next Succession to the Crowne of Ingland*, published in 1594, and Parsons was concerned to justify the deposition of Richard II and the accession of Henry IV. It seemed dangerous to Elizabeth's friends and the supporters of her government because it was sent forth in a time of discontent, when charges were being bandied about that were reminiscent of those presented as charges against Richard II. About this time Shakespeare wrote a play of Richard II which showed the deposition and murder of the king. It seems to me most natural that he should do so, for the question was uppermost in men's minds. In the play Shakespeare reiterated the charges against Richard that had been so often laid at Queen Elizabeth's door. He adjudged Richard guilty of sinful folly, but Gaunt and Richard himself and Carlisle, all the sympathetic characters, insist that "God's is the quarrel," that a subject may not give sentence on his king. Furthermore, the picture of Henry IV at the end of the play as a king whose soul is full of woe is scarcely conducive to the encouragement of would-be usurpers.

Yet the fact remains that a play on the same subject, probably Shakespeare's, was played on the eve of Essex's rebellion at the request of the conspirators. Perhaps the young Percies and their friends only recognized that there was a deposition in it, proving that such things could be. But it is also true that a book of Hayward's which told the same story was under suspicion at the same time, though the author later said he wrote it always with the interest of the true heir, King James, in mind. I do not know the answer to the riddle, though it is quite clear that Elizabeth's enemies compared her to Richard II, and that Essex's enemies compared him to Henry IV.

What seems to me more important than personalities that may or may not be involved is that Shakespeare here set forth a political problem that was engaging the interest of the nation, and that he set it forth fairly. He did not ask whether a good king might be deposed, but whether a king might be deposed for any cause. He used Richard II as the accepted pattern of a deposed king, but he used his pattern to set forth the political ethics of the Tudors in regard to the rights and duties of a king. It might equally well have served as a warning to Elizabeth and to any who desired to usurp her throne. The way of the transgressing king was shown to be hard, but no happiness was promised to the one who tried to execute God's vengeance or to depose the deputy elected by the Lord.

CHAPTER XIV

THE UNQUIET TIME OF HENRY IV

SERIES of comic interludes inter-
rupts the continuity of the historical pattern of the two parts of
Henry IV, and because these interludes have been built about
the character of Falstaff, they have obscured the history play
they were meant to adorn. It is with reluctance that I relegate
to an epilogue to this chapter the discussion of the immortal who
has been so largely responsible for keeping the play alive in the
hearts of posterity, but this is a history play, and Falstaff is historically an intruder, though certainly a "delectation."

As a history play *Henry IV* develops the pattern begun in
Richard II. In discussing that play I pointed out that Henry IV
was presented at the outset of his reign as a king with an unquiet
kingdom and an unquiet mind. From the beginning rebellion
stirred against him; his son worried him; and his conscience never
let him rest. These three disturbers of his peace are with him
throughout his life. Only at the end of his life does Shakespeare
show him as dominating his kingdom, and that fearfully. Only
on his death-bed is he reconciled with his son. And the blood
that sprinkled him to make him grow to his kingly office is never
washed from his conscience by the vowed pilgrimage to the
Holy Land.

Holinshed said of Henry IV:

But yet to speake a truth, by his proceedings, after he had atteined
to the crowne, what with such taxes, tallages, subsidies, and exactions as he was constreined to charge the people with; and what
by punishing such as mooved with disdeine to see him usurpe the
crowne (contrarie to the oth taken at his entring into this land, upon

his returne from exile) did at sundrie times rebell against him, he wan himselfe more hatred, than . . . had beene possible for him to have weeded out and remooved. And yet doubtlesse, woorthie were his subjects to tast of that bitter cup, sithens they were so readie to joine and clappe hands with him, for the deposing of their rightful and naturall prince king Richard, . . .[1]

The established pattern was one that the Elizabethans cherished as representative of the kind of arithmetical justice which they attributed to God, for here was a rebel rebelled against. The biter bitten was a favorite concept.

The problem of rebellion was, indeed, the chief concern of Henry IV, as it was the chief problem faced by the Tudors, and for the same reasons. Dr. Franklin Le Van Baumer has headed his discussion of "The Cult of Authority" in his book on *The Early Tudor Theory of Kingship* with a typical quotation from Bishop Gardiner's *De vera obedientia*:

Indeed, God, according to his exceeding great and unspeakable goodness toward mankind, . . . substituted men, who, being put in authority as his vice-gerents, should require obedience which we must do unto them with no less fruit for God's sake than we should do it (what honor soever it were) immediately unto God himself. And in that place he hath set princes whom, as representatives of his Image unto men, he would have to be reputed in the supreme and most high place, and to excel among all other human creatures. . . . By me (sayeth God) Kings reign, in so much that, after Paul's saying, whosoever resisteth power resisteth the ordinance of God.[2]

The king was responsible to God, both as a man, one of God's creatures, and as his vice-gerent, the representative of his divine justice. But he was responsible only to God. He was not to be judged by his subjects, and his subjects were not to decide the matter of their obedience upon the basis of the king's merits. A bad king was punishment meted out to the people for their sins, but the king was responsible to God for his sins. Rebellion was the rod of chastisement to the bad king, but the rebels were no

[1]III, 541.

[2]*Op. cit.* (New Haven, 1940), p. 85.

less guilty because they were used by God. Such was the Tudor philosophy, nowhere better explained than in the 1559 *Mirror for Magistrates*:

For in dede officers be gods deputies, and it is gods office which they beare, and it is he whiche ordeyneth thereto suche as himselfe lysteth, good whan he favoreth the people, and evyll whan he wyll punysh theim. And therefore whosoever rebelleth agaynst any ruler either good or bad, rebelleth against God, and shalbe sure of a wretched ende: For God cannot but maintein his deputie. Yet this I note by the waye concernyng rebelles and rebellions. Although the devyll rayse theim, yet God alwayes useth them to his glory, as a parte of his Justice. For when Kynges and chiefe rulers, suffer theyr under officers to mysuse theyr subjects, and wil not heare nor remedye theyr peoples wronges whan they complayne, than suffreth God the Rebell to rage, and to execute that parte of his Justice, whiche the parcyall prince woulde not.[3]

Richard II was guilty of many sins, but God's was the quarrel, and God used rebellion to punish him. Henry IV was a rebel and an usurper, and for his sins he, in his turn, was punished by rebellion; but still "the possession of the crown purgeth all defects," and the subject owed obedience to his king as to his God.

Dr. Baumer explains this cult of the authority of the king as a necessary development of the Tudor period in England and as one of the distinguishing political features of the sixteenth as opposed to the fifteenth century. He notes three reasons for its development. First, in an England emerging from the anarchy of the Wars of the Roses, it was natural that the dread of further disorder should result in emphasis on obedience to authority and upon the divine retribution that ensued disobedience to the king. Second, the exaltation of the king was necessary to offset the threat of foreign intervention which persisted in the reigns of Henry VIII and Elizabeth when the "Enterprise of England" was an immediate issue. Third, the Royal Supremacy could only be safeguarded when it was held that under no circumstances, "yea, even though the king were an infidel," had subjects the

[3]*Op. cit.* (1938 ed.), p. 178.

right to rebel. Dr. Baumer concludes that the doctrine of non-resistance was opportunistic, flourishing during the sixteenth century when there was need for a strong monarchy, and fading when the strong monarchy itself began to be something of a problem.[4] But the situation under Henry IV was similar to that under the Tudors, for the same uncertainty of the right of the king to reign, the same conflict over the succession, the same threat of foreign interference, and the same need for a strong central authority existed at the beginning of the Wars of the Roses as at their close.

The two official pronouncements of most importance in promulgating this doctrine in the sixteenth century were, of course, the homilies of 1547[5] and 1571. The famous *Homilie against Disobedience and Wylfull Rebellion* was issued after the Northern Rebellion and after the publishing of the papal bull which released Elizabeth's subjects from their oaths of allegiance and interdicted obedience to her laws.[6] Since the homilies were ordered to be read in all churches, this homily of 1571 was certainly familiar to almost every Englishman in the land. The theory of rebellion which it expounds is the same as that of the 1547 homily, but because of its particular significance to this study I propose to summarize each of its five parts as they were read in turn to the worshippers in all English churches. The first part explains the ordered creation of heaven and earth and the universal establishment of obedience, the first rebel being Lucifer, who lost heaven, as Adam, when he turned rebel, lost Paradise. In order to re-establish obedience in the world, God ordained not only that the wife should be obedient to her husband, the child to the parent, the servant to the master, but also that the people obey governors and rulers whom he set up. Both

---

[4]*Op. cit.*, pp. 87-92.

[5]"An Exhortation, concernyng Good Ordre and Obedience to Rulers and Magistrates" in *Certayne Sermons, or Homelies* (1547).

[6]Thomas Norton in *An Addition to the Bulls* (London, 1570) said there were two bulls, one having been circulated among Catholics since 1567. When the rebellion was arranged, the new bull of February, 1569, was issued. William Cecil, in *The Execution of Justice in England*, said the bull was the ground of the rebellions in England and in Ireland.

the Old and the New Testaments show "that kinges and princes, as well the evill as the good, do raigne by gods ordinaunce, and that subjects are bounden to obey them." Biblical passages are offered in evidence, especially the first two verses of Romans 13:

Let every soule be subject unto the higher powers, for there is no power but of god, and the powers that be, are ordayned of god. Whosoever therfore resisteth the power, resisteth the ordinaunce of God: and they that resist, shall receave to themselves damnation.[7]

The good ruler is a blessing bestowed upon the people, and the evil ruler a plague sent for their sins. The people may not, then, obey the good ruler and rebel against the evil, for what subject can judge his king? Can the foot judge the head? From attempts of the people to judge their kings come rebellions. One sentence may well be specially noted in connection with our immediate study:

Shall the subjects both by their wickednesse provoke God . . . to give them an undiscrete or evyll prince, and also rebell against hym, and withall against God, who for the punishment of their sinnes dyd geve them suche a prince?[8]

The second part of the homily cites Biblical examples of obedience to civil authorities. The third part is devoted to the sin of rebellion as violating most of the ten commandments, incorporating all the seven deadly sins, and bringing to a nation the plagues of pestilence and famine, death and destruction. The fourth part gives examples of rebels who have been destroyed. The fifth part shows rebellion to be the result of ambition on the part of some and ignorance on the part of others who are in their ignorance easily led into evil.

Looking back to Dr. Baumer's explanation of the reasons underlying the growth of the doctrine of nonresistance to the king, it will be remembered that the threat of foreign invasion in connection with the papal-inspired "Enterprise of England," and the threat to the royal supremacy were the two aspects of

[7]Quoted on fol. A3r.
[8]B2r.

rebellion discussed by Shakespeare in *King John*. They were the two threats implicit in rebellion against both Henry VIII and Elizabeth, and Shakespeare presented them inevitably about the figure of King John, who had long been the accepted English pattern of the king who defied the pope. The prime threat of rebellion was, however, the threat of anarchy and disruption brought by civil war, and it too was regularly discussed in connection with one great figure of English history, Henry IV. A history play dealing with the political problem of rebellion would, then, most properly be built about this unhappy king, who, himself a successful rebel, knew only, in the words of Halle, "an unquiet time."

Halle's chronicle had been concerned primarily with this problem of rebellion and was, it now seems, conceived as a major work of propaganda under Henry VIII.[9] The list of instances which Halle cited to prove "what mischiefe hath insurged in realmes by intestine devision" is quoted earlier, but in his history of the Wars of the Roses he conceived that "kyng henry the fourthe was the beginnyng and rote of the great discord and devision." And Halle's analysis was followed by later chroniclers.

Again and again Henry IV was used as a text for a lesson on rebellion, but never more dramatically than in the speech made from the scaffold by Sir Thomas Wyatt when he was about to die for his rebellion against Mary Tudor:

Then my lords (quoth he) I must confess my selfe guiltie, and in the end the truth of my case must inforce me. I must acknowledge this to be a just plague for my sins, which most greevouslie I therefore have committed against God, who suffered me thus brutishlie and beastlie to fall into this horrible offense of the law. Wherefore all you lords and gentlemen, with other here present, note well my words, lo here and see in me the same end which all other commonlie had, which have attempted the like enterprise from the beginning. For peruse the chronicles through, and you shall see that never rebellion attempted by subjects against their prince and countrie, from the beginning did ever prosper, or had ever better successe, except

[9]W. Gordon Zeeveld, "The Influence of Hall on Shakespeare's English Historical Plays," *ELH*, III (1936), pp. 317-52. See especially pp. 344-47.

the case of king Henrie the fourth: who although he became a prince, yet in his act was but a rebell, for so must I call him: and though he prevailed for a time, yet was it not long but that his heires were deprived, and those that had right againe restored to the king-dome and crowne, and the usurpation so sharplie revenged afterward in his bloud, as it well appeared, that the long delaie of Gods vengeance was supplied with more grevous plagues in the third and fourth generation. For the love of God all you gentlemen that be here present, remember and be taught as well by examples past, as also by this my present infelicitie and most wretched case.[10]

It will be remembered that Samuel Daniel wrote his *Civile Wars*, he testified later, "(in a time which was not so well secur'd of the future, as God be blessed now it is) with a purpose, to shewe the deformities of Civile Dessention, and the miserable events of Rebellions, Conspiracies, and bloudy Revengements, which followed (as in a circle) upon that breach of the due course of Succession, by the Usurpation of Hen. 4."[11] Whether or no Shakespeare was indebted to Daniel for the adaptations of history which their works show as common to them both is not here in point, but Daniel's choice of this period and his recognition of the fact that Henry in rebelling against his anointed king precipitated the further rebellions that led to the most disastrous of civil wars must be considered important in the history of the growth of the pattern. Shakespeare's *King John* showed foreign intervention supported by English rebels, but that is not the aspect of rebellion pictured in his *Henry IV*; here is a war between Englishmen, a civil war, reiterating Daniel's question:

> What furie, ô what madnes held you so
> Deare people to too prodigal of blood?
> To wast so much and warre without a foe, ...[12]

Anyone who wishes to understand the two-part play of *Henry IV* and the picture of rebellion there given should read and re-read two clear expositions of the plays in Shakespeare's own

[10]Holinshed, III, 1103. Also quoted in Grafton, *Chronicle*, pp. 1339-40.
[11]In his dedication of the 1609 edition to the Countess Dowager of Pembroke.
[12]*Civile Wars* (1595), Bk. I, stanza 2.

language. The first is the defiant and prophetic speech made by King Richard to Northumberland:

> Northumberland, thou ladder wherewithal
> The mounting Bolingbroke ascends my throne,
> . . . . thou shalt think,
> Though he divide the realm, and give thee half,
> It is too little, helping him to all:
> And he shall think that thou, which know'st the way
> To plant unrightful kings, wilt know again,
> Being ne'er so little urged, another way
> To pluck him headlong from the usurped throne.[13]

The second is from King Henry's dying speech to Prince Hal:

> God knows, my son,
> By what by-paths and indirect crook'd ways
> I met this crown; and I myself know well
> How troublesome it sat upon my head.
> . . . . . It seem'd in me
> But as an honour snatched with boisterous hand,
> And I had many living to upbraid
> My gain of it by their assistances;
> Which daily grew to quarrel and to bloodshed,
> Wounding supposed peace: all these bold fears
> Thou see'st with peril I have answered;
> *For all my reign hath been but as a scene*
> *Acting that argument*: . . . .
> How I came by the crown, O God forgive;
> And grant it may with thee in true peace live![14]

Keeping in mind this argument acted out by the reign of Henry IV and the general theory of rebellion which dominated Shakespeare's England, we can then turn to the two-part play to consider in some detail the way in which Shakespeare incorporated the philosophy of rebellion in character and plot.

The first part of *Henry IV* begins just one year after the

[13]*Richard II*, V, i, 55-65.
[14]*2 Henry IV*, IV, v, 183-219. The italics are mine.

events chronicled in *Richard II*. The first line of the play pictures the king,

> So shaken as we are, so wan with care,

determined to stop the "civil butchery" which has daubed the lips of England's soil with her own children's blood, and to press on to the expiation of Richard's death through the freeing of the sepulchre of Christ from the pagans. But his purgation is not to be in this manner achieved. Once more the pilgrimage has to be postponed to await peace, for Westmoreland brings news that Mortimer, erstwhile heir to Richard's throne, has been taken prisoner leading the men of Hertfordshire against the Welsh, and that Henry Percy, son of the Duke of Northumberland, is fighting the Scots. When there comes news of young Percy's victory over the Scots, the king is moved to envy as he contrasts the conduct of his own son, whose brow is stained with "riot and dishonour," with the conduct of Hotspur, "the theme of honour's tongue." But the young Percy is full of pride and refuses to yield his Scotch prisoners to the king, so that he must be summoned for a reckoning. Though the next scene demonstrates the king's reasons for sorrowing over his son, it closes with a speech by Prince Hal which may reassure the audience as to the future king of England but can do nothing for the unhappy father, who does not hear it. We return, then, to the king, facing the discontent of the rebels who have helped him to his throne, even as Richard had prophesied. Hotspur continues to defy the king about his Scotch prisoners, and the king refuses the demand of the Percies to ransom Mortimer, their kinsman by marriage. The stage is set for rebellion, the Percies joining friend and foe with them against the king: Douglas and the Scots, Glendower and his captive Mortimer, and the Archbishop of York, angry over the death of his brother Lord Scroop.

The second act reveals the conspiracy developing, the former enemies united in their common hatred of the king, but the first scene of the third act shows mistrust and suspicion growing among them, even as they plan a tripartite division of the kingdom.

The second scene of Act III takes us back to the second disquieting sorrow of the king, who sees his son's follies as a sign of God's vengeance. To the prince he says:

> I know not whether God will have it so,
> For some displeasing service I have done,
> That, in his secret doom, out of my blood
> He'll breed revengement and a scourge for me;
> But thou dost in thy passages of life
> Make me believe that thou art only mark'd
> For the hot vengeance and the rod of heaven,
> To punish my mistreadings.

In his son he can see even now the follies of King Richard threatening his fate to the heir who has cheapened himself in the public view. Hal may even join with the Percies, his father suggests. But the prince swears:

> I will redeem all this on Percy's head,
> And in the closing of some glorious day
> Be bold to tell you that I am your son;
> When I will wear a garment all of blood,
> And stain my favours in a bloody mask,
> Which, wash'd away, shall scour my shame with it:

and the king gives him charge of one of the three forces setting out to meet the rebels. To Falstaff the prince assigns "a charge of foot."

Act IV shows the mounting troubles of the rebels. They must of necessity at once meet the king's forces, but Northumberland sends word he is sick, and Glendower sends word that he cannot ready his forces for fourteen days. Hotspur and Douglas will take whatever comes, but Worcester is worried about the effect of Northumberland's absence:

>   it will be thought
> By some, that know not why he is away,
> That wisdom, loyalty and mere dislike
> Of our proceedings kept the earl from hence:
> And think how such an apprehension
> May turn the tide of fearful faction,
> And breed a kind of question in our cause; . . .

Sir Walter Blunt comes from the king to ask them to name their grievances, assuring them that the king has not forgotten their good deserts, but he is met with insulting words from Hotspur, who repeats the old story:

> My father and my uncle and myself
> Did give him that same royalty he wears; . . .

Such wrongs as the king's benefactors have endured, Hotspur says, have made them determine to "pry/ Into his title, the which we find/ Too indirect for long continuance." Meanwhile the archbishop worries over the coming battle with Northumberland and Mortimer absent and now Glendower failing them because he has been "o'er-ruled by prophecies."

Act V shows the king in his camp near Shrewsbury preparing for battle. To him come Worcester and Vernon, and to the rebels the king offers pardon if they will but yield to his grace. Prince Hal proposes that he meet Hotspur in single combat. But Worcester continues to harp on the old string and tells the tale all over again of Bolingbroke's perjuring himself, of his oppression of those who had raised him to the throne; and the king comments that insurrection has always found such excuses. Worcester will not report the king's offer of amnesty, for he knows treason is not easily forgotten, and he feels sure that he and his brother, Northumberland, would have to pay, though Hotspur might escape. Hotspur, however, would be glad to accept the prince's challenge.

Finally the battle rages over the stage with alarums and excursions, chiefly encounters between Douglas and various gentlemen dressed like the king. When at last Douglas meets the king, the king is saved only by the timely intervention of Prince Hal. And the climax of the battle is reached in the struggle between Hotspur and the prince, in which Hotspur is killed, and dead, is honored by his conqueror. The battle is won by the king's forces, for

> Thus ever did rebellion find rebuke.

Worcester is sent to his death for his deceit, Douglas is released honorably for his valor, but the king sends forces under Prince John and the Earl of Westmoreland to meet Northumberland and the archbishop, while he and Prince Hal press on hopefully to fight Glendower and Mortimer:

> Rebellion in this land shall lose his sway,
> Meeting the check of such another day:
> And since this business so fair is done,
> Let us not leave till all our own be won.

As the first part of *Henry IV* deals with the rebellion organized to overthrow the king, so the second part shows the disintegration of the rebellion. As the first part of *Henry IV* shows a wastrel son, who was to his father a part of God's revenge, finally acquiring honor at Shrewsbury, so the second part shows the father and son finally reconciled at the end of the king's short reign, and the son throwing off his unfit companions and taking upon him the virtues of a king as though virtue were as easily put on as a new garment. But the king's soul must at last meet the King of kings without his having been able to expiate his sins by the pilgrimage to the Holy Land.

The second part of the play begins just after the first ends. The very theatrically designed Rumor spreads false reports so that the "crafty-sick" Northumberland is told that the rebels have been victorious at Shrewsbury, that Hotspur has been killed in the battle, that he is alive and victorious, that he is dead, until the audience must grow weary of the lesson concerning rumor. As Northumberland staggers under the blow of the final knowledge of his son's death, he hears from Mortimer of the forces which are being sent against him and is comforted by the news that the archbishop "with well-appointed powers" is rising, a man whose forces will be more determined than those supporting Hotspur:

> But now the bishop
> Turns insurrection to religion:
> Supposed sincere and holy in his thoughts,
> He's followed both with body and with mind;
> And doth enlarge his rising with the blood

> Of fair King Richard, scraped from Pomfret stones;
> Derives from heaven his quarrel and his cause;
> Tells them he doth bestride a bleeding land,
> Gasping for life under great Bolingbroke; . . .

Yet as we see the archbishop counselling with his leaders, we sense their uncertainty. They are relying on Northumberland for their supplies, and upon the king's having to divide his forces into three for the adequacy of their own troops. They need to survey their resources for such a task, "Which is almost to pluck a kingdom down/ And set another up," and both the king's plans and their own support from the people are not assured. The archbishop is fearful of the commons, fickle when it applauded Bolingbroke, fickle when it would have Richard die, fickle when it would have him live again.

In the midst of the comic scenes of the second act there is only one short scene that has to do with the historic characters, but in it we hear Northumberland deciding at the urging of his women folk not to go to the aid of his fellow rebels but to escape to Scotland:

> Fain would I go to meet the archbishop,
> But many thousand reasons hold me back.
> I will resolve for Scotland: . . .

In Act III the king, a melancholy king, envying the ship-boy his easy sleep and viewing sadly his diseased and threatened kingdom, talks of the past and recalls the words of Richard,

> "Northumberland, thou ladder by the which
> My cousin Bolingbroke ascends my throne;"

and Warwick replies with a speech which echoes the whole Renaissance philosophy of history:

> There is a history in all men's lives,
> Figuring the nature of the times deceased;
> The which observed, a man may prophesy,
> With a near aim, of the main chance of things
> As yet not come to life, which in their seeds
> And weak beginnings lie intreasured.

> Such things become the hatch and brood of time;
> And by the necessary form of this
> King Richard might create a perfect guess
> That great Northumberland, then false to him,
> Would of that seed grow to a greater falseness;
> Which should not find a ground to root upon,
> Unless on you.

But the king is sick, and reluctantly he agrees to let his forces fight on without him, wishing only that these wars were over, so that he might make his journey to the Holy Land.

In Act IV the rebels receive the news of Northumberland's disaffection and his good wishes. With their hopes thus dashed they listen to Westmoreland, who comes from Prince John, the general of the army marching against them. He offers a just and lasting peace, though he takes occasion to reprove the archbishop for having used his peaceful and religious office to lead men to war. The archbishop justifies the war as having offered the best hope of removing the infection of the times and creating a peace in more than name, but he is willing to consent to a peace by which the wrongs of the rebels shall be righted. To Lord Mowbray, who would revive his father's wrongs, and who maintains that there can be no enduring peace with the king, he answers that the king is weary of bickering:

> For he hath found to end one doubt by death
> Revives two greater in the heirs of life,
> And therefore will he wipe his tables clean,
> And keep no tell-tale to his memory . . .

The peace-making which follows has brought disillusion to many modern readers, but it would, I think, have seemed quite orthodox to the Elizabethan audience. Prince John himself appears with Westmoreland to negotiate the terms. To the archbishop he speaks harshly as to one who has been the voice of God, who has been the go-between for heaven and men's minds:

> You have ta'en up,
> Under the counterfeited zeal of God,
> The subjects of his substitute, my father,

> And both against the peace of heaven and him
> Have here up-swarm'd them.

As the peace is agreed to, shouts of joy are heard without from the armies receiving the news, and the enemies drink together in happy celebration. But the rebel army is disbanded while that of the prince awaits orders, and the blow falls. Hastings, the archbishop, and Mowbray are arrested as traitors. Mowbray questions the justice and honor of such an action, and the archbishop demands, "Will you thus break your faith?" Prince John replies:

> I promised you redress of these same grievances
> Whereof you did complain; which, by mine honour,
> I will perform with a most Christian care.
> But for you, rebels, look to taste the due
> Meet for rebellion and such acts as yours.

And he commands:

> Some guard these traitors to the block of death,
> Treason's true bed and yielder up of breath.

Then we are shown the king, sick unto death but still planning his holy war, once peace is assured, and still fearful for the future of his countrymen when Prince Hal shall rule them:

> The blood weeps from my heart when I do shape,
> In forms imaginary, the unguided days
> And rotten times that you shall look upon,
> When I am sleeping with my ancestors.

The news of peace comes from everywhere: the archbishop, Mowbray, and Hastings have been seized; Northumberland with his English and Scotch supporters has been overcome. But the king is very ill, and there are omens which precede the death of kings.

With this scene, the fourth scene of the fourth act, Shakespeare closes his account of the rebellion of the Percies and turns to portray the death of Henry IV and the accession of the new king. And that is another story. I propose, then, to pause at this point to consider the significance of the picture of the rebellion which Shakespeare has had enacted before us.

The differences between Shakespeare's account of the life and death of Henry IV and that of Holinshed have been well studied, and I shall consider here only those which are of special significance.[15] In the first place, Shakespeare excludes practically everything but the rebellion of the Percies from the nine acts which portray the story of the reign of Henry IV. The troubles with Wales, with Scotland, with France, with the Lollards—all these matters and more are recorded by the chroniclers, but they are excluded as irrelevant to the theme with which Shakespeare is dealing here. In the second place, the rebellion that Shakespeare presents is really one rebellion, a rebellion which reached its climax at Shrewsbury and died a death of attrition thereafter, largely because of the defection of Northumberland. Holinshed, like Halle, records that after the battle of Shrewsbury in 1404, the Earl of Northumberland made a politic peace with King Henry; that a second rebellion initiated by Northumberland, Archbishop Scroop, and Mowbray was undertaken the next year, the archbishop and the earl marshal being tricked into submission, while Northumberland escaped to Berwick, thence to Scotland, and afterwards to Owen Glendower in Wales; and that a third rebellion was led by Northumberland from Scotland, where he had returned after having gone to France and Flanders to seek aid. Northumberland was slain in battle with the sheriff of Yorkshire before the king's forces had time to arrive to put down this third rebellion. Shakespeare has, therefore, combined these three rebellions into one, and he has made it the major concern of the years of Henry's reign.

Two other significant changes have been made by Shakespeare

[15]*The New Variorum Edition of Shakespeare: Henry the Fourth; Part 1*, ed. S. B. Hemingway (Philadelphia and London, 1936), pp. 356-94, and *The Second Part of Henry the Fourth*, ed. M. A. Shaaber (1940), pp. 521-57, reproduce source texts and comments on Shakespeare's use of them. Boswell-Stone's remains the most detailed account, but the various editors of the play have almost invariably analyzed the relationship of Shakespeare's play to its sources. See especially the English Arden edition of the *First Part of King Henry the Fourth*, ed R. P. Cowl and A. E. Morgan (London, 1930), pp. xii-xxii.

that have not, I think, been accorded their full significance by critics. First, Shakespeare represents Henry as vowing after the death of King Richard to make a voyage to the Holy Land to wash away the blood of the murdered king. In Holinshed the pilgrimage is proposed only in the last year of the king's life and is not connected with the death of Richard or with Henry's desire to make expiation. Daniel had, however, anticipated Shakespeare in making this change,[16] though Moorman did not note it. Second, the king's worry over Prince Hal is much exaggerated by Shakespeare, and the acceptance by the king of his son's misdeeds as divine retribution for his own sins is a new interpretation. Telescoping times and events, making Hal and Hotspur into contemporaries, giving credit to Hal for saving the life of his father in battle—such changes are important in tracing sources and analyzing dramatic technique. But making Henry, the rebel, to be plagued by rebellion; showing Henry, the regicide, as hoping vainly to placate an avenging King of kings by a pilgrimage to the Holy Land; picturing Henry, the usurper, as sorrowing over his disobedient son and fearful that he may try to supplant him: these changes indicate the moral universe in which Shakespeare set his characters and give meaning to the plot.

In *King John* it is possible to see the adaptations of history motivated by the desire to make the story serve as a mirror of a particular situation in Shakespeare's England. In *Richard II* the story has become more universalized and can easily be taken to mirror one of several situations. In *Henry IV*, as Shakespeare's understanding of the political world grows, the story is still more universalized and still less confined to mirroring one particular situation. But if Shakespeare was using an Elizabethan rebellion to focus the Elizabethan teachings concerning rebellion, it would have to be the Northern Rebellion, for no other rebellion passed beyond threat into actuality during the reign of Elizabeth until the Essex uprising, which had not yet occurred when *Henry IV*

[16]*Civile Wars*, Bk. 3, stanza 127. Daniel represented the voyage as having two purposes: (1) to appease God, and (2) to busy the minds of the people. Cf. F. W. Moorman, "Shakespeare's History-plays and Daniel's 'Civile Wars,'" *Shakespeare Jahrbuch*, XI (1904), pp. 69-83.

was written. There were always plenty of rebellious subjects who could have sat for their individual portraits, but there had been only one rebellion.

Richard Simpson, whose study of Shakespeare's historical plays has been so often referred to in these pages, did, indeed, assert that the Northern Rebellion was unmistakably pictured in *Henry IV* and suggested that Shakespeare worked up his account with the aid of someone with personal knowledge of the rebellion. As to the identity of this person he said:

One of the Percies, Sir Charles, was settled at Dumbleton in Gloucestershire, and in a letter of 1601 speaks familiarly of himself as Justice Shallow. This man, who refers to the very plays, may have furnished some of the matter.[17]

Whether Simpson was right in his guess I do not know or care, but modern research has made it seem very probable that Sir Charles Percy was known to the men of the Lord Chamberlain's company, for he was one of those friends of Essex who arranged for the company to put on the special performance of *Richard II* by way of prologue to Essex's rebellion. However, there would have been no need for Shakespeare to have drawn from private sources his knowledge of the rebellion, since information concerning it was plentiful and public. Indeed, it was in 1597 that Thomas Beard wrote in his *Theatre of Gods Judgements* of this rebellion as the chiefest of those treasons from which God had so remarkably preserved Elizabeth. I quote his short summary of the rebellion:

First therefore to begin with the chiefest, the Earle of Northumberland and Westmerland in the eleventh year of her raign began a rebellion in the North, pretending their purpose to bee sometimes to defend the Queens person and government from the invasion of strangers, and sometimes for conscience sake to seeke reformation of religion: under colour whereof they got together an army of men to the number of six thousand souldiors: against whom marched the Earle of Sussex leiutenant of the North, and the Earle of Warwick sent by the Queen to his aid: whose approch stroke such a

[17]*Op. cit.*, pp. 411-16.

terror into their hearts, that the two Earles with diverse of the Arch-rebels fled by night into Scotland, leaving the rest of their companie a prey unto their enemies, whereof threescore and sixe or there-abouts, were hanged at Durham. As for the Earles, one of them (to wit) of Northumberland, was after taken in Scotland and beheaded at Yorke. Westmerland fled into another countrie, and left his house and family destroied and undone by his folly.[18]

Whether or not he did use this rebellion as the pattern by which to adapt history to the teaching of the causes and the re-sults of rebellion, there are certain striking parallels between the rebellion that Shakespeare drew and the rebellion of 1569, and it was the Northern Rebellion that furnished the occasion for the homily that was the familiar and official pronouncement on rebellion. Intrigue with foreign enemies marked the rebellions against Henry IV as well as those against Elizabeth, but as I have said, Shakespeare does not present such intrigues in *Henry IV*. The background of foreign intervention was there also in 1569, for the Northern Rebellion was the first great festering of the sore that remained until after the death of Mary Stuart, but it was primarily an attempt of the Catholic lords of the northern counties of England to support her cause, and there was actual-ly no foreign invasion and no use of foreign troops to support the Englishmen. It was essentially a civil war.

The first and most obvious likeness between the two rebel-lions is to be found in the group of rebels who center the opposi-tion to the king. Against Henry IV stand Henry Percy, the Earl of Northumberland; Henry Percy (Hotspur), his son; Thomas Percy, Earl of Worcester, brother of Northumberland and uncle to Hotspur. It is his uncle, Worcester, who pours fuel on the flame of Hotspur's wrath, and who keeps rebellion burning. Against Elizabeth stood Thomas Percy, Earl of Northumber-land; Charles Neville, Earl of Westmoreland; and Christopher Neville, uncle to Westmoreland. Christopher Neville has come down in history as a man of violent temper who was said to have

[18]*Op. cit.*, pp. 221-22.

been largely responsible for the actions of his nephew.[19] Indeed, George Bowes writes at the close of the rebellion that many of the rebels have fled, and that the Countess of Westmoreland

braste owte agaynste them with great curses, as well for their un- happy counselling as nowe, their cowerd flyghte. But all the evyll counsellors be not yett gone, for [in] trewth, Mr. Christopher Nevill hath doyne more harme to that noble younge Erle, hys nephewe, than can be thoughte, and doeth yet remayne about hym. I wyshe he were further off.[20]

Also, as the leader of the last phase of the rebellion, in the second part of the play, there is the Archbishop of York, whose role during the Northern Rebellion was played by the Catholic Bish- op of Ross, one of Mary's most powerful agents, whom Cecil called "the principal instrument of this late rebellion,"[21] and of whom Lord Hunsdon wrote to Elizabeth, "al this rebellion and practice with foreign nations proceeds from him."[22]

But there were also in the background of the play Mortimer, pretender to the throne, whom Henry refused to ransom, and Archibald, Earl of Douglas, taken prisoner by Hotspur, whom that brash young man refused to yield to the king. The for- tunes of the two were the means of fanning into flame the smouldering resentment of the Percies against the king. In the places of these two stands Mary of Scotland, pretender to the throne of England, who, when she fled from her own distracted kingdom to take refuge in England, stirred up wrath compar- able to Hotspur's. George Chalmers in his life of Mary best sum- marizes the struggle (though his commas are distracting):

The Scotish Queen had scarcely arrived, in England, when an acrimonious dispute arose between individuals, with regard to the appropriate person, who had a right to detain her. The Earl of Northumberland claimed her, as she had landed, within his liberty,

[19][Sir Cuthbert Sharp], *Memorials of the Rebellion of 1569* (London, 1840), Appendix, contains interesting information on the leaders of the rebellion.

[20]*Ibid.*, pp. 33-34. See also the *Dict. Nat. Biog.* article on Christopher Neville by W. A. J. Archbold.

[21]*Cal. S. P., For., 1569-1571*, p. 171.

[22]*Ibid.*, p. 176.

as his prisoner; as she had come within his charge, without a pass-port. The earl obtained, from the council at York, an order upon Mr. Lowther, to deliver the Scotish Queen to the earl, which he refused to obey. Sir Francis Knollys, hearing on the journey north-ward, of this dispute, wrote to that high minded earl, that he would do well not to press his pretensions, till they were settled, by Eliza-beth, to whom the authority of deciding such a question belonged. The earl, however, came to Carlisle, and demanded the Scottish Queen, to be delivered to him, which, being refused by Mr. Low-ther, the haughty noble called him *varlet;* saying that he was too low a man, to pretend to such a charge. It is possible, that the earl's disappointment, on this occasion, may have been one of the ingredi-ents, which formed the mass of discontent, that induced this ill fated noble, to go into his unsuccessful rebellion.[23]

The *Annals of the House of Percy* records Northumberland's demand to Cecil for Mary's custody:

seeing she hath happened unto my handes, I trust you, and other my dear frendes, will be meyne that my credit be not so much impared in the face of the country as she should be taken from me and de-lyvered to any other person in these parts.[24]

These same northern lords had been as insistent in their demands that Elizabeth rescue Mary from her incarceration by the Scots before her escape and flight to England as they were now to be insistent that she be released from her imprisonment in England. It is thus apparent that the combined wrath of the Percies over Henry's failure to ransom Mortimer, the pretender, and over his demand that they hand over the Scotch prisoners may well be patterned by the demands of the northern lords that Mary, the pretender, be released, and that Mary, the Scotch prisoner, be left in the keeping of the Elizabethan Percy.

As to the main action of the play, I have already pointed out that Shakespeare compressed the events of years into a short space of time, and three rebellions into two phases of a single

[23]George Chalmers, *The Life of Mary, Queen of Scots* (Philadelphia, 1822), I, 206.

[24]Edward Barrington de Foublanque, *Annals of the House of Percy* (London, 1887), II, 16-18.

rebellious surge against the king. The rebellion which Shakespeare showed spent itself at Shrewsbury, and in spite of the renewed effort under the Archbishop of York, flickered out in an atmosphere of weakness and discouragement and disaffection on the part of the rebels when they met determined resistance from the king's forces. The picture is not a true picture of the rebellions against Henry IV, but it is a true picture of the rebellion of 1569 against Elizabeth, for after the battle for Bernard's Castle, which was seized by the rebels, the queen's forces were successfully organized, and the rebellion died a death of attrition. The compiler of the *Annals of the House of Percy* says of the last phases of the rebellion, when the rebels were forced to go ahead without the promised support of the other lords and foreign powers:

The conduct of the ensuing campaign, if a series of desultory marches and purposeless manoeuvres, can be dignified by the term, does not admit explanation upon any principles of the art of war.[25]

The leaders of the rebellions against Henry IV and the leaders in the Rebellion of the North against Elizabeth are, then, similar enough to invite comparison. The rebellion which Shakespeare drew was motivated and carried out with greater resemblance to the rebellion of 1569 than to the three rebellions under Henry IV, which it telescopes. But in addition to these likenesses, it must be remembered that as Worcester justified the rebellion against Henry IV as a necessity because of the oppressions and wrongs which the king was heaping upon the ancient nobility which had been the ladder by which he ascended the throne, so the Earls of Northumberland and Westmoreland proclaimed that they intended to do no harm to the queen or her good subjects but only to amend and redress the wrongs included under the following *whereas* in one of the proclamations:

Whereas, divers newe sette upp nobbles about the Queene's Majestie, have and doe dailie not onlie goe about to overthrow and put down the ancient nobilitie of this realme, but also have misused the Queene's Majesties personne, and alsoe have by the space of twelve

[25]*Ibid.,* II, 57.

years now past, sett up and mayntayned a new found religion and heresie, contrary to God's word; . . .[26]

Elizabeth's attitude was well expressed in the reply of Henry IV:

> And never yet did insurrection want
> Such water-colours to impaint his cause . . .[27]

Furthermore, it must be remembered that, as I have said earlier, the Bishop of Ross was a central figure in the thoughts of the English loyalists, since in him they saw the root of the trouble. Of him in relation to the none too reliable followers of the northern lords, it might have been said as it was of the followers of the rebel leaders under Henry IV:

> For that same word, rebellion, did divide
> The action of their bodies from their souls;
> . . . . But now the bishop
> Turns insurrection to religion:[28]

and Ross might well have been made to listen to the reproof spoken by Prince John to Scroop:

> O, who shall believe
> But you misuse the reverence of your place,
> Employ the countenance and grace of heaven,
> As a false favorite doth his prince's name,
> In deeds dishonourable? You have ta'en up,
> Under the counterfeited zeal of God,
> The subjects of his substitute, my father,
> And both against the peace of heaven and him
> Have here up-swarm'd them.[29]

There is another resemblance between the rebellion of the north against Henry IV as it is represented by Shakespeare and the Northern Rebellion of 1569 which has struck me as particularly interesting. I know of no historic authority for the conspicuous and important part played by rumor in the opening

[26]*Ibid.*, II, 46.
[27]*1 Henry IV*, V, i, 79-80.
[28]*2 Henry IV*, I, i, 194-201.
[29]*Ibid.*, IV, ii, 22-29.

prologue and the early scenes of the second part of *Henry IV*. "Rumor painted full of tongues" is an arresting theatrical device, and indeed, has seemed to many almost too stridently theatrical. But if rebellion in the time of Henry IV was used to mirror rebellion in the time of Elizabeth, there is ample reason for the use of this symbolic figure. No one can, I think, read the letters and contemporary accounts dealing with the 1569 rebellion without having his attention drawn to the part played by rumor. Wright's *Queen Elizabeth and Her Times* discusses the rumor-mongering at length,[30] and the evidence is, as I have said, to be found in all the letters and records of the time. Northumberland professed to have acted because of a false rumor, Sussex acted on rumor, the privy council was much concerned because of the rumors that were coming to it, and Wright quotes an account "of the diligence of the disaffected in spreading rumors and news" which I quote here, but I quote from the original work, adding a paragraph which precedes that used by Wright. The passage is found in Thomas Norton's *Warning agaynst the Dangerous Practises of Papists, and Specially the Parteners of the Late Rebellion*, first published by John Daye in 1569. The author has been speaking of seditious books, and continues:

An other companie of good sure men at home, receive these goodly bookes, sprede them abroade, rede them in audiences and corners, commend them, defend them, geve them great praises for learning and substantialnesse, as matters unanswerable, they amplifie them, they set them out, much like to false seditious talebearers that during this late rebellion spred rumors in the quiet partes of the Realme, what numbers of thousandes these rebelles were, how armed, how horsed, what rank riders, what mighty strong, active and couragious fellowes, what Giantes, as if all the rest of England were but shepe: what wonderous confederates, what aydes, by land, by sea, from Hierusalem, and no man knoweth whence, I thinke even out of Purgatorie . . . And all this was no more but to discourage the Queenes true subjectes and soldiers, and to raise up in doutfull men inclined to papistrie, a daring to joyne themselves to such a supposed strong side and faction. And yet these be not taken for seditious, as they are: the reason is because they are not yet hanged as they ought.

An other knot of such good companie be common rumorspreders, of whom the publike fame is that there be or have bene certaine notable and noted walkers in Paules and such places of resort, so common that the very usuall places of their being there, are ordinarily knowen by the name of Papists corner, and liers bench, saving that I heare say now of late many of them flocke more into the middle isle, which is supposed to be done partly for better harkening, and partly for more commodious publishing. The suspition, grudge and talke goeth among the Quenes good subjectes, how such fellowes be the coyners of newes; In the beginning of the rebellion, how lustie they were, how their countenances, their fleering, their flinging paces, their whisperinges shewed their hartes; how they had newes of everie encrease, of every going forward, and of everie avantageable doing of the Rebelles; how they have newes out of Fraunce and Flaunders . . . how they had newes of the late horrible murder ere it were done . . . how they write letters at home directed to themselves . . . and . . . they deface (as men say) all that can be brought or reported never so truly of any good successe to the Quene or her frendes.[31]

There can thus be made a very good case for Shakespeare's having designed the rebellion against Henry IV upon the pattern of the Elizabethan rebellion of 1569. But there was never in Elizabethan England any lack of models to sit for the portraits of ireful gentlemen who were ready to turn into rebellious subjects. While Shakespeare was writing of Henry IV, Essex was frequently displaying his Hotspur qualities, and it is quite possible, as has been suggested, that Shakespeare was thinking of him when he wrote of Hotspur. Certainly Essex defied the queen as bitterly as did Hotspur the king. Certainly both young men became rebels because of the personal affronts they imagined themselves to have suffered as well as because of their proclaimed desire to right England's wrongs. Both were apt to confuse the urgings of a hot temper with the demands of honor and to win others to think of them as the "theme of honour's tongue." Lodge

[31]*Op. cit.*, fol. G1-G2 (published with no date). The date 1569 is assigned by the *STC;* another edition was published in 1570.

quotes a letter from Sir Christopher Hatton to Essex, written in 1591, which might well have been addressed to Hotspur:

Your Lordship best knoweth that true valour consisteth rather in constant performinge of that which hathe been advisedly forethought than in an aptnes or readines of thrusting your person indifferently into every danger.[32]

It is even possible to see resemblances between the yet unborn Essex rebellion and that depicted by Shakespeare as led by the Percies. But it must be remembered that it was because men are eternally the same, rulers and subjects, tyrants and rebels, that history can be useful as a mirror of political conduct.

The fourth scene of the fourth act of the second part of *Henry IV* is, as I have said, a transition scene, closing the account of the rebellion of the Percies and beginning the account of the new king. All of the matters that have concerned the king are again brought into focus. He is again planning to take the "sanctified" swords of Englishmen to battle for the Holy Land as soon as the rebels have come "underneath the yoke of government." He is again worrying over his wayward son and skeptical of Warwick's kindly assurance that

> The prince will in the perfectness of time
> Cast off his followers; . . .

Westmoreland brings the news that "There is not now a rebel's sword unsheathed" among the archbishop's forces, and another brings the news of the victory over Northumberland and the Scots. But the king can only ask why such good news should make him sick, and confess "now I am much ill." Then we hear a recital of the marvels that as omens herald the death of kings.

One of Henry's troubles has now ceased to occupy his thoughts, for the rebellion that has been his chief concern throughout his reign is quelled. But in his last illness his most extreme suspicion of his son is roused. Prince Hal, sitting all alone at the bedside of his dying father, watching him as he sleeps, apostrophizes the crown, vowing:

[32]Edmund Lodge, *Portraits of Illustrious Personages of Great Britain* (London, 1835), vol. III, "Sir Christopher Hatton," p. 7.

> Lo, here it sits,
> Which God shall guard: and put the world's whole strength
> Into one giant arm, it shall not force
> This lineal honour from me: this from thee
> Will I to mine leave, as 'tis left to me.

As he carries the crown with him from the room, the king wakes, and at once his mistrust of his son is roused. When the prince is recalled to the king, he is peremptorily rebuked for having thought the king was dead:

> Thy wish was father, Harry, to that thought:
> I stay too long by thee, I weary thee.
> Dost thou so hunger for mine empty chair
> That thou wilt needs invest thee with my honours
> Before thy hour be ripe? . . . .
> Thou hast stolen that which after some few hours
> Were thine without offence; . . .

But alas, the king sees only misfortune for the state when the time comes indeed for his son to put on the crown:

> Harry the fifth is crown'd: up, vanity!
> Down, royal state! all you sage counsellors, hence!
> And to the English court assemble now,
> From every region, apes of idleness!

Finally the erring son is allowed to explain, and a final reconciliation is affected. Again the political significance of the play is summed up by Shakespeare in the king's farewell to his son. Confessing the deviousness of the ways by which he acquired the crown and the discomfort with which he wore it, he tries to persuade himself that it can be worn with more assurance by his son and that it can bring greater happiness to him:

> God knows, my son,
> By what by-paths and indirect crook'd ways
> I met this crown; and I myself know well
> How troublesome it sat upon my head.
> To thee it shall descend with better quiet,
> Better opinion, better confirmation;
> For all the soil of the achievement goes
> With me into the earth.

But yet he feels that his heir is not firmly enough established, needing the support of the rebels too newly made harmless. He recalls that he purposed to lead many to the Holy Land to avoid future restlessness. It is a new purpose for his crusade, but he links it to advice to his son "to busy giddy minds/With foreign quarrels." And the prince echoes his father's hopes for the crown as he promises:

> You won it, wore it, kept it, gave it me;
> Then plain and right must my possession be:
> Which I with more than with a common pain
> 'Gainst all the world will rightfully maintain.

As the king dies in the chamber called *Jerusalem*, rather than in the Holy Land toward which his eyes have for so long been turned, the second of the worries that have beset him has already ceased, for he dies reassured as to the worthiness of his son to rule his kingdom. But he has not washed away the blood of Richard that sprinkled him to make him grow. The rebel has conquered rebellion. The usurper has not been parted from his crown till death. But the primal sin of murder has not been expiated. It is necessary to recite these facts again and again if the moral significance of the plot is to be understood.

However, aside from the general moral significance of the events recorded, I cannot but feel that an English audience of the last years of the sixteenth century must have heard overtones of contemporary political events. As I have indicated in discussing *Richard II*, Shakespeare was certainly aware of the conflict waged in its greatest intensity during the nineties over the succession to the crown. And the fears of those loyal to Elizabeth aroused by the Essex rebellion gave sure evidence that the successor might not patiently await his heritage. Whether Shakespeare intended it or not, the hasty snatching of the crown before the death of the king was a symbolic representation of the unseemly activity of would-be heirs, and particularly James of Scotland. Camden says that definite attempts were made to sow discord between Elizabeth and James in 1598, and he reports:

Whilest these rumors were fresh, she privily advised him to weigh these things seriously, *Whether there were any other besides her, that could more profit him, or hurt him. Whether any other were more bountifull unto him. Whether any other expected lesse from him then she, who looked for nothing else, but that he would advance the glory of God, and not be wanting to himselfe.* And wanting certainely he was not: For, to blow over such feigned rumors, men were sent forth farre and neere throughout *England* and *Ireland*, to winne the hearts of the multitude to love him, by extolling his constancy in Religion, his Wisedome, Justice, Clemency, and other Royall Vertues. There were Bookes also dispersed, both to maintaine his title of succession to the Crowne of *England*, . . . and also to shew that the admission of him would be more beneficiall to both kingdomes, then the intrusion of any other whosoever, . . . There were set forth also the lamentable ends not onely of usurpers, but also of advancers of usurpers; . . . What Queene ELIZABETH thought hereof, I finde not; . . .[33]

James had been ready to ally himself with France, with Denmark, with Spain, if he could thereby be sure of the crown of England; he had been ready to be consoled for his mother's execution if he could be assured of the crown of England; he was to be ready to ally himself with English rebels in the years to come for the crown's sake; and as Camden points out, he was in 1598 waging a war of propaganda in his own interests. He commenced his correspondence with Essex immediately after the death of Leicester, determined to prepare himself a welcome when the great day arrived. His troops were on the border when Essex's insurrection took place. The whole story of his determination to be Elizabeth's successor and of his restlessness during the long period of waiting was the subject of much gossip and rumor, and the picture of the prince snatching away the crown before its wearer was dead must have seemed a suggestive one to many in the audience. But the king dies at peace with his successor as Elizabeth was to do only a few years after the play was written.[34]

Act V shows the new king putting on his garment of virtue

[33]Camden, *The Historie of the . . . Princesse Elizabeth*, Bk. IV, pp. 133-34.
[34]See Helen Stafford, *James VI of Scotland*.

and becoming at once the ideal king. As Hardyng said, "The houre he was crouned and anoynt/ He chaunged was." He becomes, in fact, the chief example of the proverb much quoted by the Elizabethans, "Honors change manners." His first acts as king are those exercising the first of all kingly qualities, justice. He rewards the chief justice who has meted out justice to him; and he banishes Falstaff, the companion and guide of his wayward years. Like the execution of justice upon the archbishop and the other leaders of the rebels after they have submitted to Prince John, this administration of justice has caused much distress to many modern critics with good hearts. But I do not think the Elizabethans would have disagreed at all with this same Prince John's comment on his brother's action, and certainly the chief justice did not:

> I like this fair proceeding of the king's:
> He hath intent his wonted followers
> Shall all be very well provided for;
> But all are banish'd till their conversations
> Appear more wise and modest to the world.

Perhaps a quotation from a rather curious book called *Newes from the North* and published in 1579 will illustrate the popular idea. After a long discussion of Saul's transformation, the author continues:

The like examples we have of many Kings and Prophets in the holy Scripture. But to come nearer, bothe for the time and also the place, in our English History we read of that noble King H. the fifth, who in his Fathers life was of evill government, and kept company with riotors and unthrifts, so that there was small hope of him, but after the death of H. the fourth, when this young man was placed in his kingdom: he sent for all his olde companions, who were not a little glad therof, but when they weare come into his presence: he sharply rebuked them, and giving them small rewards, yet better then he thought them woorthy, he forbad them during their lives to come within xii. miles of the Court, and that upon great penaltie. All these examples doo manifestly proove, that liberall reward of vertue, and high and Honorable calling doo increase vertue in them in whom it is already, and causeth them in whom it is not save only in appearaunce yet for pure shame to imbrace it, seeing that otherwise hot

coales are heaped uppon their heads, through their shameless un-
thankfulnes unto them that have so thorowly provoked them with
the greatnes of their benefits.[35]

Whether Shakespeare had in mind the probable reformation
of the hopeful heir to Elizabeth's throne when he wrote this
scene, it is impossible to say. But James's favorites were as notorious as was his preoccupation with hunting and gaming. And
James was at this time engaged in gaining the good will of his
prospective subjects by publicly protesting his good faith and
by penning noble sentiments concerning the office of a king, addressed to his son and published for all to read. (The *Basilikon
Doron* was first published in Edinburgh in 1599.) However, the
supporters of almost any of the candidates for the succession
might have advanced the claims of their chosen leader by arguing that honors change manners.

When Prince John has approved the justice of the new king
he confides to the chief justice that

> I will lay odds that, ere this year expire,
> We bear our civil swords and native fire
> As far as France: I hear a bird so sing,
> Whose music, to my thinking, pleased the king.

The only bird the audience has heard so sing was the king in
his dying admonition to the future king:

> Be it thy course to busy giddy minds
> With foreign quarrels; . . .[36]

When in the next play we see Henry V going to France, Shakespeare seems to have forgotten the reason urged by Henry IV
for so doing. But of that, more later.

[35]Fols. D₁ᵛ-D₂ʳ. The work is said to be by Francis Thynne.
[36]Daniel combines the purposes of atonement and political expediency in the
King's advice to Prince Hal (*Civile Wars*, Bk. 3, stanza 127):

> And since my death my purpose doth prevent
> Touching this sacred warre I tooke in hand,
> (An action wherewithall my soule had ment
> T'appease my God, and reconcile my land)
> To thee is left to finish my intent,
> Who to be safe must never idly stand;
> But some great actions entertaine thou still
> To hold their mindes who else will practise ill.

The play of *Henry IV*, then, is primarily a play of rebellion and the end of rebellion.[37] The arch-rebel Henry is scourged by God for his sins, and the rebellion against him is put down, for

Thus ever did rebellion find rebuke.

But *Henry IV* is most remembered because a great part of it is given over to the revelries of the prince and his merry crew. Much of the interest of both parts is diverted from the historical plot to the Falstaffian episodes, so much that the working out of divine justice in the fate of the usurping king is almost forgotten in the delight of the comic episodes. As I have already said, the place of Falstaff in the plays resembles that of the bastard Faulconbridge in *King John*, and the two plays are structurally in a class by themselves. Falstaff does not comment on or reflect the political events of *Henry IV*, however, in any such important fashion as does Faulconbridge in *King John*. He, it is true, views honor with a realism that contrasts with the exaggerated unreality of Hotspur's speeches on the subject and so enables Shakespeare to present the happy temperance of Prince Hal's conception. He mocks the office of king and of the representative of justice. He makes a mockery of duty and courage. He mocks death on the battlefield by the thrust in the thigh given to the dead Hotspur and the claim which he makes to have conquered him, as well as by his own feigning of death until danger has passed. He mocks the glory of the conqueror by his actions with Colville. He reaches in his discussion of his mock soldiers and his mock leadership a degree of cynicism which can only be accounted for by conditions which were recognized by the audience. Since it is in mirroring the problem of the soldier that he comes into the political picture presented by *Henry IV*, I append a consideration of his wartime activities. I am, however, not unaware that the comic Colossus who is not only witty in himself "but the cause that wit is in other men" acquired his preeminence otherwise than as a political problem.

[37]In connection with the possible relations of *2 Henry IV* to Essex, see Alfred Hart, *Shakespeare and the Homilies*, pp. 154-218, "Was the Second Part of *King Henry the Fourth* Censored?"

THE UNQUIET TIME OF HENRY IV

AN EPILOGUE ON FALSTAFF
THE PROBLEM OF THE SOLDIER

IT HAS long been recognized that Falstaff in *Henry IV* exhibited an attitude toward his "charge of foot" which was the object of reproach in Elizabethan England.[38] Barnabe Googe, addressing his "very loving friend Captain Barnabe Riche" on the occasion of the captain's publishing his *Allarme to England* in 1578, took the opportunity to generalize the situation. He wrote:

But our countrey hath alwayes had that faute (and I am afrayde will never be without it) of being unnaturall and unthankfull to such as with their great hazard, paynes and charges have fought to attayne to the knowledge of armes, by which shee is chiefly mainteyned, succoured and defended. To bring one example amongst thousands. What a number was there of noble Gentlemen, and worthy souldiours, that in the dayes of that victorious prince King Henry the fifth (after the honourable behaving of themselves, as well at *Agincourt*, as other places, to the discomfiture and utter overthrowe of the whole Chivalry of Fraunce) returning to their countrey, were pitifully constrained (and which was indeed most miserable) in their olde and honourable age for very want and necessitie to begge, whyle a great number of unworthie wretches that lyved at home, enjoyed all kindes of felicities. That Noble Gentleman Syr William Drurie a Paragon of armes at this day, was wont (I remember) to say, that the souldiers of England had alwaies one of these three endes to looke for: To be slayne, To begge, or To be hanged.[39]

Captain Barnabe Riche became the most prolific writer of the period on the soldier and the soldier's wrongs. In the *Allarme to England* he pointed out that one reason for the Englishman's being unwilling to give much consideration to the soldier was that wars had always been considered the worst of all evils:

for warre, pestilence, and famine, are the three dartes, which the almightie God is wont to shoote against the earth, when he is dis-

---

[38]The latest work on this general subject is the paper by F. S. Boas, "The Soldier in Elizabethan and Later English Drama" in *Essays by Divers Hands, Being the Transactions of the Royal Society of Literature* (N.S. XIX: London, 1942), pp. 121-56.

[39]Address prefaced to *op. cit.*

pleased: and is holden so yrcksome amongst us, that in our letanie we daily use this praier, *From plague, pestilence, famine, battell, and murther, good Lord deliver us.*[40]

Its professors are most often considered ruffians, roisterers, blasphemers, refuse of the commonwealth. Seeing how badly soldiers thrive, therefore, many men prefer to become courtiers, lawyers, or lovers. For such a condition Riche found many causes, certain of which are pertinent to the study of Falstaff's military career. Captains are often chosen for favor rather than knowledge and ability. And soldiers are chosen even more unworthily:

Our maner of appointing of souldiers, is yet more confused than the rest, they be appointed in the countrie as it pleaseth Maister Constable: for if there be any within his circuit, that he is in displeasure withall, he thinkes it some part of revenge, if he sets him forth to be a souldier, but if Maister Constable be in love and charitie with his ncighbours, then some odde fellowe must be picked out that doth least good in the parish, it is no matter for his conditions, thcy thinke he cannot be too yll to make a souldier of. In London when they set foorth souldiers, either they scoure their prisons of theeves, or their streates of roges and vagabondes, for he that is bound to find a man, will seeke suche a one as were better lost then found: but they care not, so they may have them good cheape, what he is, nor from whence he comes, . . .[41]

Geoffrey Gates in his *Defence of Militarie Profession*, published in 1579, argued that virtue is more necessary to the soldier who is to execute God's justice than it is to anyone else:

Foolishe therefore and beastely is the common speach, used of the base and humble mynded sort of our natione, that doe not onely saye, but also affirme in their doinges, that the worst sort of men, (and such as for the vilenes of their conditiones the earth is not able to susteyne) are fit for the warres: and accordingly doe call out the refuse of the people to be soldiers for the service of their Prince and countreie, where indeede the worthiest people ought to be chosen, and preferred: as to a state most honorable, and of most credite and importance.[42]

[40]*Ibid.*, fol. A1r.
[41]*Ibid.*, fol. K3.
[42]*Op. cit.*, p. 18.

In the same year, 1579, Thomas Digges wrote in his *Stratioticos* that in the time of peace England should not rest careless of war but prepare the minds and bodies of soldiers for any future military orders; yet he bewailed:

the corruption of Millitarie Discipline, and licentious living of the Souldyoure of oure time, hath made them odious, who of all other should most be imbraced and loved, if these Errors were refourmed, and this their Art dulie practised.[43]

The same degradation of the soldier's profession was decried throughout Elizabeth's reign and after. In 1604 Captain Riche was still refashioning the same ideas into new pamphlets, often without much change of wording. He still was ruing the fact that when soldiers are to be chosen:

the election is made of Rogues, Runnagates, Drunkards, and all sorts of Vagabonds and disordered persons, such as are fitter to garnish a prison, then to furnish a Campe:[44]

and in 1604 Dudley Digges, the son of Thomas, was also asserting that oftentimes condemnation of wars for murdering men and wasting money fruitlessly could be accounted for by the "poore hunger-starved snakes halfe dead ere they go out of England," who would have cumbered the armies of the ancient Romans themselves and made victory difficult. He blamed the corruptness and the ignorance of the leaders for such a state of affairs:

such decayed unthriftie gallants as to gett a little money by the sale, spoile or slaughter of their Companies make meanes to be favorable sent from the Court to the Camp, as Commanders, before they knowe how to obey . . .[45]

These commanders, Digges says, are the cause of the extraordinary spoil of treasure in the wars and the apparent dilatoriness

---

[43]Leonard Digges, *An Arithmeticall Militare Treatise, Named Stratioticos,* fol. A1v. For an account of this book begun by Leonard Digges but completed by Thomas Digges, see below, pp. 299-300.

[44]*A Souldiers Wishe to Britons Welfare,* p. 61.

[45]*Foure Paradoxes, or Politique Discourses,* p. 80.

and fruitlessness of their prosecution. Such officers and such soldiers "only use the warres as naughty men doe learning to increase their wickedness."

The wars in the Low Countries and in France especially left their military flotsam and jetsam on English shores. Both pay and discipline seem to have been blamed. The defenders of the military profession pointed out again and again (1) that commanders were often appointed because of their influence with someone at court; (2) that these commanders and their subordinate officers were sometimes not only incapable but also corrupt in their dealings; (3) that the soldiers were chosen as means to private gain on the part of the officers or constables; and (4) that the choice of begging or stealing for a living on their return from the wars was not one to make men enthusiastic about becoming soldiers.

Evidence as to the unfortunate status of the soldier is provided by many proclamations of Queen Elizabeth. On August 20, 1588, when the army gathered to meet an expected invasion at the time of the Armada was being sent home, a proclamation was issued which began:

The Queenes Majestie being given to understand, that divers Souldiers upon the dissolving of the Campe at Tilberie in the countie of Essex, have in their way homeward solde divers their Armors and weapons, which have bene delivered unto them by the Officers of those Counties where they have bene levied and set out; and besides the sale of their said Armour and weapons, have most falsely and slanderously given out, that they were compelled to make sale of them for that they received no pay, which is most untruely reported. . .[46]

Therefore she ordered all buyers of such military equipment to turn it in to authorities of the city, while the soldier-salesmen were to be apprehended.

In 1589 there was issued *A Proclamation Against Vagrant Souldiers and Others* which provided means of relief for conditions which had come to the attention of the queen, who had

[46]STC 8174.

heard "of the great outrages that have bene, and are daily committed by Souldiers, Mariners, and others that pretend to have served as Souldiers," and who had learned that servants on returning from the army and being refused work by their former masters, "goe up and down begging, contrary to the Lawes and statutes of this realme."[47]

In February, 1592, members of the privy council appointed certain justices of the peace to examine such persons as are described in the *whereas* clause:

Whereas the Queenes Majestie doth understand, that notwithstanding her late Proclamation concerning such persons as wander abroad in the habite of Souldiers, there are divers persons pretending to have served in the late warres and service as Souldiers, that remain within and about the Cities of *London* and *Westminster*, . . . And some amongst these have neither bene maymed nor hurt, nor yet served at all in the warres, but take that cloake and colour, to bee the more pitied, and do live about the Citie by begging and in disorderly manner: . . .[48]

In April, 1593, another proclamation[49] by members of the council gave orders for the execution of an act of parliament which provided relief for those maimed and hurt in the wars but sent them back to reside in the counties where they were born, decreeing explicitly that no one receiving relief or found unworthy of relief should stay within three miles of Southwark or London or Westminster.

Such official documents as these surely attest the fact that writers like the scholarly Digges and the somewhat whining journalistic Riche were picturing real conditions, conditions which set a troublesome political problem for the state. Shakespeare dramatized the situation with irony and without sentimentality, even without sympathy; rebellion in *Henry IV* is apparently put down with brilliant leaders and cannon-fodder soldiers.

---

[47]*STC* 8188.

[48]*STC* 8218.

[49]*STC* 8227.

Now it should be noted that Prince Hal is as yet very much unredeemed when, after having proved Falstaff a coward and a liar over the Gadshill robbery, he announces to Peto:

We must all to the wars, and thy place shall be honourable. I'll procure this fat rogue a charge of foot; and I know his death will be a march of twelve-score.[50]

Peto's being provided with an honorable place is surely not due to his military prowess, and it is a princely joke that sends Falstaff to the wars on foot, as he himself attests when the prince informs him of his "charge of foot": "I would it had been of horse."[51] Bardolph is sent off with messages to Lancaster and Westmoreland.[52] Such a way of taking care of the crew of wastrels is a perfect example of military preference coming by court preferment.

Falstaff immediately proceeds to act as officers so chosen are reputed to have acted. Riche listed[53] many ways by which the elect abused their offices. Sometimes they took pay for a whole company and enlisted only a half-company. Sometimes they made all others afraid to cross them because of the great favor they enjoyed at court. Sometimes they pressed men, honest householders of wealth and ability, who could be dealt with as merchandise. But no one better described the possibilities than did Falstaff in his proud confession to Bardolph:

I have misused the king's press damnably. I have got, in exchange of a hundred and fifty soldiers, three hundred and odd pounds. I press me none but good householders, yeomen's sons; inquire me out contracted bachelors, such as had been asked twice on the banns; such a commodity of warm slaves, as had as lieve hear the devil as a drum; . . . and they have bought out their services; . . .[54]

In Hakluyt's *Principal Navigations* the account of "the memorable defeate of the Spanishe huge Armada, Anno. 1588, and

[50]*1 Henry IV*, II, iv, 543-45.
[51]*Ibid.*, III, iii, 187-88.
[52]*Ibid.*, ll. 196-97.
[53]In all his works, but see particularly *A Souldiers Wishe to Britons Welfare* (London, 1604).
[54]*1 Henry IV*, IV, ii, 11-33.

the famous victorie atchieved at the citie of Cadiz, 1596," included the record of punishments imposed as deterrents upon viola-
tors of the articles of war while the forces were gathering at
Plymouth. One of these cases, previously noted by editors of
the play, is in point here:

a certain Lieutenant . . . was by sound of Drumme publikely in all
the streates disgraced, or rayther after a sort disgraded, and cashiered
for bearing any further Office at that time, for the taking of money
by way of corruption, of certaine prest souldiers in the Countrey,
and for placing of others in their roomes, more unfit for service, and
of lesse sufficiency and abilitie.[55]

Shakespeare dramatizes such an exchange in the second scene
of Act III in the second part of *Henry IV*, where Shallow is trying to secure for Falstaff the four men that he is ordered to provide. Of the six men called, four are to be chosen. Bardolph explains in an aside to Falstaff that he has three pounds to free
Mouldy and Bullcalf. The following conversation ensues:

SHAL. Come, Sir John, which four will you have?

FAL. Do you choose for me.

SHAL. Marry, then, Mouldy, Bullcalf, Feeble, and Shadow.

FAL. Mouldy and Bullcalf: for you, Mouldy, stay at home till you
are past service: and for your part, Bullcalf, grow till you
come into it: I will none of you.

SHAL. Sir John, Sir John, do not yourself wrong: they are your like-
liest men, and I would have you served with the best.

FAL. Will you tell me, Master Shallow, how to choose a man?[56]

Wart is given a caliver to try, and Falstaff proclaims himself
pleased in spite of Shallow's remonstrance that "he is not his
craft's master; he doth not do it right."

Such misuse of the press brought about conditions which disturbed authorities and caused protests from the defenders of the
military profession. Even Falstaff confesses himself ashamed of

[55]London, 1598, p. 607. This voyage was deleted from the second issue.
Quoted in part in the Arden ed. of *1 Henry IV* (p. 155n.) from Steevens.
[56]*2 Henry IV*, III, ii, 242-52.

his soldiers, and no one has done better than he in describing the sad state of Englishmen chosen to fight for their country:

> now my whole charge consists of ancients, corporals, lieutenants, gentlemen of companies, slaves as ragged as Lazarus in the painted cloth, . . . and such as indeed were never soldiers, but discarded unjust serving-men, younger sons to younger brothers, revolted tapsters, and ostlers trade-fallen; the cankers of a calm world and a long peace, . . . : and such have I, to fill up the rooms of them that have bought out their services, . . .

He refuses to march through Coventry with such scarecrows. Furthermore, they are not equipped even with shirts, though the prince has arranged money for their furniture, and Falstaff trusts to their being able to find the necessary linen on the hedges as they pass by:

> There's not a shirt and a half in all my company; and the half shirt is two napkins tacked together and thrown over the shoulders like a herald's coat without sleeves; and the shirt, to say the truth, stolen from my host at Saint Alban's, or the red-nose innkeeper of Daventry. But that's all one; they'll find linen enough on every hedge.

In 1574 Riche had indicated that soldiers were wont to provide themselves with barterable goods as well as shirts from the hedges:

> Fyrst by the way as they travayle through the Countrey, where they chaunce to lye all nyght, the godwyfe hath spedde well if shee fynde hyr sheetes in the morning, or if this happe to fayle yet a coverlet, or Curtins from the bed, or a Carpet from the table, some table clothes, or table Napkins, or some other thing must needes pack away with them, . . .[57]

The four worthies from Justice Shallow's domain are, however, provided with coats on Falstaff's orders.

Falstaff's opinion of his soldiers is endorsed by Prince Hal, who comments, "I did never see such pitiful rascals," but Falstaff's attitude remains consistent:

---

[57]Riche, *A Right Exelent and Pleasaunt Dialogue, Betwene Mercury and an English Souldier,* fol. G6ᵛ.

Tut, tut; good enough to toss; food for powder, food for powder; they'll fill a pit as well as better: tush, man, mortal men, mortal men.[58]

And he sees that his men reach their predestined end, for he tells us later at Shrewsbury:

I have led my ragamuffins where they are peppered: there's not three of my hundred and fifty left alive; and they are for town's end, to beg during life.[59]

Such is the picture of the common soldier as Shakespeare portrays him in *Henry IV*. His immediate superiors complement the picture. Offices have been handed out to Prince Hal's companions as a matter of court favor. Peto was promised an honorable place and apparently was the companion of the prince as he rode to war. Pistol's captaincy is adequately commented on by Doll:

You a captain! you slave, for what? for tearing a poor whore's ruff in a bawdy-house? He a captain! hang him, rogue! he lives upon mouldy stewed prunes and dried cakes. A captain! God's light, these villains will make the word as odious as the word "occupy," which was an excellent good word before it was ill sorted: therefore captains had need look to't.[60]

The end of the captain is recorded in *Henry V*. Bardolph is addressed as "Corporal Bardolph" by Pistol and feeds the money to Falstaff by which Mouldy and Bullcalf free themselves.

But above and beyond all there is Falstaff, who opposes his preference for longer life to the honor so much vaunted by Hotspur and so gloriously achieved by Prince Hal; who pretends death to avoid fighting; who tries or pretends to try to receive compensation for a dead Hotspur whose corpse he has wounded; who is valorous in taking a prisoner who gives himself up without a fight; who places his men in battle where they are peppered, and where a hundred and forty-seven out of a hundred and fifty are lost.

[58] *1 Henry IV*, IV, ii.
[59] *Ibid.*, V, iii, 36-39.
[60] *2 Henry IV*, II, iv, 140-47.

That the common soldiers and their lesser leaders were used for comic relief while the royal and noble gentlemen of the high command fought their great battles with their royal and noble opponents on the stage furnishes a text for the discussion of Shakespeare's democracy, but I do not propose to deliver the sermon here. It must be noted, however, that it is the business of the same characters and their fellows to furnish the comedy for *Henry V*.[61]

When Falstaff demands recognition of his capture of the yielding Colville, he threatens:

or, by the Lord, I will have it in a particular ballad else, with my own picture on the top on't, Colville kissing my foot:[62]

and it is interesting to note that Riche later bemoaned the lack of reward for the most honorable action of the soldier,

unlesse perhaps a little commendations in a Ballad: or if a man be favored by a Play maker, he may sometimes be Canonized on a stage.[63]

Falstaff reaped better than a ballad when the greatest of play-makers chose to canonize him as the greatest of comic characters. But when Shakespeare gave him immortality, he also confirmed the picture of conditions in the English army and the picture of the aftermath of war for the soldier.

---

[61]See chap. xv.
[62]*2 Henry IV*, IV, iii, 46-48.
[63]In *The Fruites of Long Experience* (London, 1604), p. 21.

CHAPTER XV

THE VICTORIOUS ACTS OF KING HENRY V

THE ARDEN editor of Shakespeare's *Life of King Henry the Fifth*, H. A. Evans, sums up the common view of the play when he says that "its interest is epic rather than dramatic; it is the nearest approach on the part of the author to a national epic."[1] The historical mirrors that Shakespeare held up to England before he wrote of Henry V were mirrors in which the Elizabethans could see their own national problems being acted out on the stage before them, and in which they could witness the eternal justice of God in the affairs of the body politic. They showed the conflicts of the age which endangered the state, threatening its peace and security. But in *Henry V* the English are mirrored triumphant in a righteous cause, achieving victory through the blessing of God. A mood of exultation pervades the play. Henry V stands as the ideal hero in contrast with the troubled John, the deposed Richard, the rebel Henry IV; for the traditional conception of Henry V was of a hero-king, and about his dominant figure Shakespeare chose to fashion a hero-play. The theme of the play is war, and the progress of the warrior-hero is the progress of the play. Thus the play becomes in form and content epic.

This traditional view of Henry V as the hero-king of England, Kingsford traces to the official biography by Tito Livio, written by that Italian historian at the suggestion of his English patron, Humphrey Duke of Gloucester, brother of Henry V and protector during the minority of Henry VI.[2] Tito Livio dedicated

[1] *Op. cit.* (London, 1917), p. xli.
[2] C. L. Kingsford, *The First English Life of King Henry the Fifth* (Oxford, 1911), pp. xiv-xv, and xlvi.

his work to the young king, offering it as a guide by which he might follow in his father's footsteps. Yet since it was, perforce, an account of Henry V's wars that he had written, he felt called upon to explain:

Not that I preferr and laude warr and discention, rather than tranquillitie and peace; but if thou maiest have none honest peace, that then·thou shalt seeke peace and rest with victorie to both thie realmes by thy vertue and battaile, and by those feates by which thie Father attamed both his adversaries and thine.[3]

In 1513 or 1514 a translation of the work of Tito Livio was offered by an unnamed writer to King Henry VIII because he had "now of late entered into semblable warr against the Frenchmen."[4] The translator inserted moralizations throughout the course of the narrative, and Kingsford says of these insertions:

They are the endeavour of an historian to draw instruction from the past for the benefit of the present. Their didactic purpose was not purely moral; there is in them a deliberate design to apply the political lesson of the life of Henry V to the times of Henry VIII.[5]

It is thus evident that the life of Henry V was first written as a mirror of victorious deeds for his son, and that it grew into "the first English life of King Henry the Fifth" in order that it might serve as a mirror to Henry VIII in a "semblable warr." Holinshed and Stow both consulted Tito Livio, Kingsford says, and Halle did not.[6] But the theme of all the chroniclers was the same, for Halle took as the title for the section of his chronicle dealing with this hero-king "The victorious actes of kyng Henry the V." The play upon which Shakespeare drew for a selection of incidents had likewise the title of *The Famous Victories of*

[3]*Ibid.*, p. 7. The quotation is from the 1513 English translation.

[4]*Ibid.*, p. 190.

[5]*Ibid.*, p. xiii.

[6]*Ibid.*, p. xlvi.

[7]See *ibid.*, pp. xlvii–lvi for a discusssion of the relation of the first *Life* to this play and to Shakespeare's *Henry V*. The most complete study is B. M. Ward's "*The Famous Victories of Henry V*: Its Place in Elizabethan Dramatic Literature," *Review of English Studies*, IV (1928), pp. 270–94.

Henry V.[7] It was pre-determined that in writing about Henry V Shakespeare should write about war and victory in war, as it had been that in writing about Henry IV he should write about rebellion. In the midst of his wooing of the Princess Katherine of France, Henry V, indeed, explains his stern visage by the fact that his father "was thinking of civil wars when he got me."[8]

The Elizabethan period was, by and large, a time of peace, for there were no wars with foreign invaders fought on English soil; yet the English fought in Scotland and in Ireland, in France on behalf of Henry IV, and in the Netherlands on behalf of the Lowlanders against Spain. Elizabeth had an army as well as a navy ready to meet invasion at the time of the Armada, and she continued to be troubled by fears of an invasion long afterward, especially during 1598, when Henry IV of France was making peace with Spain in spite of English protests, and in 1599, when Camden says an army was called up, ostensibly at least to meet a Spanish threat.[9] Professor Dietz estimates that Elizabeth, up to 1588, spent for military purposes £1,517,351, and from that time on very much more. Between 1585 and 1596 she spent in aiding the Netherlands £1,186,119, and Henry IV of France was in her debt £445,125 when she tried to effect a settlement with him.[10] If we consider the value of money at that time and the comparatively small population, we realize that such expenditures for war, added to the constant raising of forces to fight on land and on sea, must have kept war to the forefront of English interests throughout the reign, as indeed it did. The useful bibliography of English and continental books on military matters by Captain Cockle gives ample proof that England was not only reading but quarreling about the theories and the arts of war.[11]

When Shakespeare wrote *Henry V*, then, does not concern us

---

[8]*Henry V*, V, ii, 238-39.

[9]Camden, *Historie of the . . . Princesse Elizabeth*, Bk. IV, pp. 142-43. Camden implies that the rumors concerning the Earl of Essex constituted the real reason.

[10]F. C. Dietz, *English Public Finance, 1558-1641* (New York and London, 1932, for the American Historical Association), pp, 59, 455, 459.

[11]M. J. D. Cockle, *A Bibliography of English Military Books up to 1642 and of Contemporary Foreign Works* (London, 1900).

if we regard it as simply a political play about war, war viewed from the Elizabethan point of view. But from Simpson[12] onward there has been a tendency to associate the play with Essex. The facts are these. The first quarto, a "bad" quarto, was published in 1600. Meres failed to mention *Henry V* in his *Palladis Tamia* in 1598, and he did mention *Henry IV*. The chorus that precedes the fifth act of *Henry V* makes obvious reference to the expected victorious return of Essex from Ireland, where he had gone to quell rebellion in March, 1599, and must have been written after that date and before September of that year, when the harried earl made his very unvictorious appearance in England. But the choruses, certain scenes, and many passages of dialogue did not appear in the quartos, being first printed in the folio of 1623. Chambers thinks that the play, choruses and all, was probably written in 1599, but any conclusions that go beyond these facts must remain tentative.[13] Those who regard Henry V as Essex, however, make two mistakes, it seems to me. In the first place, Shakespeare does not compare Essex to Henry V; what he compares is the greeting which would be given to Essex if he should return from Ireland, "Bringing rebellion broached on his sword," to the greeting which Henry V received from the populace when he returned victorious from France. In the second place, even though Essex were compared to Henry V in the chorus, it would be a mistake to assume that he must therefore be Henry V throughout the play. It is the mistake which critics have made, who, finding Duessa certainly presenting the case of Mary Stuart in the trial scene of Book V of the *Faerie Queene*, try to make Duessa represent Mary Stuart throughout the whole poem. The result is confusion, for that is not the way of the artist who holds his mirror up to nature. Undoubtedly Shakespeare here as elsewhere had specific and contemporary situations in mind, but he does not simply label a contemporary character with an historical name. Even the situations and the roles of Mary and her son

---

[12]Simpson, *op. cit.*, pp. 416-19; see E. M. Albright, "The Folio Version of *Henry V* in Relation to Shakespeare's Times," *PMLA*, XLIII (1928), 722-56.

[13]For a full discussion of these matters see E. K. Chambers, *William Shakespeare*, I, 395.

James of Scotland were merged in the picture of Arthur in *King John*, by far the most specific of the historical mirrors.

Henry V is apparently based on Holinshed and covers the period from Lent, 1414, to May, 1420. The character and the achievements of the king remain true to tradition, though both persons and times are frequently telescoped. During this period the dauphin of France was first Lewis, then John, then Charles. To Shakespeare he is merely the dauphin. Henry's war upon France is abridged and compressed. The Battle of Agincourt in 1415 is followed by the peacemaking at Troyes in 1420, only the chorus to Act V bridging the years. This chorus takes the king to London by way of Calais and boldly declares that the play omits "All the occurrences, whatever chanc'd,/ Till Harry's back-return again to France." The great battles fought on his return to France in 1417 are, however, omitted, so that we are left to infer that the French made peace because of the victory at Agincourt. The peace parley at Troyes in 1420 is apparently telescoped with the meeting at Meulan in 1419, where Henry fell in love with the Princess Katherine.[14] There is also much in the play that is not in the chronicles, but, as I have said, the general picture remains true to the pattern set by Tito Livio and continued in all the English chronicles.

The first act of the play is given over to the decision of Henry V to make war on France. Henry IV had advised his son "to busy giddy minds/ With foreign quarrels;" but that advice is passed over in the new play, and both Shakespeare and Henry V are justifying the war on high moral grounds, instead of as a means of quieting rebels at home. In the opening scene the Archbishop of Canterbury and the Bishop of Ely are discussing the new king and his reformation. It is perhaps worthy of note in passing that while Holinshed praised Henry V for commanding the clergy to preach the word of God and the laity to obey it, for appointing the men best learned in the laws to the "offices of justice," Shakespeare represents the praise of the churchmen

[14] W. G. Boswell-Stone, *Shakspere's Holinshed* (New York, 1896), pp. 165 et seq.

as bestowed on the king, not because of his wise choice of men for office but because of his own academic achievements. They praise him because he is able to reason in divinity like a prelate, to debate commonwealth affairs as though they were his chief study, and to discourse so admirably of war

> that, when he speaks,
> The air, a charter'd libertine, is still,
> And the mute wonder lurketh in men's ears,
> To steal his sweet and honey'd sentences;
> So that the art and practic part of life
> Must be the mistress to this theoric.

These are words which find parallels in comments on King Henry VIII and Queen Elizabeth, and very often King James, but spoken of King Henry V they are as curious as praise given to an enthusiastic rooter in the bleachers for his football prowess. This praise of the king is, however, only incidental to the churchmen's discussion of a bill urged by Commons which would deprive the higher clergy of important revenue. The archbishop is certain that the king will take the part of the church, since he has offered from Convocation "a greater sum/ Than ever at one time the clergy yet/ Did to his predecessors part withal." The sum has been offered in aid of the projected wars in France, but Shakespeare does not indicate, as does Holinshed, that the archbishop's purpose in the offer has been to turn Henry's mind to making war in France in order to get it off church revenues. Instead, Shakespeare makes the king the prime mover in the matter, representing him as seeking advice from the archbishop as his moral and spiritual mentor.

The second scene gets down to the real business of justifying Henry's war against France. Henry asks that the archbishop argue his right "justly and religiously." He does not want to go to war without the assurance of justice on his side, for the horrors of war are too terrible to be risked in an unworthy cause. The archbishop then sets forth the exposition of the Salic law which is so wearying to the reader and so stimulating to the identifiers among the critics. There is no question that it was a law that drew the attention of Elizabethan writers, but critics who have found grounds in its genealogical intricacies for identifying Essex as Henry V ignore the fact that upon the right of the woman to inherit depended also the right of Mary and Elizabeth Tudor to the throne, the right of the Tudors to rule, and the right of Mary and James of Scotland to inherit.

When the archbishop has finished his harangue, the king renews his urgent demand:

> May I with right and conscience make this claim?

And the archbishop replies:

> The sin upon my head, dread sovereign!

The Bishop of Ely and the noblemen present join him in urging war, and the king makes his decision even as the ambassadors from France enter. Warnings concerning the collaboration of the French and the Scotch and suggestions for the protection of the homeland while the king leads an army abroad are uttered.

The French ambassadors bring a scornful reply from the dauphin to Henry's demand for certain dukedoms by right of his descent from Edward III, and offer their prince's gift, a tun of tennis balls. Indignation and a more resolute decision for war are Henry's answer.

The chorus tells of the bribing of Richard Earl of Cambridge, Lord Scroop, and Sir Thomas Grey by the French as it gives new words to the theme which dominated *King John:*

> O England! model to thy inward greatness,
> Like little body with a mighty heart,
> What might'st thou do, that honour would thee do,
> Were all thy children kind and natural!

In Act II we hear of Falstaff's sickness, for "The king has killed his heart." Then we see the king at Southampton, again executing justice. He orders freed one who has been taken up for railing against the king's person and hands out to the traitors Cambridge, Scroop, and Grey warrants for their arrest instead of the commissions they are expecting. It is a grim joke, not much to the modern taste, but Henry finds in the detection of the treason before the voyage is undertaken an omen of success. After hearing the tale of Falstaff's death, we are transported to the French king's palace, where the French leaders are discussing the coming of the English, and the dauphin is advising against underestimating the enemy. To them comes a messenger announcing the ambassadors from England, and Exeter treads upon the messenger's heels to make demands and formally declare the war that is their only alternative to granting these demands.

The chorus to the third act carries the king's forces to Harfleur and announces that Henry has spurned the offer of the hand of the Princess Katherine, with some petty dukedoms as her dower. Then we hear him addressing his troops before Harfleur, urging them to do their utmost. A comic scene intrudes before the governor of Harfleur is addressed by the English king, who makes formal demand for surrender, threatening the horrors of war. As the governor yields, Henry commands, "Use mercy to them all." After meeting Katherine—and Shakespeare's French— we hear the French high command speaking of certain victory. King Henry, talking to his soldiers, is interrupted by Montjoy, coming from the French king to demand satisfaction for the wrongs of France and defy him to come further. Though his troops have suffered illness and are decimated, Henry trusts to God and presses on. The French are then shown, despising the enemy, interested in effeminacies, and counting the enemy dead before they have killed them.

The chorus again serves to carry us to the English camp at Agincourt to let us watch the English king comforting his men the night before the battle. In the first scene we see him eavesdropping on their conversation, playing a joke upon an unsuspecting common soldier, philosophizing upon the cares of kingship, and praying his desperate prayer:

> Not to-day, O Lord!
> O! not to-day, think not upon the fault
> My father made in compassing the crown.

THE VICTORIOUS ACTS OF KING HENRY V

The Constable of France addresses his soldiers, bidding them on, for their enemies are ready to be blown over with a breath. Henry makes his grand oration before the battle, and after he has refused new offers from the French to ransom himself, the battle is waged with alarums and excursions. They do well, the English, though the Duke of York and the Earl of Suffolk are slain. But a new alarum sounds, and Henry, aware of French reinforcements, orders every soldier to kill his prisoners. Montjoy asks permission to bury the French dead, and the victory is yielded to the English. The king plays out his joking wager with the soldier and then reckons the dead on both sides. Triumphant, he gives praise for victory to the God of battles.

The chorus before the last act bears the king to Calais, takes him to the English beaches crowded with the multitudes of anxious watchers, then to London, where the Emperor [Sigismund] comes on behalf of France, and returns him to France, omitting "All the occurrences, whatever chanc'd," between times. After a scene with the comic characters, the great making of the peace at Troyes is presented on the stage, the Duke of Burgundy acting as the peacemaker. The king delegates the treaty making to five of the greatest among the English and turns his attention to wooing the French king's daughter.

The chorus returns to the scene of matchmaking and peacemaking with a somber note, reminding us of the great cycle of history of which this is but a part:

> Small time, but in that small most greatly liv'd
> This star of England: Fortune made his sword,
> By which the world's best garden he achiev'd,
> And of it left his son imperial lord.
> Henry the Sixth, in infant bands crown'd King
> Of France and England, did this king succeed;
> Whose state so many had the managing,
> That they lost France and made his England bleed; . . .

As I have said, the first act of the play is taken up with the decision to make war on France, not as a means of busying giddy minds, but on the high moral grounds of righting wrongs and

263

regaining lost rights. Holinshed records that Henry V on his deathbed

protested unto them, that neither the ambitious desire to inlarge his dominions, neither to purchase vaine renowme and worldlie fame, nor anie other consideration had mooved him to take the warres in hand; but onlie that in prosecuting his just title, he might in the end atteine to a perfect peace, and come to enjoie those peeces of his inheritance, which to him of right belonged: and that before the beginning of the same warres, he was fullie persuaded by men both wise and of great holinesse of life, that upon such intent he might and ought both begin the same warres, and follow them, till he had brought them to an end justlie and rightlie, and that without all danger of Gods displeasure or perill of soule.[15]

This apology provides the theme for the first act, and rightly so, for justifying war and justifying a particular war were matters of prime concern in the Tudor philosophy of war, as well as in Tudor practice.

The sixteenth century saw the development of a crisis in the conflict between the authority of the church and that of the state, between Catholics and Reformers, and between sect and sect. Fundamental problems arose to be argued: whether a Christian state might make war, whether it might war on another Christian state, and whether it might make war for religion's sake. Furthermore, the problem of who should be responsible for the waging of war was at issue, as well as the question of the individual soldier's responsibility in engaging in battle. The philosophy of war was rationalized to answer these and other questions on the basis of national needs and ambitions. One of the clearest and most comprehensive of these philosophic rationalizations is found in a translation by Walter Lynne dedicated to King Edward VI in 1549:

A Treatise or Sermon of Henry Bullynger, most fruitfull and necessarye for this tyme, concernynge magistrates and obedience of subjectes. Also concernyng the affayres of warre, and what scryptures make mension thereof. Whether christen powers may war against

[15]Holinshed, *op. cit.*, III, 583.

their enemies. And whither it be laufull for a christyan to beare the office of a magistrate, and of the duety of souldiers with many other holsom instructions for captaynes and souldiers both.

This "treatise or sermon" argues that Christians may make war: for Moses fought battles at God's command; John the Baptist, when soldiers came to him to be baptized, did not order them to lay down their arms; Christ commanded that those things which are Caesar's should be given unto Caesar and "therefore be tributs payd, whereby warres may be waged, and souldiers mainteined for necessities of war."[16]

However, the causes of war must be just, for the evils of war are great, and Bullinger gives a typical list of the evils:

Fyrst by warre spryngeth dearth and utter scasety of al thynges. For the wayes be stopped, the corn trodden downe, townes set on fyre, vitalle distroied and wasted, all occupations and marchandise cease, both rich and poore decayeth. In warre the most valiante sonest destroyed, the cowards thei retyre and save themselves whyles greater afterclappes do fal upon them. The most vile ruffynes, most avaunted, which abuse men more lyke beastes than other. All is full of murning on everye syde. Wydowes bewayle: fatherles children lament and be destitute, Great riches provided for nede to come, cleane spoyled, hole cities set afyre, vyrgynes and unmared maydens defyled: Al shame al honesty set asyde: no reverence to age. All maner of ryght all lawes unregarded: al holy religion and studies cleane under foote, vyle vacaboundes and desperate breuylles rule all the roste. And therefore in scripture warre is called the scourge of god.[17]

Thus war may be undertaken, but only for good cause. War for religion's sake is justified, war against a foreign state that despoils the citizens of another state is justified, and war in defence of "confederat frendes and ayders" is justified. But war may never be undertaken for private revenge, it must be directed to the execution of justice, and it may not be undertaken until "allmaner of wayes" of avoiding it have been tried.

[16]*Op. cit.*, fol. A7.

[17]*Ibid.*, fols. A8-B2.

The magistrate (or ruler) is the instrument of public vengeance. To him God gives the sword of his justice. The sword so given is to be used to punish trespassers and to destroy open enemies, foreign enemies as well as rebellious and seditious subjects, for the magistrate must not only execute justice upon thieves and murderers, but also upon those evil men who come as ravening wolves.

In 1598 Stephen Gosson preached before the mayor and aldermen of London at Paul's Cross a sermon entitled *The Trumpet of Warre* which shows as well as anything can the persistence of the fundamental ideas enunciated by Bullinger. War, Gosson says, is good and lawful in reason, in religion, and in the practice of the church. The calamities of war are so great that it should not be undertaken lightly, but only when the occasion is proportionable to the cost. He explains further:

As warre must have a just title to make it lawfull, so it must also be undertaken by lawfull authoritie . . . The reason of it is this, that as in a common weale it is requisite there should be an authoritie, to punish offences, and to keepe the same in order: so in the wide worlde, that all kingdomes and commonweales might be preserved, it is requisit there shuld be a power and authority to punish injuries, this power resting in no Prince in the world as superior to al other Princes, warre steppes in in the place of just vindicative judgement, and hath left no other meanes unto Princes to hie unto.[18]

The prince must, then, make war even on his own behalf, while the private person is forbidden private revenge, inasmuch as he may not be both judge and advocate in his own cause. But the authority of the prince is public and administered by a public council, "whereby the affections of Princes are easily restrained." The common soldiers are instruments by which God punishes offenses. As to the "execution of war" Gosson repeats that in the beginning there must be counsel taken and deliberation to begin the weightiest of all human affairs. War must be undertaken to

---

[18]The quotation is from the copy generously lent by Princeton University for my perusal at the Huntington Library. I have not been able to recheck it.

secure peace and not for the sake of pride, ambition, or any similar passion.[19]

Choosing almost at random from the very great number of writers who argue about war, we may look at three who present the widely different points of view of churchman, militarist, and theorist. Calvin, the great Genevan, took the same fundamental position that the magistrate is to be regarded as God's executioner, as the public avenger of wrongs. War must not be undertaken lightly or for private vengeance, but kings and peoples are justified in warring when public justice is to be executed. Guillaume du Bellay's *Instructions for the Warres*, translated by Paul Ive, the famous military engineer who has been mentioned as one of Marlowe's sources, discussed first the question "whether it be lawful for Christians to make warres, or not," and came to the same conclusions. Bertrand de Loque's *Discourses of Warre and Single Combat*, translated in 1591, was particularly concerned with meeting the objections of the Anabaptists, but followed Bullinger's arguments and came to the same general position upon the justifications for war.

Queen Elizabeth declared that "by the bond sealed to the people at the Coronation; every Prince covenants with the people, to defend them from all injuries, domesticke and forraigne," and King James wrote to his son in 1599:

Ye have also to consider, that yee must not onely bee careful to keepe your subjects, from receiving anie wrong of others within; but also yee must be careful to keepe them from the wrong of any forraine Prince without: sen the sword is given you by God not onely to revenge upon your owne subjects, the wrongs committed amongst themselves; but further, to revenge and free them of forraine injuries done unto them: And therefore warres upon just quarrels are lawful: but above all, let not the wrong cause be on your side.[20]

However, the matter was anything but academic, especially in the last two decades of Elizabeth's reign. In 1585, after twenty-

[19]See William Ringler, *Stephen Gosson* (Princeton, 1942), p. 14.

[20]*The Political Works of James I*, ed. C. H. McIlwain (Cambridge, 1918), p. 28.

seven years of at least technical peace, Elizabeth intervened openly against Spain on behalf of the Netherlands and sent troops
under the Earl of Leicester to aid the Dutch. The venture was
not undertaken without an attempt at securing moral and religious sanction for the undertaking. Strype, in his life of Archbishop Whitgift, gives a good deal of space to recounting events
of this summer of 1585, and I think it is worth while to consider
his account in connection with *Henry V*. His first sentences explain the situation:

A weighty motion was made this summer, about the month of July,
to the Archbishop by the Earl of Leicester; namely, to declare what
his judgment was for the Queen's assistance of the inhabitants of the
Netherlands, so grievously now oppressed by Philip, King of Spain:
. . . This great affair had been already concluded upon at Court by
the great men about the Queen; though she herself was very tender
of entering into this open breach with Spain. The lofty Earl expected
this mighty addition to the rest of his honours and titles, to lead and
govern her forces in those countries for their relief. But now, that
the Queen might be fully fixed and determined, and that he might go
with the greater glory and hope of success, he wanted the Archbishop's approbation of the lawfulness and expediency of this counsel, to be opened by him to the Queen; . . .[21]

The archbishop was discreet and made a wary answer. But,
Strype says, Piers, Bishop of Sarum and the queen's almoner,
had previously been consulted, the question being put as a question of divinity, not of policy, "Whether a prince may defend
the subjects of another prince from being forced to commit
idolatry." He had replied that it might be right to do so, but that
first all possible remedies must be tried, and that covetousness
and ambition must not enter into the decision. In addition, Strype
records an answer left in manuscript which he thought was written by the archbishop, and which dealt with the difficulties of
aiding the Netherlanders if they were really subjects of Spain,
since England did not recognize the right of Spain to aid the

[21]John Strype, *The Life and Acts of John Whitgift, D.D.* (Oxford, 1822),
Vol. I, Bk. III, p. 434.

Irish. However, he seemed to think that the Netherlanders might be helped if it could be decided that they were not Spanish subjects.[22]

Making King Henry V take the initiative in seeking advice from the Archbishop of Canterbury as to his moral justification for going to war is thus seen to have Elizabethan precedent. But in order to see the aptness of the picture of the archbishop's offering aid to Henry V for his wars in France, in confirmed expectation of Henry's saving the church from the difficulties of the bill urged by the Commons, it must be recalled that the years from 1584 onward were years of great difficulty for the established church of England. Parliament was threatening to concern itself with many ecclesiastical matters. George Paule in his life of Archbishop Whitgift waxed particularly indignant because these hecklings of the church reached their climax in the year of the Armada. But Strype in his life of Whitgift explains how the tactful churchman met the difficulties of the dangerous years:

This year, 1588, was the most dangerous year of the Queen's whole reign, both for her own and the kingdom's safety, and of the present Church of England. For a dreadful invasion of this land was now resolved upon, and vast preparations making for that purpose by the Pope, and the enraged proud King of Spain, and other Popish princes in league.

All the nation did their best for defense, and the archbishop determined that the church should not be behindhand. He wrote a circular letter to his bishops urging them to have the clergy find arms, assuring them that "their readiness herein would be a good means to stop the mouths of such, as did think those temporal blessings which God had in mercy bestowed upon them, [the Bishops and Clergy,] to be too much." Strype adds that Whitgift said he acted for certain considerations, and that "some of them surely were, to preserve the liberty of ecclesiastical persons, who had the privilege of taxing themselves; and to hinder

[22]*Ibid.*, Bk. III, pp. 434-39.

occasions of a *melius inquirendum*, and of racking the Clergy."[23] The Convocation of 1586 had granted a benevolence as well as a subsidy, but the Convocation of 1588 granted two subsidies. Strype records:

This was very well taken, and (for their readiness) got the ecclesiastics a reputation: the matter, no doubt, managed by the Archbishop's wisdom, industry, and influence with the Bishops and the rest of the Clergy. Sergeant Puckring, March the 17th, and the Attorney General, came from the Lords to the Lower House, and brought a bill from the Lords, for confirmation of this subsidy granted by the Clergy, . . . together with a bill likewise from the said Clergy, for horses, armour, and weapons: and gave a very special commendation of the same bills as things of very great importance.[24]

The story of the parliamentary and the Puritan attacks upon the established church is not in place here, but it should be noted that Convocation again granted a double subsidy in 1593, and the *quid pro quo* nature of the Convocation's generous contribution to war in *Henry V* must have seemed familiar to the Elizabethan.

When Henry asks the archbishop to argue his right "justly and religiously" since he does not want to go to war without the assurance of right and justice on his side, he speaks in the best Tudor tradition:

> And God forbid, my dear and faithful lord,
> That you should fashion, wrest, or bow your reading,
> Or nicely charge your understanding soul
> With opening titles miscreate, whose right
> Suits not in native colours with the truth; . . .

The horrors of war are too terrible, he continues, to be risked in an unworthy cause:

---

[23]*Ibid.*, Bk. III, pp. 524-26. Don Bernardino de Mendoza addressed the king of Spain in his *Theorique and Practise of Warre* (trans. by Sir Edward Hoby, 1597) and urged him first to give ear to the divines who are "to approve whether your cause bee just or no."

[24]Strype, Bk. III, p. 538.

> For God doth know how many now in health
> Shall drop their blood in approbation
> Of what your reverence shall incite us to.
> Therefore take heed how you impawn our person,
> How you awake our sleeping sword of war:
> We charge you, in the name of God take heed;
> For never two such kingdoms did contend
> Without much fall of blood; whose guiltless drops
> Are every one a woe, a sore complaint
> 'Gainst him whose wrongs give edge unto the swords
> That make such waste in brief mortality.[25]

Again he presses his question:

> May I with right and conscience make this claim?

And the archbishop replies:

> The sin upon my head, dread sovereign![26]

This model dramatization of the treatises on war is continued when the king addresses the French ambassadors who have asked whether they may speak their message from the dauphin plainly, for these treatises were insistent that the ruler must make war as the agent of public justice and not as passion's slave. Rightly Henry replies:

> We are no tyrant, but a Christian king;
> Unto whose grace our passion is as subject
> As are our wretches fetter'd in our prisons:
> Therefore with frank and with uncurbed plainness
> Tell us the Dauphin's mind.[27]

To the consequent demands made by the ambassadors with their taunting gift of the tennis balls from the dauphin, he replies with his decision "to put forth/ My rightful hand in a well-hallow'd cause." The justification of the war against France is thus established, and the conviction that his is a righteous war should be fixed in the mind of every playgoer.

[25] I, ii, 13-28.
[26] I, ii, 96, 97.
[27] I, ii, 241-45.

Though Canterbury might, in his ardor, exclaim, "The sin upon my head, dread sovereign!" the king could not so easily cast off his burden of responsibility, and it is the king who at the end of the first act ultimately decides for war. The king was the responsible agent of God's justice, and the whole Tudor philosophy of the state made such an assignment of power and responsibility inevitable. Thus Elizabeth in 1585 caused to be published *A Declaration of the Causes Mooving the Queene of England to Give Aide to the Defence of the People Afflicted and Oppressed in the Lowe Countries*, which began:

Although Kinges and Princes Soveraignes, owing their homage and service onely unto the Almightie God the king of al kings, are in that respect not bounde to yeeld account or render the reasons of their actions to any others but to God their only Soveraigne Lord: yet (though amongst the most ancient and Christian Monarches the same Lorde God having committed to us the Soveraignetie of this Realme of *Englande* and other our dominions, which wee holde immediately of the same Almightie Lord, and so thereby accountable onely to his divine Majestie) wee are notwithstanding this our prerogative at this time specially mooved . . . to publish not onely to our owne naturall loving Subjectes, but also to all others our neighbours, . . . what our intention is at this time, and upon what just and reasonable grounds we are mooved to give aid to our Neighbours the naturall people of the lowe Countries, . . .

The necessity for the king's having such authority was variously rationalized. Sarpi's *Free Schoole of Warre* argued:

God hath together with the *Majestie*, given unto the *Soveraigne* alone, the authority to make peace, warre, leagues, and allyances, as hee shall conceive it necessary and convenient: neither can any but hee know the circumstances of opportunities and needs, as nothing can governe and actuate the body but the Soule which *God* and *Nature* hath given it.[28]

The translator of Chelidonius' work *Of the Institution and Firste*

---

[28][Paola Sarpi], *The Free Schoole of Warre, or, A treatise, whether it be lawfull to beare armes for the services of a prince that is of a divers religion* (London, 1625), fols. G2ᵛ, G3ʳ.

THE VICTORIOUS ACTS OF KING HENRY V

Beginning of Christian Princes developed the analogy implied in this passage from *The Free Schoole of Warre:*

The anciente Philosophers . . . have ben of opinion, that the natural bodie of Man with the offices and duties of the parts thereof joyned and united togythere to a common function, do represent the lyvely image and very figure of a good and perfect commonwealth . . .[29]

As the soul determines the movements of the body, so, he said, the king or prince must determine the movements of the parts of the commonwealth. It is a figure commonplace in the literature of the time, and it is the figure connoted in Exeter's advice to the king about Scotland:

> While that the armed hand doth fight abroad
> The advised head defends itself at home:
> For government, though high and low and lower,
> Put into parts, doth keep in one consent,
> Congreeing in a full and natural close,
> Like music.[30]

Canterbury further embroiders the theme by the long analogy between state and beehive, an analogy likewise developed by Chelidonius from Pliny in the work already instanced, as well as in the well-known passage in Lyly's *Euphues.*[31] My sole interest in such analogies as present is, however, to show how they expressed the Tudor idea of the state in which the king was the sole responsible head and the sole responsible agent for making war.

The matter of the king's responsibility was of practical as well as theoretical importance in Elizabethan England, for it answered one of the most controversial questions of the day, the question of the soldier's responsibility for the justice of the cause in which he fought. This answer is given explicitly and at length by

[29]*Op. cit.*, trans. by James Chillester (London, 1571), in dedication to Queen Elizabeth.

[30]I, ii, 178-83.

[31]For an exposition of this analogy see James E. Phillips, *The State in Shakespeare's Greek and Roman Plays* (New York, 1940), pp. 3-8 *et passim.*

Shakespeare later on in the play, but it must be discussed here in connection with the king's responsibility. It was the principle at issue in 1587 when Sir William Stanley surrendered the town of Deventer to the Spanish. The case became a *cause célèbre*. I quote Martin Haile's account of the event:

Appointed governor on the 24th November, 1586, Stanley seems to have lost little time in entering into communication with J. B. de Tassis, the former Spanish ambassador in Paris, and through him with the Duke of Parma. His explanation, as given in the presence of Tassis to the assembled townspeople in the marketplace of Deventer, being that he did not hold the town for the Queen of England, but for the States, whom he knew in his conscience to be rebels to their king, and that therefore, he felt bound to "render unto Caesar the things that were Caesar's," and to deliver up the town to the King of Spain.[32]

Cardinal Allen at once proceeded to defend Stanley in a book published in Antwerp in 1587 as *The Copie of a Letter Written by M. Doctor Allen: Concerning the Yeelding Up, of the Citie of Daventrie, unto his Catholic Majestie, by Sir William Stanley, Knight*. It sermonized on the text of Stanley's own defense. Allen accepted the traditional concepts. The causes of war must be just. War is the prince's responsibility. The subject must obey his king, though any actions other than military actions are his private responsibility, and he must account for them to God. He has no right to surrender himself or the king's property. But, the Catholic spokesman argued, these principles are not here in question. The present war of England in the Low Countries is not just; it is not being fought in defense of England. A subject is not bound to obey his king in opposition to his God. The soldier may die at any moment and must be ready to answer for the justice of his cause. Ever since the publication of Queen Elizabeth's excommunication and deprivation by the pope no war could be proclaimed by her, however just, because war must be proclaimed by one with supreme power to do so. He turned to England for examples of those who had refused to obey their

[32]Martin Haile, *An Elizabethan Cardinal: William Allen*, pp. 290-91.

nominal rulers from King John to Jane Grey. In regard to King John he asked:

what disgrace, or shame was it, for al the chiefe Lordes of our countrie, to revolt from King John, in his dayes? and absolutely to denie him ayde, and assistence, even in his lawful warres, until he returned againe to the obedience of the Sea Apostolike, and were absolved from the censures of the same, which he justly incurred?[33]

The important conclusion at which Cardinal Allen arrived is succinctly stated:

For that to revolt, is of itselfe, lawful or unlawful, honorable or otherwise, according to the justice, or injustice of the cause, or difference of the person, from or to whom the revolt is made.[34]

Furthermore, he asserted that whatever is unjustly obtained must be returned to its rightful owner, and Spain was the rightful ruler of the Low Countries. Therefore in returning Deventer to Spain, Stanley had been acting justly. Ultimately he thus made the pope the arbiter over the nation's rulers and made the individual soldier the supreme judge of the cause in which he fought.

The most direct answer to Cardinal Allen was made in *A Briefe Discoverie of Doctor Allen's Seditious Drifts, Concerning the Yeelding Up of the Towne of Deventer*, the address to the reader of which was signed "G.D." The author argued that Sir William Stanley and his fellows did not obtain Deventer from the King of Spain. Moreover, he continued:

howsoever the towne and fortes were obteined, yet the subject being tyed to his *Prince* by allegeance and oth, and having upon that othe received from his Prince, or her lawfull deputy, any place of charge to keepe and hold to her use, is not to enquire into her right, how justly or unjustly she hath gotten or keepeth it, but to looke into his owne charge and othe, whereof he is bound to give account. Yea suppose the Queenes Majestie had by violence, fraude, or in-

---

[33]*Op. cit.* (Antwerp, 1587), reprinted as *Cardinal Allen's Defence of Sir William Stanley's Surrender of Deventer January 29, 1586-7*, ed. T. Heywood (Chetham Society, XXV; 1851), p. 26.

[34]*Ibid.,* pp. 26-27.

justice entred upon those places, and so deteined them from the k. of Spaine: yet the same *justice*, which giveth unto every man his owne, and in such case tyeth her to restitution of whatsoever she wrong-fully withholdeth, yet the same *justice* (I say) giveth her subjectes no such authoritie over her, as to be judges of her just or unjust dealing, much lesse to make themselves correctors, or executors of justice against her upon their owne judgement, and at their owne pleasure.[35]

The author answered the points made by Cardinal Allen, one by one, but this quotation gives the bases of his argument.

Now in the first scene of Act IV of *Henry V* Shakespeare represents the king, unrecognized, mingling with his common soldiers and exploring with them this fundamental problem raised by the dispute over the surrender of Deventer. Simpson in 1874 said that this conversation of the king with his soldiers "casuistically refuted" the scruples which Cardinal Allen had striven to sow about fighting Catholic enemies in an unjust war and made a distinction between political and religious obligation by laying down the principle that "Every subject's duty is the King's; but every subject's soul is his own." He then went on to point out that the historical Henry had not been noted for his religious tolerance as this Henry of Shakespeare's creation might have been. But actually the problem that both Allen and Shake-speare's Henry V discussed had nothing to do with religious tolerance. Nor does Shakespeare answer in this play Allen's basic contention that the queen had no authority to make war because she had been excommunicated and deprived by the pope. What Shakespeare's Henry V discusses is the general problem of the king's responsibility for deciding to make war and the subject's duty to obey his king. Thus we hear:

KING HENRY. . . . methinks I could not die anywhere so contented as in the king's company, his cause being just and his quarrel hon-ourable.

WILLIAMS. That's more than we know.

BATES. Ay, or more than we should seek after; for we know enough

---

[35]*Op. cit.* (London, 1588), pp. 13-14.

if we know we are the king's subjects. If his cause be wrong, our obedience to the king wipes the crime of it out of us.

WILLIAMS. But if the cause be not good, the king himself hath a heavy reckoning to make; when all those legs and arms and heads, chopped off in a battle, shall join together at the latter day, and cry all "We died at such a place"; some swearing, some crying for a surgeon, some upon their wives left poor behind them, some upon the debts they owe, some upon their children rawly left.[36]

So far the argument has served but to emphasize the Tudor position, a position which opposed that of Allen. The responsibility is the king's; the duty of the subject is to his king.

But Shakespeare represents Williams as posing a further question when he continues:

I am afeard there are few die well that die in battle; for how can they charitably dispose of any thing when blood is their argument? Now, if these men do not die well, it will be a black matter for the king that led them to it, who to disobey were against all proportion of subjection.[37]

King Henry replies by making clear the distinction between the private and the military crimes of soldiers. Perhaps the simplest statement of this distinction was made by Sir William Segar in his famous work on *Honor, Military and Civill*, where he said:

First it is to be knowen, that some crimes be common, and punishable in all men: and some are proper to men of war onely: of the first are forgeries, adulterie, publique and private violence, sedition, manslaughter, burning of houses, treason, sacrilege and other enormities: for whosoever committeth any such offence, whether he be a man of warre or not, the punishment due is all one. Crimes proper to souldiers, are such only as are committed contrarie to discipline Militarie, . . . whereby men are made obedient, and instructed in all such qualities as are required in a souldier.[38]

Segar listed cowardice, treason, and disobedience as military

---

[36]IV, i, 127-43. F. S. Boas, "The Soldier in Elizabethan and Later English Drama," discusses this passage from much the same point of view as Simpson.
[37]IV, i, 143-49.
[38]*Op. cit.* (London, 1602), p. 13.

crimes but reserved special condemnation for going over to the enemy or yielding a stronghold to the enemy.

There is, therefore, no religious tolerance in question in King Henry's words when he concludes that "Every subject's duty is the king's; but every subject's soul is his own." He is merely stating the difference between the soldier as a man responsible to God and as a soldier responsible only for obedience to his king. The king's argument in the play makes clear his meaning:

the king is not bound to answer the particular endings of his soldiers, the father of his son, nor the master of his servant; for they purpose not their death when they purpose their services. Besides there is no king, be his cause never so spotless, if it come to the arbitrement of swords, can try it out with all unspotted soldiers. Some, peradventure, have on them the guilt of premeditated and contrived murder; some, of beguiling virgins with the broken seals of perjury; some, making the wars their bulwark, that have before gored the gentle bosom of peace with pillage and robbery.

He continues his philosophizing by showing God as eternally taking vengeance for sin:

Now, if these men have defeated the law and outrun native punishment, though they can outstrip men, they have no wings to fly from God: war is his beadle, war is his vengeance; so that here men are punished for before-breach of the king's laws in now the king's quarrels: . . .

After his long exposition of the nature of private sin, for which each man is responsible to God, he then concludes:

Then, if they die unprovided, no more is the king guilty of their damnation than he was before guilty of those impieties for the which they are now visited. Every subject's duty is the king's; but every subject's soul is his own.[39]

The king then introduces another matter discussed by Cardinal Allen, the need for the soldier to be prepared to meet death and to see that his conscience is washed clean. Cardinal Allen had made this necessity an excuse for advocating the subject's right

[39]IV, i, 159-83.

to judge his king and the cause for which he fought. Shakespeare does not let any such idea intrude, going back rather to the warning that was common in the books dealing with the philosophy of war, the warning to the soldier to be ready to meet his God:

Therefore should every soldier in the wars do as every sick man in his bed, wash every mote out of his conscience; and dying so, death is to him advantage; or not dying, the time was blessedly lost wherein such preparation was gained: and in him that escapes, it were not sin to think that, making God so free an offer, he let him outlive that day to see his greatness, and to teach others how they should prepare.[40]

Williams shows that he has been a good pupil, and it is to be hoped that the reader has by this time already learned the lesson that Shakespeare through King Henry took so much time and pains to teach, for Williams summarizes: "'Tis certain, every man that dies ill, the ill upon his own head; the king is not to answer it."[41] The soldier is thus responsible to the king as a soldier, but as a man he is responsible to God. Conversely, the king is responsible for the cause in which he orders his soldiers to fight, but he is not responsible for their sins as private persons.

The horrors of war make the king's responsibility for waging war a heavy one, and his chief concern must be the righteousness of his cause, for God determines the outcome. Geoffrey Gates in his *Defence of Militarie Profession* gave long consideration to this matter, affirming that "it is he onely that beareth the sword of vengeance, that striketh in the battell, and giveth the victory to himselfe."[42] De Loque asserted that victory "dependeth not of the multitude of fighting men, but of the grace and favour of God."[43] It was a commonplace in the military books of the Elizabethan period, this assertion that the king proposes war, but God gives the victory, not to numbers of soldiers

[40]IV, i, 183-92.

[41]IV, i, 193-94.

[42]*Op. cit.*, p. 16. Gates calls God the "high generall of all warres."

[43]B. de Loque, *Discourses of Warre and Single Combat*, trans. J. Eliot (London, 1591), p. 21.

but to the righteous cause. War is the scourge of God, they quoted over and over again. It is no wonder, then, that Shakespeare's Henry V out-Henries the historical Henry in his recognition of his dependence upon God as the giver of victory. At times his references to God seem a little out of place in the context. For instance, as he returns taunt for taunt to the dauphin anent the tennis balls, the cynical and angry speech closes with a reference that could only apply to a personally vindictive God:

> many a thousand widows
> Shall his mock mock out of their dear husbands;
> Mock mothers from their sons, mock castles down;
> And some are yet ungotten and unborn
> That shall have cause to curse the Dauphin's scorn.
> But this lies all within the will of God, . . .[44]

Before the battle of Agincourt we hear him taking the name of God in vain as he speaks greedily of honor:

> The fewer men, the greater share of honour.
> God's will! I pray thee, wish not one man more.
>
> .   .   .   .
>
> No, faith, my coz, wish not a man from England:
> God's peace! I would not lose so great an honour
> As one man more, methinks, would share from me,
> For the best hope I have.[45]

Yet after the battle his gloating becomes a *Jubilate*. Ten thousand Frenchmen slain, one hundred and twenty-six princes and nobles dead; eight thousand and four hundred knights, esquires, and gentlemen killed. He recites the names of the greatest. And of the English only four "of name" slain. Then he chants the response:

> O God! thy arm was here;
> And not to us, but to thy arm alone,
> Ascribe we all.

[44]I, ii, 284-87.
[45]IV, iii, 22-33.

Again he gloats:

> When, without stratagem,
> But in plain shock and even play of battle,
> Was ever known so great and little loss
> On one part and the other?

And again comes the response:

> Take it, God,
> For it is none but thine!

But the final triumph of piety comes as the king proclaims death to anyone who would steal the honor from God:

> And be it death proclaimed through our host
> To boast of this or take that praise from God
> Which is his only.[46]

The drastic order is given without benefit of Holinshed, but Henry's ordering the *Non nobis* and the *Te deum* after battle is recorded in the chronicle, as is his insistence upon his return to England that the people give thanks only to God. This emphasis upon God as the God of battles, the justicer among nations, was the basic premise in the philosophy of war which made a just cause the best hope of victory.

But the consideration of war must inevitably bring also a consideration of peace. "The Lord will bless his people with peace" was a promise as comforting to the Elizabethans as to other God-fearing peoples. Peace builds and war destroys. Peace conserves and war corrupts. Peace brings plenty and war dearth. Peace is the nurse of arts and sciences; war leads to brutishness. Peace brings happiness; war mourning and misery. The tale is old; the reality ever new. Always the blessings of peace are more prized as the horrors of war become more imminent. I could quote almost innumerable passages to illustrate the praises of peace written or read in sixteenth-century England, but an inclusive description quoted from the translation of Chelidonius' "Treatise of Peace and Warre" will serve to represent them:

[46]IV, viii, 108-18.

Being as it were the spring and fountaine of all humaine felicitie, governer and nursse of all that the universall worlde containeth. Peace I say giveth being and strengthe to all things: shee keepeth and conserveth them in suche sorte, as without hir aide and helpe in one instante they would be overthrowne, destroyed and spoyled: for by hir aide the lande is tilled, the fieldes made flourishing and greene, the beastes feede quietly, Cities be edified, things ruinate be repaired, antiquities be augmented, lawes be in their force, the common wealth flourisheth, religion is maintained, equitie is regarded, humanitie is embraced, handie craftes men be set a woorke, the poore live at ease, the riche men prosper, learning and sciences be taught, with all libertie, youthe learne vertue, olde men take their rest, virgines be happely married, Cities and Townes be peopled, and the world is multiplied.[47]

In a play about war it was inevitable that Shakespeare too should hymn the praise of peace, and it was fitting that to the peacemaker of the play, the Duke of Burgundy, the part should be given. Of the kings of England and France he demands:

> Why that the naked, poor, and mangled Peace,
> Dear nurse of arts, plenties, and joyful births,
> Should not in this best garden of the world,
> Our fertile France, put up her lovely visage?

Peace has long been chased from France, he mourns:

> Her vine, the merry cheerer of the heart,
> Unpruned dies; . . . .
> The even mead, that erst brought sweetly forth
> The freckled cowslip, burnet, and green clover,
> Wanting the scythe, all uncorrected, rank,
> Conceives by idleness, and nothing teems
> But hateful docks, rough thistles, kecksies, burrs,
> Losing both beauty and utility.
> And as our vineyards, fallows, meads, and hedges,
> Defective in their natures, grow to wildness,
> Even so our houses and ourselves and children
> Have lost, or do not learn for want of time,
> The sciences that should become our country,

[47]The treatise is "annexed" to the *Most Excellent Hystorie of the Institution . . . of Christian Princes* as chap. xii. See p. 156.

> But grow like savages, as soldiers will
> That nothing do but meditate on blood,
> To swearing and stern looks, defus'd attire
> And every thing that seems unnatural.[48]

But no matter how excellent the beauties of peace, the Elizabethan realist recognized that peace at any price was not to be desired. Barnabe Riche might have been writing in 1938 rather than in 1604 when he admonished:

This olde Canticle, *Da pacem in diebus nostris*, hath sometimes bene too much imbraced, and the bare motion and sound of *Peace*, is so sweete and pleasing to the fearefull and faint harted, that to patch and peece it up, they neglect and set aside all occasions, giving an enemie those advantages, that many times are not to be redeemed. . . .

I will not say but in the time of Parlies, perswasion may doe much, but it is best then to perswade, when there is force to command: for in the time of Parlies and Treaties of peace, the Conquerour and he that is of greatest power, doth rather give than receive conditions.[49]

And Riche's *Allarme to England* had pointed out in 1578 the corroding and corrupting power of long-continued peace.

This realist's view of peace was shared by most of the writers on the military art, but it was also pointed out that God used peace as well as war as the instrument of his avenging justice. Geoffrey Gates warned:

When the Lord meaneth to plague a wicked nation for sinne and to translate them to the power and scepter of another nation: then he filleth them with the fatnesse of the earth, and geeveth them peace that they may rotten in idlenesse, and become of dulle wittes, slowe of courage, weak handed, and feeble kneed: . . .[50]

And we remember Sidney's description of Helen, Queen of Corinth, who so remarkably resembled Queen Elizabeth:

she using so straunge, and yet so well-succeeding a temper, that she made her people by peace, warlike; her courtiers by sports, learned,

---

[48]V, ii, 34-48.
[49]*The Fruites of Long Experience*, pp. 69-70.
[50]*Op. cit.*, p. 20.

her Ladies by Love, chast. For by continuall martiall exercises without bloud, she made them perfect in that bloudy art.[51]

Ironically Shakespeare makes the dauphin the spokesman for the canonical doctrine:

> It is most meet we arm us 'gainst the foe;
> For peace itself should not so dull a kingdom,
> Though war nor no known quarrel were in question,
> But that defences, musters, preparations,
> Should be maintain'd, assembled, and collected,
> As were a war in expectation.[52]

It is the dauphin too who advises:

> In cases of defence 'tis best to weigh
> The enemy more mighty than he seems: . . .[53]

And it is the dauphin who whines out the truth:

> By faith and honour,
> Our madams mock at us, and plainly say
> Our mettle is bred out; and they will give
> Their bodies to the lust of English youth
> To new-store France with bastard warriors.[54]

The seventh scene of the third act, the pre-battle scene among the French, where we hear the dauphin praising his horse and desiring to recite the sonnet he once made in honor of that favored darling, gives us, however, a revealing picture of the weakness and effeminacy of the French, of their too great concern with the frivolities of peace, and of their consequent degeneration. And the constable exhorting his armies makes light of their task, despising the English, and contradicting in every word the principle expounded by the dauphin of not under-estimating the enemy:

---

[51]The 1590 *Arcadia*, ed. A. Feuillerat (Cambridge, 1922), Bk. II, chap. xxi, p. 283.

[52]II, iv, 16-20.

[53]II, iv, 43-44.

[54]III, v, 27-31.

> Do but behold yon poor and starved band,
> And your fair show shall suck away their souls,
> Leaving them but the shales and husks of men.
> There is not work enough for all our hands;
> Scarce blood enough in all their sickly veins
> To give each naked curtle-axe a stain, . . .[55]

To the righteous cause God gives the victory. He had indeed plagued a wicked nation by filling them with the fatness of the land until they waxed rotten in idleness, dull of wit, slow of courage, weak-handed, and feeble-kneed. The French did ill to despise their hungry and disease-ridden enemies; they did ill to neglect the arts of war for the enticements of peace. For their sins God translated them to the power and sceptre of another nation. Shakespeare's *Henry V* acts out the thesis of Geoffrey Gates and the other Elizabethan expounders of war.

But as a war play, *Henry V*, while developing in plot and dialogue the Elizabethan philosophy of war, also makes conspicuous use of the formal procedures of war. However just the war, nearly all writers insisted upon one formality as essential to the right conduct of war; this was the formal "denouncing" or declaration of war. Alexander Leighton went so far as to insist that a war might be lawful in itself and yet be unlawfully undertaken if the warring power failed 1) to declare the causes of the war, 2) to demand reparation for wrongs, and 3) to denounce the war.[56] Queen Elizabeth, it should be noted, conformed to this prescribed course of action. On October 1, 1585, she caused to be published *A Declaration of the Causes Mooving the Queene of England to Give Aide to the Defence of the People Afflicted and Oppressed in the Lowe Countries* in which all the machinations of the Scots and the Guises and the continuous plotting of the Spanish were recounted, together with the history of the attempts of the queen to keep the peace, even though she prefaced this declaration by insisting that she was responsible to God alone, as I have already pointed out. Likewise in 1596

---

[55] IV, ii, 16-21.

[56] [Alexander Leighton], *Speculum belli sacri* (n.p., 1624), p. 38.

there was published *A Declaration of the Causes Moving the Queenes Majestie of England, to Prepare and Send a Navy to the Seas, for the Defence of Her Realmes against the King of Spaines Forces*, though in this case Lord Howard and the Earl of Essex spoke jointly for the queen.

Halle had given credit to Henry V for adhering to this formality of denouncing the war, saying:

The kyng like a wise prince and pollitique governor, entendyng to observe the auncient ordres of famous kynges and renoumed potentates used aswel among Paynimes as Christians, whiche is, not to invade another mannes territory without open war and the cause of the same to hym published and declared, dispatched into Fraunce his uncle the duke of Excester, . . .[57]

Holinshed represents the king as sending Antelope, his pursuivant at arms, to the French king to demand restitution of his rights and to announce his determination to fight for his rights, though he asks that the French king save the shedding of blood by yielding to his demands. Shakespeare follows Halle rather than Holinshed by making Exeter the messenger who demands that the French king divest himself of

> The borrow'd glories that by gift of heaven,
> By law of nature and of nations, longs
> To him and to his heirs; . . .[58]

Presenting a manuscript pedigree to substantiate the English claims, Exeter then proclaims the determination of King Henry, even as he pleads that the horrors of war may be avoided

> And bids you, in the bowels of the Lord,
> Deliver up the crown, and to take mercy
> On the poor souls for whom this hungry war
> Opens his vasty jaws; and on your head
> Turning the widows' tears, the orphans' cries,
> The dead men's blood, the pining maidens' groans,
> For husbands, fathers, and betrothed lovers,
> That shall be swallow'd in this controversy.[59]

[57]Halle, *op. cit.*, fol. 41.
[58]II, iv, 79-81.
[59]II, iv, 102-9.

THE VICTORIOUS ACTS OF KING HENRY V

To make sure that the formalities have been observed and the war denounced Exeter concludes:

> This is his claim, his threat'ning, and my message.

Again, before Harfleur, the demand for surrender follows the formal denouncing of war as King Henry discharges himself of all responsibility and appeals to the men of Harfleur to submit:

> If not, why, in a moment look to see
> The blind and bloody soldier with foul hand
> Defile the locks of your shrill-shrieking daughters;
> Your fathers taken by the silver beards,
> And their most reverend heads dash'd to the walls;
> Your naked infants spitted upon pikes,
> Whiles the mad mothers with their howls confus'd
> Do break the clouds, as did the wives of Jewry
> At Herod's bloody-hunting slaughtermen.

Against these pictures of the horrors of war, he demands:

> What say you? Will you yield, and this avoid?
> Or, guilty in defence, be thus destroy'd?[60]

It may be noted that the men of Harfleur yielded to a mercy which was not recorded of Henry V, but which was much praised in the behavior of the Earl of Essex toward the people of Cadiz in 1596.

Another formal procedure much admired in the records of Thucydides and other historians and generally recommended by the military theorists was the oration addressed by the general to his troops on the eve of battle. It was not, of course, considered legally and morally necessary, as was the "denouncing" of war, but it was generally thought to be the best way to keep up what we should call the morale of the troops. In his *Path-way to Military Practise*, dedicated to Queen Elizabeth in 1587, Barnabe Riche, discussing devices to keep troops advancing, ranked the general's oration even higher than burning the ships behind them. His encomium is descriptive of the ideal oration:

[60]III, iii, 33-43.

it kindleth the mind and humaine passions of a man, it taketh away feare, it ingendreth obstinacie to fight, it discovereth deceiptes, it showeth perrilles and the way to avoide them, it prayeth, it promiseth rewardes, it reprehendeth, it threateneth, it incourageth the mindes eyther of hope, eyther else of dispaire.[61]

The French Academie, discussing the requisites for a good general, said:

there is no doubt but that in a matter of great importaunce, the grave exhortations of a Generall, grounded upon good reasons and examples greatlie encourage and hearten a whole armie, in so much that it will make them as hardie as Lions, that before were as fearfull as sheepe.[62]

Richard Crompton dedicated his *Mansion of Magnanimity* to the Earl of Essex in 1599 with special praise for the achievements of the earl in his late valiant service at Cadiz, opening his work with "an oration to be made by the general to the whole armie afore the battel."

Shakespeare uses this device of the oration of the general to his troops before battle to emphasize the rightness of the English cause and the valor of the English armies in contrast with the over-confidence of the French, which is but a cloak to hide their weakness. King Henry delivers two formal orations in the play, the first before the final attack on Harfleur, the second before the battle of Agincourt. A whole scene is given to the speech before Harfleur, in which the king encourages, inspires, and exhorts his soldiers:

> Once more unto the breech, dear friends, once more,
> Or close the wall up with our English dead.
> In peace there's nothing so becomes a man
> As modest stillness and humility:
> But when the blast of war blows in our ears,
> Then imitate the action of the tiger;
> . . . . . . On, on, you noblest English!
> Whose blood is fet from fathers of war-proof;

[61]*Op. cit.*, fol. H2ʳ.
[62]Peter de la Primaudaye, *op. cit.*, trans. T. B. (1586), p. 775.

> Fathers that, like so many Alexanders,
> Have in these parts from morn till even fought,
> . . . . The game's afoot:
> Follow your spirit; and upon this charge
> Cry, "God for Harry, England, and Saint George!"[63]

Before Agincourt the king's oration is ostensibly addressed to Westmoreland, who is commanded to speak the king's message to the troops:

> Rather proclaim it, Westmoreland, through my host,
> That he which hath no stomach to this fight,
> Let him depart; his passport shall be made,
> And crowns for convoy put into his purse:
> We would not die in that man's company
> That fears his fellowship to die with us.
> This day is call'd the feast of Crispian:
> He that outlives this day, and comes safe home,
> Will stand a tip-toe when this day is nam'd,
> And rouse him at the name of Crispian.

Old men will yearly recall their feats to their neighbors; the names of the leaders will be freshly remembered. Till the end of the world the day shall be remembered. Today all those fighting are fighting as brothers:

> We few, we happy few, we band of brothers;
> For he to-day that sheds his blood with me
> Shall be my brother; . . .

Those at home will feel deprived and humble when any speak who fought in this battle. It is a great speech to rouse men to prowess, and at the end Henry says farewell:

> You know your places: God be with you all![64]

In sharp contrast is the speech of the Constable of France to his men before the battle. He despises the enemy and belittles the task before his troops. There is nothing in what he says to make them lions:

[63]III, i.
[64]IV, iii, 34-78.

> To horse, you gallant princes! straight to horse!
> Do but behold yon poor and starved band,
>
> . . . .
>
> There is not work enough for all our hands;
> Scarce blood enough in all their sickly veins
> To give each naked curtle-axe a stain,
>
> . . . .
>
> A very little little let us do, ...
> And all is done.[65]

And Grandpré continues the disdainful oration which contradicts all the requirements of the approved exhortation to the troops:

> Why do you stay so long, my lords of France?
> Yon island carrions, desperate of their bones,
> Ill-favour'dly become the morning field: . . .[66]

Shakespeare, as was his custom, has here used the prescribed vehicle to make clear the characters of those who tread his stage. He has, incidentally, it may be said, incorporated into these orations the descriptions of conditions as Holinshed wrote of them.

It is, of course, as general of his armies and not as king that Henry addresses his troops, though it is as king that he declares war. The distinction should be kept in mind as we consider the next aspect of war dealt with in *Henry V*, army discipline. In addressing the governor of Harfleur, Henry speaks of himself as a soldier, "A name that in my thoughts becomes me best," and wooing the French princess in proud humility, he says, "I speak to thee plain soldier." Shakespeare describes him in the fourth prologue mingling with his soldiers:

> For forth he goes and visits all his host,
> Bids them good-morrow with a modest smile,
> And calls them brothers, friends and countrymen.

But nevertheless Henry V is far from democratic in the modern

[65]IV, ii, 15-34.
[66]IV, ii, 38-40.

sense of the word. He reckons the losses of the French as high at Agincourt because, of the ten thousand men lost, only sixteen hundred are mercenaries:

> The rest are princes, barons, lords, knights, squires,
> And gentlemen of blood and quality.[67]

He reckons the English losses as light because only four "of name" have been slain and "of all other men/ But five and twenty." Nor is his much-quoted speech before Agincourt democratic in the modern sense:

> We few, we happy few, we band of brothers;
> For he to-day that sheds his blood with me
> Shall be my brother; be he ne'er so vile
> This day shall gentle his condition;[68]

for it is not a declaration of the brotherhood of man, but of the brotherhood of soldiers. It does, however, recognize that brotherhood and accepts the mingled blood of great and small on the battlefield as a common offering.

This picture of the soldier king is the more impressive by contrast with the picture of the leaders of the French armies. The Constable of France despises his common soldiers. Addressing the peers before Agincourt he comments that

> 'Tis positive 'gainst all exceptions, lords,
> That our superfluous lackeys and our peasants,
> Who in unnecessary action swarm
> About our squares of battle, were enow
> To purge this field of such a hilding foe, . . .[69]

And Montjoy, come to ask leave to bury the French dead, desires with the same arrogance

> To sort our nobles from our common men;
> For many of our princes—woe the while!—
> Lie drown'd and soak'd in mercenary blood;

[67]IV, viii, 91-92.
[68]IV, iii, 60-63.
[69]IV, ii, 25-29.

> So do our vulgar drench their peasant limbs
> In blood of princes; . . .[70]

It is a far cry from Henry's "he to-day that sheds his blood with me/ Shall be my brother;" and it must have been written to mark the sharp contrast.

However kindly Henry's mingling with his soldiers, he is presented as a stern disciplinarian. We first see him in this role when, on the eve of his departure for France, he is called upon to deal with treason, the greatest of military sins. Shakespeare represents the three traitors—the Earl of Cambridge, Lord Scroop, and Sir Thomas Grey—as having accepted pay from France to kill their king. As a matter of fact, the Earl of Cambridge seems to have been led by his hopes of securing the succession to his own heirs rather than by avarice, but Shakespeare has him say merely:

> For me, the gold of France did not seduce,
> Although I did admit it as a motive
> The sooner to effect what I intended: . . .

Henry's grim humor in handing the traitors warrants instead of commissions seems like something out of the *Spanish Tragedy*, but he is quite in the best tradition when he disavows private vengeance as a motive:

> Touching our person seek we no revenge;
> But we our kingdom's safety must so tender,
> Whose ruin you have sought, that to her laws
> We do deliver you.

The articles of war which have come down to us from different times and different nations are remarkably alike. Leicester's preamble to the *Lawes and Ordinances* established in 1586 for the government of his forces in the Low Countries announced realistically the reasons underlying all such regulations:

seeing that martial discipline above all things (proper to men of warre) is by us at this time most to be followed, as well for the advancement of Gods glorie, as honourablie to governe this Armie in

[70]IV, vii, 76-80.

good order: And least the evil inclined (pleading simplicitie) should cover any wicked facte by ignorance: Therefore these martiall Ordinances and Lawes following are established and published.[71]

Henry V's army in France was governed by articles of war which Shakespeare probably knew. But because soldiers are much the same in every generation and the "evil inclined" commit the same wicked deeds, the soldiers of Henry V were very like Elizabethan soldiers, and the articles of war are very like Elizabethan articles of war. What is most interesting in the play of *Henry V* as a war play, however, is the use of the violations of the articles of war to round out the careers of Prince Hal's merry men. Shakespeare allowed Falstaff to go to Arthur's bosom like any "christom child," but he was not so kind to the others. There is tenderness in the comedy of Falstaff's death, but no pity tempers the comedy of Bardolph and Pistol and Nym.

The camp boy introduces them as military characters;

For Bardolph, he is white-livered and red-faced; by the means whereof a' faces it out, but fights not. For Pistol, he hath a killing tongue and a quiet sword; . . . For Nym, . . . a' never broke any man's head but his own, and that was against a post when he was drunk. They will steal anything and call it purchase. Bardolph stole a lute-case, bore it twelve leagues, and sold it for three half-pence. Nym and Bardolph are sworn brothers in filching, and in Calais they stole a fire-shovel; . . .[72]

They are, in the words of Gower, "slanders of the age."[73]

The articles of war generally give first consideration to the spiritual welfare of the soldier and to the preservation of churches and other religious institutions. The first of Henry's laws for his army was unusually specific, however, decreeing that anyone removing without the permission of the constable of the army any church goods was to be hanged, and the stolen goods returned to the church. A special provision was added:

[71]*STC* 7288.
[72]III, ii, 32-47.
[73]III, vi, 82.

we moreover ordain, that no one, under pain of death, shall dare irreverently to touch the sacrament of the Eucharist, nor the pyx or box in which the said sacrament is contained.[74]

It is Bardolph who is chosen to add to the gayety of war by stealing the pix, and he is hanged for it. Pistol described the stolen object as a *pax* or *packs*, but editors have identified it properly and described it just as it was described in Henry V's articles of war, though no one seems to have investigated the articles of war as a source.

Like most articles of war, those of Henry V also tried to legislate temptation into keeping its distance. Whores must stay away —a league at least—said Henry. Nevertheless Bardolph was said to be "a bawd, a cut-purse."[75]

Failing to turn over his prisoner was also a crime in the England of Henry V as well as in that of Elizabeth. Shakespeare gives a whole scene to Pistol's compounding with his French prisoner and pocketing the redemption money.[76] In commenting on this scene the camp boy gives us word of the third of the old trio:

Bardolph and Nym . . . are both hanged; and so would this be if he durst steal any thing adventurously.[77]

Actually Pistol escapes hanging and steals away to England to do some more stealing, he hopes.

It is an unkind end that Shakespeare gives to these former boon companions of the king, and there is no indication that the king acknowledges them in any way as old acquaintances.

Striking an officer is another offence reckoned with in the articles of war, and Shakespeare makes more comedy about the violation of this law as the king talks unrecognized with the

[74]Francis Grose, *Military Antiquities Respecting a History of the English Army* (London, 1778), II, 65-83, contains a translation of the statutes of Henry V in time of war. W. Y. Baldry, "Early Articles of War," *Journal of the Society of Army Historical Research*, IV (Sheffield, 1925), 166-67 offers a bibliography of articles of war.

[75]III, vi, 62.

[76]IV, iv.

[77]IV, iv, 71-75.

soldier Williams and then exchanges glove for glove with him to be redeemed at a future encounter. The king does not let Williams meet the fate which the disciplinarian Fluellen would prescribe, for to Fluellen "if there is any martial law in the world," Williams should answer with his life for having struck that worthy captain while he wore the king's glove in his cap at the king's command. This practical joke at poor Williams' expense does not amuse the modern reader much more than the king's handing out warrants instead of commissions to the traitor nobles, but the king evidently feels that filling a glove with crowns is ample repayment for having put a man in jeopardy. Williams does not join the king in his hilarious laughter, how-ever.[78] And incidentally, I would point out that the king's action is not democratic. The unbloodied Williams has not yet entered the brotherhood of those who shed their blood in a common cause.

Other extra-historical scenes introduced by Shakespeare are those relating to wordy battles between the captains of divers nationalities—Irish, Scotch, Welsh, English. I agree with the Arden editor that it is not likely that these gentlemen were intro-duced "to symbolize the union of the component parts of the United Kingdom." They certainly are not united, and they much better illustrate the condition which Leicester spoke of in his articles of war, though he was not referring to the same nations. Leicester ordered that

whereas sundrie nations are to serve with us in these warres, so as through diversitie of languages occasion of many controversies may arise or happen to growe:

therefore all private revenge was expressly prohibited, and all complaints ordered to be referred to the captain for settlement.[79] But having made the violations of the articles of war the occa-sion for comic interludes which rid Henry V of the companions who were with him when he himself was a part of the comic

---

[78]IV, i, 209-226; IV, vii, 124-69; IV, viii, 24-74.

[79]No. 17 of the *Lawes and Ordinances*. See Grose, II, 66, note.

interludes of *Henry IV*, Shakespeare also builds a set of comic episodes to present a parody of the battle of the books which was being waged over "the school of war." Even in the 1590's the fight between the defenders of the long-bow and the admirers of the weapons brought into being by the introduction of gunpowder was not yet a thing of the past. And there were new quarrels over new issues, most notably the dispute as to whether the ancients or the moderns were the better authorities on military affairs, and the dispute as to whether theory or practice was to be preferred as a school of war. Generally speaking, the advocates of the long-bow and classical authority favored the study of theory as a preparation for the military man, while the defenders of weapons which used gunpowder and knowledge of current Spanish and French military practice urged experience as the best teacher in war. There was some crossing of the line, but in general the opposing ranks were aligned in this fashion. Shakespeare did not bring up the matter of gunpowder for discussion in the supposed time of Henry V, but the other two issues are the subject of much discourse, and it was Fluellen against the field.

To understand the battle waged by Fluellen, however, it is necessary to digress to the consideration of the conflicting thinking about war in Elizabethan England. The ancient historians, as I have stated in an earlier chapter, were studied for their practical usefulness from the very beginning of the Revival of Learning. But there were also ancient writers on military matters who were given recognition as professionals, and whose works were carefully studied and often interpreted by drawings and diagrams. Three such works may be mentioned as particularly influential. The earliest of these to be translated was Frontinus' *Stratagems, Sleyghtes, and Policies of War*, dedicated to Henry VIII in 1539, a work familiar to architects and engineers in Latin also. To this translation were appended the general rules of war taken from Vegetius. The second to be translated was Onosander's *Of the General Captain, and of His Office*, a comprehensive but generally philosophic treatment of the art of war, dedicated by the translator to the Duke of Norfolk in 1563. This work commented interestingly upon the Turks' rapid rise to power and noted that there was no nation with which they warred that "so much resembleth, and imitateth the famous antiquitie," as did the Turks. The last of these great authorities to be mentioned here was Vegetius, whose *Foure Bookes of Martiall Policye* was translated by John Sadler and published in 1572. The translator claimed that Vegetius was "the chiefest writer of war," and it is probably true that he was so regarded. I have already noted that his general rules were appended to the translation of Frontinus, and Lathrop says that the mediaeval work of Christine du Castel, published by Caxton as *The Book of Fayttes of Armes and of Chyvalrye* contained long passages from Vegetius as well as extracts from Frontinus.[80]

There were great wars waged during the sixteenth century, however, that inevitably produced books which made the study of war something more than an antiquarian pursuit. Oman's introduction to Cockle's *Bibliography of English Military Books up to 1642* says:

The men who wrote in the age of Elizabeth had seen all their service in Flanders and France, and were set on teaching their fellow-countrymen the Art of War that had been developed by Spanish and Italian captains since the commencement of the great struggle between Charles V, and Francis I. The military books of the period . . . are very largely compilations from the continental authors. When they are original compositions, they are still mainly inspired by foreign experience and foreign necessities . . . It is natural, therefore, that all our early English military books, with very few exceptions, are echoes from the great wars of the continent.

This bibliography appends to the list of English books a list of foreign works for the same period, and the indebtedness of the English to the continental works is amply demonstrated by the comparison of the two lists. Many of the English works are professed translations, such as Nicholas Lichefield's translation from

[80]Lathrop lists him as Christine de Pisan.

the Spanish of the work of Gutierrez de la Vega, *De re militari*, which was dedicated to Sir Philip Sidney in 1582; or Guillaume du Bellay's *Instructions for the Warres*, translated from the French by Paule Ive, the famous military engineer, and dedicated to Secretary Davison, who Ive says delivered it to him with his own hands to be translated. One of the rare original works also shows the inevitable indebtedness of such works to foreign instruction in its very title, *The Arte of Warre: Beeing the onely rare booke of the myllitarie profesion: Drawn out of all our late and forraine services, by William Garrard Gentleman, who served the King of Spayne in his warres fourteene yeeres and died Anno Domini 1587*. This work was dedicated by Thomas Garrard to the Earl of Essex. As I have said, allegiance was divided between such works as these and the works of ancient and long-recognized authorities.

But there was a concurrent struggle between those who thought that an hour in the field taught a soldier more about war than a year in the study, and those who considered it necessary that experience should at least be supplemented by the study of military theory. Professor Francis R. Johnson has shown the growing desire in England before 1588 for the establishment "of some kind of scientific school or lectureship backed by government support" in London, where many scholars were then coming to be "in closer contact with artisans, technicians, and instrument-makers" who could give them better advantages for experimental investigation. It was desired to give a better scientific education to these craftsmen. Professor Johnson says:

The crisis was the arrival of the Spanish Armada off the coast of England in the summer of 1588. In great haste a militia was organized for the defense of London, and even after the defeat of the Armada these troops remained in training for fear of another Spanish attack. Then it was that a final victory was quickly won by the new plea that the effective defense of the capital required providing instruction in mathematics for the untrained leaders of the volunteer forces. Urged by Queen Elizabeth's Privy Council, a group of London merchants and the city authorities raised the funds for creating the first public lectureship in the mathematical sciences in London.[81]

The plea for the "learned soldier," later to be voiced by Dudley Digges, was in fact urged by all those who saw that the new weapons of warfare and the old problems of strategy and tactics could be better handled by leaders with a greater knowledge of mathematics as well as history and geography.

Perhaps the best statement of the general position was given in the work begun by Leonard Digges but completed by Thomas Digges as *An Arithmeticall Militare Treatise Named Stratioticos* which applied mathematical methods to problems of military fortification and ballistics. Thomas Digges dedicated the work to the Earl of Leicester in 1579. He argued:

as in all other Artes and Sciences we ayde ourselves with Precedents from Antiquitie, so in this Arte of Discipline Militare, so corrupted, or rather utterly extinguished, we should repaire to those Fountaines of perfection, and accomodate them to the service of our time.[82]

But just as he had met with a lack of interest in many "masters and mariners" when he had tried to show them by mathematical computation the imperfection in navigation, so he found most military men

if they had been in a few skirmishes, or taken any degree in Fielde, they thought it so great a disgrace, that any thing should be desired in a Souldiour that wanted in themselves, that presentlie they would give their Definitive Sentence, that the Time was chaunged, the Warres were altered, . . . As though the Heavens and Elementes had chaunged their Natures, or Men and Weapons so altered, as no humaine reason might attaine to consider the difference.[83]

Professor Leslie Hotson has suggested that before writing *Henry V* "Shakespeare had observed Digges' peculiarities and had also

---

[81]Francis R. Johnson, "Thomas Hood's Inaugural Address as Mathematical Lecturer of the City of London, 1588," *Journal of the History of Ideas*, III (1942), 96-97.

[82]In "The Preface to the Reader."

[83]*Ibid.*

glanced over his military treatise," which was reprinted in 1590 by Richard Field. Thomas Digges had been muster-master general under Leicester and had peculiarities which Hotson thinks may have been in Shakespeare's mind when he drew his picture of Fluellen. It is certainly quite possible that Shakespeare did know his book—and many others. The issue was a live issue in London in the nineties.[84]

The bitterest if not the most important quarrel was taking place, however, between Sir John Smythe and Sir Roger Williams. Sir Roger is or was in 1912 Professor Dover Wilson's candidate for Fluellen,[85] with what disregard of that noble soldier's attitude will be evident. Sir John Smythe was a son of a sister of Jane Seymour and hence a cousin of Edward the Sixth. He had received some favors from the crown, and had performed ambassadorial services for the crown. But his interest was in war. He had served in foreign wars, and Sidney Lee says he was noticed by the Emperor Maximilian II for his fighting in Hungary against the Turks in 1566.[86] He was given some soldiers to train for service in 1588 when the Earl of Leicester was lieutenant general of the armies brought into being to repel the expected Spanish invasion. When he expressed his opinion about the state of the army Leicester was assembling, the lieutenant general was displeased, though he himself was expressing much the same dissatisfaction at the same time. In 1596 Smythe made a treasonable appeal to the militia training near Colchester to desert to "mr Seymour" of royal blood and have Smythe as captain. As a result he was committed to the Tower and later detained in his own house, where, he said, he wrote about the military profession for the benefit of the nation. In 1590 this turbulent gentleman had published *Certaine Discourses . . . Concerning the formes and effects of divers sorts of weapons, and other verie important matters militarie*, with a proem to the nobility which

---

[84]Leslie Hotson, *I, William Shakespeare* (New York, 1938), pp. 118-22.

[85]J. D. Wilson, "Martin Marprelate and Shakespeare's Fluellen," reprinted from *The Library* (London, 1912), pp. 36-37.

[86]Sidney Lee in the *Dict. Nat. Biog.* article. See also Cockle, *op. cit.*, pp. 40-43.

explained his attitude as well as justified his own right to speak with authority. He argued that the greatest of moderns had been content to recognize the superiority of the ancients and to learn from them, but that the young men of the last twenty years were so vain as to think themselves wiser in the arts and sciences, especially in the military art, than the greatest of the ancients and even the older living men who had seen service "in the well ordered warres of Emperours or Kings." Who are these young men? Are they newly fallen from heaven to bring us the military art? he asked. And he answered his own question scornfully, saying that they were merely the children we have known, children grown young men who argue hotly but improperly, with no recourse to reason and example. What wars have they served in to know so much?

Certainlie, all men knowe, that the chiefest warres that they ever served in, where they have learned anie experience, hath bene in the disordered and tumultuarie warres of the Lowe Countries under the States, or (peradventure) some little divers yeres past, in the intestine and licentious warres of *France*.[87]

Those who have known but hell think there is no other heaven, but these wars which have been their schools "have beene altogether without anie formed *Milicia* and discipline militarie, and therefore farre different from the well ordered wars that have bin in former times, betwixt Emperors, Kings, and formed common wealthes." Peace and civil war are the two great destroyers of a state, Smythe asserted. Bad conditions brought about disorder in the wars in France and the Low Countries, he thought, and he chose to show them up. He made drastic charges also concerning the English armies under Leicester, accusing their leaders of incompetency, fraud, waste of soldiers' lives, and other sins. His book was promptly suppressed.

But in 1590 there was also published *A Briefe Discourse of Warre* by Sir Roger Williams, dedicated to the Earl of Essex. Sir Roger was a great soldier and many times a thorn in the flesh of Leicester. Cockle says the book "succeeded in establishing a

[87]*Op. cit.*, Fol. *3ᵛ.

case for the new system of warfare against that advocated in England by the elder generation of military men, headed by Sir John Smythe." It attacked many of the men and actions in the Dutch wars, explained the superior discipline and organization of the Spanish army, though made up of inferior men, and stressed the importance of experience as a teacher for leaders in military undertakings. In spite of its critical attitude the book was not suppressed, and Sir John Smythe wanted to know why. He wrote to Burghley to ask.

Humphrey Barwick, "Gentleman, Souldier, Captaine," undertook in *A Briefe Discourse* to adjudicate the affair of Smythe versus Williams but really proceeded to refute Smythe's arguments for the long-bow. The book was suppressed also but was reprinted in 1594, when, according to the author, it had been found not to contain such matter as was supposed.

The battle over the school of war was much more extensive than I have been able to indicate in so short a space, but the issues were always the same: weapons, discipline, methods of training. The long-bow versus the new guns and cannon; the ancient military discipline versus the modern; historical and theoretical training versus experience—these were the grounds of personal feuds and much spilling of ink as well. When Fluellen wages battle, therefore, on the subject of the authority of the ancients and is insistent upon the "disciplines" of the Romans, he is taking sides in a quarrel raging in Elizabeth's day but not in Henry V's, and he is taking the side espoused by Sir John Smythe against Sir Roger Williams.

In the second scene of Act III Fluellen is dissatisfied with the mines as "not according to the disciplines of war," and he blames Captain Macmorris:

he has no more directions in the true disciplines of the wars, look you, of the Roman disciplines, than is a puppy-dog.

But of Captain Jamy he speaks well as a great arguer from ancient authority:

Captain Jamy is a marvellous falorous gentleman, that is certain; and of great expedition and knowledge in th' aunchient wars, upon my particular knowledge of his directions: by Cheshu, he will maintain his argument as well as any military man in the world, in the disciplines of the pristine wars of the Romans.

What Fluellen wants is a chance to debate the question, preferably with the Irishman as an opponent:

Captain Macmorris, I beseech you now, will you voutsafe me, look you, a few disputations with you, as partly touching or concerning the disciplines of the war, the Roman wars, in the way of argument, look you, and friendly communication; partly to satisfy my opinion, and partly for the satisfaction, look you, of my mind, as touching the direction of the military discipline: that is the point.

Captain Jamy is interested in the project, but Captain Macmorris does not consider the time apt for discourse on the theory of war:

The town is beseeched, and the trumpet call us to the breach; and we talk, and, be Chrish, do nothing: 'tis shame for us all; . . .

Captain Jamy vows good service before he sleeps, but he would have liked to have heard some discourse between the two. Macmorris is readier to fight than argue theory, and Gower has to step in, but Fluellen goes off with his unspent words, muttering:

Captain Macmorris, when there is more better opportunity to be required, look you, I will be so bold as to tell you I know the disciplines of war; and there is an end.

In the first scene of Act IV, Fluellen is again at it, this time with Gower, who calls his name too loudly for the Welshman's sense of decorum, and he bids him speak lower, giving his authority:

It is the greatest admiration in the universal world, when the true and aunchient prerogatifes and laws of the wars is not kept. If you would take the pains but to examine the wars of Pompey the Great, you shall find, I warrant you, that there is no tiddle taddle nor pibble pabble in Pompey's camp; I warrant you, you shall find the ceremonies of the wars, and the cares of it, and the forms of it, and the sobriety of it, and the modesty of it, to be otherwise.

King Henry, listening to this authoritarian, passes judgment:

> Though it appear a little out of fashion,
> There is much care and valour in this Welshman.

But it is Fluellen's estimate of Gower which best evaluates the speaker, "Gower is a good captain, and is good knowledge, and literatured in the wars."[88]

Fluellen remains the stickler for observing the laws of war, and he consistently judges the moderns by reference to the ancients. The Duke of Exeter is as magnanimous as Agamemnon. Pistol is as valiant as Mark Antony—for a moment—but Pistol's interceding for Bardolph is fruitless, "for discipline ought to be used." The French action in killing the boys and the lackeys guarding the luggage is horrible because "'tis expressly against the law of arms," but the action of King Henry in ordering every English soldier to cut his French prisoner's throat brings only a comparison of the king with Alexander the Great. Alexander was born at Macedon; Henry at Monmouth. Macedon is on a river, and Monmouth is on the River Wye. Alexander killed his best friend Cleitus, and Henry—Gower may interrupt to protest that the king never killed any of his friends, but Fluellen presses the point:

> as Alexander killed his friend Cleitus, being in his ales and his cups, so also Henry Monmouth, being in his right wits and his good judgments, turned away the fat knight with the great-belly doublet; . . .[89]

Sir John Falstaff, it was. Thus the comparison becomes two-edged. Modern critics seem to have missed the allusion, but let anyone read the popular Tudor translation of *The Historie of Quintus Curcius, Conteyning the Actes of the Greate Alexander*[90] or the derivative accounts, and he will find that the killing of Cleitus was the act of Alexander the Great which turned many of his friends and followers against him and gave him cause

---

[88]IV, vii, 153-54.

[89]IV, vii, 47-50.

[90]Lathrop, *op. cit.*, pp. 86-87, says that this translation was the best of the translations of classical historians before Golding, and that almost alone it held its popularity into the seventeenth century.

for repentance. Fluellen speaks "but in the figures and comparisons of it," but the flaw in Henry V's conduct which every reader has tried to rationalize is exposed by the king's fellow-Welshman who belonged to those "literatured in the wars."

This weaving of the comic episodes into the texture of the play by making them all contribute to the development of the theme of war makes *Henry V* a much more unified play than *Henry IV*. Discussing the philosophy of war, picturing the accepted procedures of war, building comic scenes about the violations of the articles of war and the current Elizabethan dispute over the preferred "school of war," it is a great war play, but there is little of the shock of battle on the stage. The horrors of war are talked about, but they are not there to confound the senses as they are in *Henry VI*. War is here a victorious progress of a hero whose cause God has blessed, but in his supreme moment before Agincourt the king shows that he knows his father's sins must yet be paid for. Praying that the Lord will not that day "think upon the fault/ My father made in compassing the crown," reciting his attempts to atone for that fault by interring anew the body of the murdered Richard, keeping in his pay five hundred of the poor to ask heaven daily "to pardon blood," and building two chantries where the priests sing for Richard's soul, he is yet aware that the guilt is not washed away:

> Though all that I can do is nothing worth,
> Since that my penitence comes after all,
> Imploring pardon.[91]

The Lord is good to Henry the Fifth, and he dies victorious, but his "penitence comes after all" and is "nothing worth" in averting the judgment which finally descends upon his house. The chorus at the end of Shakespeare's play reminds us of the record of that judgment in the plays of Henry VI that had been written earlier, but were indeed the end of the story and the record of the final fulfillment of the forces set at work by the seizing of the crown from Richard II. In them the cycle ends, for the wheel has come at last the full round.

[91]IV, i, 309-11.

CHAPTER XVI

THE TRAGICAL DOINGS OF KING RICHARD III

THE PLAY of *Richard III,* antedating in its composition the historical dramas that we have been studying, is of special interest for two reasons: first, it shows where tragedy and history meet; and second, it reveals an author writing without a clear distinction between these genres in mind. The play can with justification be classed as either tragedy or history, and Shakespeare's first editors did not resolve the dilemma. It was first published in quarto in 1597 with the title:

The Tragedy of King Richard the Third. Containing, his treacherous plots against his brother Clarence: the pittiefull murther of his innocent nephews: his tyrannicall usurpation; with the whole course of his detested life, and most deserved death.

The five subsequent quartos which preceded the folio gathering of the plays bore the same title. The editors of the First Folio put it with the "Histories," though in this unique instance they departed from custom by retaining the term *tragedy* when printing the head-title:

The Tragedy of Richard the Third: with the landing of Earle Richmond, and the battell at Bosworth Field.

In order to understand this play, then, it is necessary to distinguish the elements of tragedy from those of the history play with which they are combined, and to do so we must again recall the fundamental distinctions between the two genres. An earlier chapter[1] pointed out that the plays listed by Shakespeare's editors as histories are derived from the same chronicles that furnished material for *Lear* and *Macbeth.* Furthermore, Shakespear-

[1]Chapter II.

ean tragedy, like most Elizabethan tragedy, deals with those of high estate and is therein not differentiated from history, for it remained true that, as Raleigh said, "the markes, set on private men, are with their bodies cast into the earth; and their fortunes, written only in the memories of those that lived with them." In his histories and his tragedies alike Shakespeare patterned a moral universe in which the wages of sin is death; in both genres he acted as a register of God's judgments. Yet Macbeth kills his king and usurps a throne, and his tale is classified as a tragedy by Shakespeare's editors: Bolingbroke usurps a throne, his king is killed, and the story is classed as a history. We think of Macbeth as a murderer; of Henry IV as a rebel who usurped a throne. Neither the source material, the characters, nor the divine vengeance which the plays record can, therefore, be held to account for the difference between tragedy and history. For that difference, as I have earlier indicated, we must look to the old division of morals into private and public, a division most clearly explained among the poets by Spenser in his letter to Raleigh, for Spenser proposed to portray in the first twelve books of *The Faerie Queene* the twelve private moral virtues in Arthur before he became king and "to frame the other part of polliticke vertues in his person, after that hee came to be king." He also proposed to present Queen Elizabeth both as the Faerie Queene and as Belphoebe, "considering she beareth two persons, the one of a most royall Queene or Empresse, the other of a most vertuous and beautifull Lady."[2] This was the distinction laid down by philosophers and observed by poets, a distinction between private and political virtue, which marked the difference between the realms of ethics and of politics. Tragedy deals with an ethical world; history with a political world. In tragedy God avenges private sins; in history the King of kings avenges public sins, those of king and subject alike.

In classifying Shakespeare's *Richard III*, then, we need to consider the over-all impression. The killing of the little princes in the Tower, rather than the illegal seizing of the throne, haunts

---

[2] All quotations from Spenser are from the Oxford edition (1916).

the play-goer. Clarence's dream of divine vengeance, rather than the right of the House of York to rule, fills the mind and stirs the emotions. We accept Richard's labeling of himself as a villain, and when Richmond describes him as "a bloody tyrant and a homicide,"[3] we think more of the shed blood than of tyranny. These are impressions left by a tragedy rather than a history play. We need to ask why and wherefore.

One answer to these questions is to be found in Richard's own words when, waking from his last night of dreams, in which the ghosts of his murdered victims have passed before him, he cries out:

> Perjury, perjury, in the high'st degree:
> Murder, stern murder, in the dir'st degree;
> All several sins, all us'd in each degree,
> Throng to the bar, crying all, Guilty! Guilty![4]

Now perjury and murder are sins which brand Richard or any man a villain, a sinner against the moral order; but they are not sins which identify him as a traitor, a regicide, an usurper, a tyrant. Perjury and murder are, moreover, not only the sins which Richard commits with each of his victims in turn; they are also the sins which doom the other sinners in the play to divine vengeance. So much do these two sins dominate the play that the moral pattern becomes repetitious and at times almost loses its cumulative horror.

Also there is in *Richard III* the same portrayal and analysis of passion which characterize Shakespearean tragedy elsewhere. Ambition compels Richard, as it does Macbeth,[5] to murder that he may gain a throne. Fear compels him, as it does Macbeth, to murder to keep the throne. Even the murderer becomes surfeited with his own crimes. The *Mirror for Magistrates* had represented Richard as saying:

[3]V, iii, 247.

[4]V, iii, 197-200.

[5]For a discussion of passion in *Macbeth*, see my *Shakespeare's Tragic Heroes* (Cambridge, 1930), chap. xv.

> But what thing may suffise unto the bloudy man,
> The more he bathes in bloud, the bloudier he is alway:[6]

and Shakespeare later wrote the same idea into words for Macbeth:

> I am in bloud
> Stepp'd in so far, that, should I wade no more,
> Returning were as tedious as go o'er.[7]

He writes like words here for Richard III:

> But I am in
> So far in blood that sin will pluck on sin.[8]

But each step in blood brings new perturbation to Richard's soul. Like Macbeth, he has murdered sleep, and his queen complains:

> For never yet one hour in his bed
> Did I enjoy the golden dew of sleep,
> But with his timorous dreams was still awak'd.[9]

Yet fear urges him on to new crimes. He arranges with Tyrrel to kill the little princes in the Tower:

> two deep enemies,
> Foes to my rest and my sweet sleep's disturbers . . .[10]

And Tyrrel, like another Exton, promises, "I'll rid you from the fear of them." His last night is a night of dream-riding ghosts, and roused by Ratcliff to the day of battle, he protests, "O Ratcliff, I fear, I fear!" Answering Ratcliff's plea not to be afraid of shadows, he confesses:

> By the apostle Paul, shadows to-night
> Have struck more terror to the soul of Richard
> Than can the substance of ten thousand soldiers
> Armed in proof, and led by shallow Richmond![11]

[6]*Op. cit.*, p. 364, ll. 120-21.
[7]*Macbeth*, III, iv, 136-38.
[8]IV, ii, 63-64.
[9]IV, i, 82-84.
[10]IV, ii, 72-73.
[11]V, iii, 215-20.

In contrast, the Richmond whom he must encounter has had

> The sweetest sleep and fairest-boding dreams
> That ever entered in a drowsy head,

and his heart "is very jocund" in the remembrance.[12] The picture of the destructive power of passion in *Richard III* is a cruder one than Shakespeare was later to achieve in *Macbeth*, but in the other characters as well as in Richard himself its corrosive effect is exhibited and analyzed.

Emphasizing moral rather than political sins and revealing passion as both motivating sin and punishing it by the perturbation of the soul, *Richard III* also shares with the other Shakespearean tragedies a deep concern with the problem of revenge. The contemporary discussion of revenge, as I have shown elsewhere, was built upon the Biblical authority for a jealous God who had said "Vengeance is mine." Three kinds of vengeance were posited on the basis of this Biblical authority: God's vengeance for sin; public vengeance executed by the ruler or his representative acting as the agent of God in administering justice and punishing sin; and private vengeance which usurps the authority of God and is, therefore, forbidden.[13]

In *Richard III* the murder of Clarence and the execution of Hastings are made the occasions for long discussions of private revenge in relation to divine vengeance and public vengeance. Clarence, it will be remembered, was condemned by his brother, King Edward IV, but "the order was revers'd," and Clarence is actually killed by the hirelings of Richard, who sees in him an impediment in his path to the throne. The murderers at first pretend to come on an order from the king, and I quote from the impassioned debate between them and their victim Shakespeare's most detailed statement of the whole Elizabethan philosophy of vengeance. Clarence makes clear from the first the difference between private vengeance and public vengeance, delegated by

---

[12]V, iii, 228-35.

[13]See my "Theories of Revenge in Renaissance England," *Modern Philology*, XXVIII (1931), 281-96.

God to his vice-gerent to be executed under law for the public weal:

> CLARENCE. Are you drawn forth, among a world of men,
> To slay the innocent? What is my offence?
> Where is the evidence that doth accuse me?
> What lawful quest have given their verdict up
> Unto the frowning judge? or who pronounc'd
> The bitter sentence of poor Clarence' death?
> Before I be convict by course of law,
> To threaten me with death is most unlawful.
> I charge you, as you hope to have redemption
> By Christ's dear blood shed for our grievous sins,
> That you depart and lay no hands on me!
> The deed you undertake is damnable.

> FIRST MURD. What we will do we do upon command.

> SECOND MURD. And he that hath commanded is our king.

> CLARENCE. Erroneous vassals! the great King of kings
> Hath in the table of His law commanded
> That thou shalt do no murder. Will you then
> Spurn at His edict, and fulfil a man's?
> Take heed; for He holds vengeance in His hand,
> To hurl upon their heads that break His law.

> . . . .

> FIRST MURD. How canst thou urge God's dreadful law to us,
> When thou hast broke it in such dear degree?

> CLARENCE. . . . .
> If God will be avenged for the deed,
> O, know you yet, He doth it publicly.
> Take not the quarrel from His powerful arm;
> He needs no indirect or lawless course
> To cut off those that have offended Him.

Even the king has no right to exact private revenge, but as the murderers reveal the fact that not Edward, but Richard, is the author of their deed, Clarence calls upon them to relent and save their souls, asking

> **And are you yet to your own souls so blind**
> **That you will war with God by murdering me?**

The murderers do not relent, but no sooner is the deed committed than the Second Murderer cries, as does many another murderer in Shakespeare's tragedies:

> How fain, like Pilate, would I wash my hands
> Of this most grievous murder—[14]

The case of Hastings is also presented at length to show the heinousness of private revenge, here disguised as public revenge. Hastings, betrayed by Catesby, is reported unwilling to see young Edward V deprived of his throne. Without due process of law and on the obviously trumped-up charge that he has succeeded Edward IV as the protector of Jane Shore, who is accused along with Queen Elizabeth of having through witchcraft brought harm to his deformed body, Richard orders the death of Hastings. Anticipating the suspicion which his action may cause, he justifies the hugger-mugger execution to the Lord Mayor of London:

> What, think you we are Turks or infidels?
> Or that we would, against the form of law,
> Proceed thus rashly in the villain's death,
> But that the extreme peril of the case,
> The peace of England, and our persons' safety,
> Enforc'd us to this execution?

The mayor is amenable to such reasoning, but Buckingham feels it wise to share the blame with lesser folk who do their master's bidding too enthusiastically:

> Yet had we not determin'd he should die,
> Until your lordship came to see his end;
> Which now the loving haste of these our friends,
> Something against our meanings, have prevented: . . .[15]

The audience is already aware of the reason why Hastings has been hurried to his death, but a scrivener is introduced to enforce

---

[14]I, iv, 180-273.
[15]III, v, 41-46 and 52-55.

the lesson by explaining that the writing out of the precedent and the indictment had anticipated the accusation and seizure of Hastings by many hours, and he queries:

> Who is so gross,
> That cannot see this palpable device?
> Yet who so bold, but says he sees it not?[16]

The introduction of the long dialogue between Clarence and his murderers and the intrusion of the scrivener with his undramatic but pointed speech make evident Shakespeare's special interest in revenge in this play.

The matter of the divine vengeance which is inexorably meted out for sin is, moreover, associated with the unstinted use of the supernatural in divers ways throughout the play. The wounds of King Henry VI bleed in the presence of his murderer. Prophecies contribute to the imprisonment of the Duke of Clarence, and his terrible dream warns him of his doom. Stanley dreams of Hastings' downfall. Hastings' horse stumbles three times. The littler of the princes senses the presence of the ghost of his uncle Clarence in the Tower. Richard accuses Jane Shore and the queen of witchcraft. The ghosts of those whom he has murdered disturb Richard's dreams and give comfort to his foe the night before Bosworth Field. Most important of all, the plot of the play is woven as a web of curses and their fulfilment, and the sense of a divine vengeance exacting a measured retribution for each sin is ever present.

However, God may and often does make use of an evil instrument in the execution of his divine vengeance, and Richard, like Tamburlaine, functions as the scourge of God.[17] His first murder in the play is that of his brother Clarence. The third part of *Henry VI* showed Clarence going over to the side of King Henry in support of Warwick against Edward IV and marrying Warwick's younger daughter. It showed him later forsworn as

---

[16]V, vi, 10-12.

[17]See R. W. Battenhouse, *Marlowe's Tamburlaine* (Nashville, 1941), where the Elizabethan conception of God's use of a wicked man as a scourge is discussed at length.

he rejoined his brother's forces. Now we hear Richard, pretending pity for him and commenting unctuously:

> Poor Clarence did forsake his father, Warwick;
> Ay, and forswore himself, which Jesu pardon!—[18]

Margaret tries to close his speech with a curse before Richard
can finish it, and she apparently makes herself heard in heaven—
or hell—with her "Which God revenge," for Clarence dreams of
a descent "Unto the kingdom of perpetual light":

> The first that there did greet my stranger-soul
> Was my great father-in-law, renowned Warwick,
> Who spoke aloud, "What scourge for perjury
> Can this dark monarchy afford false Clarence?"

Then appeared the slaughtered Prince of Wales, son of Henry
VI, "A shadow like an angel, with bright hair," who "squeak'd
out aloud":

> "Clarence is come, false, fleeting, perjur'd Clarence,
> That stabb'd me in the field by Tewksbury:
> Seize on him Furies, take him into torment!"

Shattered by his dream, Clarence sorrows to his keeper:

> I have done those things,
> That now give evidence against my soul,
> For Edward's sake; and see how he requites me!
> O God! If my deep prayers cannot appease Thee,
> But thou wilt be aveng'd on my misdeeds,
> Yet execute Thy wrath in me alone; . . .[19]

Clarence is murdered before an Elizabethan audience that knew
his last prayer had not been answered, for the destruction of his
wife and children by Henry VII and Henry VIII, who feared
their possible claims to the throne, was an oft-told tale.

King Edward IV, learning of the death of Clarence, which he
had commanded and then unavailingly countermanded, cries out
in horror:

[18]I, iii, 135-36.
[19]I, iv, 46 *et seq.*

> O God, I fear thy justice will take hold
> On me, and you, and mine, and yours for this![20]

Like King John and King Henry IV he bitterly chides those who have failed to advise him and check him, but he acknowledges his own sin, and Richard assents, "God will revenge it." King Edward dies, and those who heard his words are soon themselves experiencing the justice of God administered through Richard's malice.

Anne calls down the wrath of God upon the wife of Richard III and thereby curses her future self. Buckingham calls upon God to take vengeance if he be not true to England's queen and so curses himself. Edward on his death-bed warns the rival factions gathered about him to swear peace:

> Take heed you dally not before your king;
> Lest He that is the supreme King of kings
> Confound your hidden falsehood, and award
> Either of you to be the other's end.[21]

Both factions perjure themselves, heedless of the warning, and upon them both the supreme King of kings takes vengeance through Richard's evil acts.

The poor, distracted Margaret, queen to Henry VI, is taunted by Richard as one who suffers the fate to which she was doomed by his father's curses:

> The curse my noble father laid on thee,
> When thou didst crown his warlike brows with paper,
> And with thy scorns drew'st rivers from his eyes,
> And then, to dry them, gav'st the duke a clout
> Steep'd in the faultless blood of pretty Rutland—
> His curses, then from bitterness of soul
> Denounc'd against thee, are all fall'n upon thee;
> And God, not we, hath plag'd thy bloody deed.[22]

[20]II, i, 131-32.
[21]II, i, 12-15.
[22]I, iii, 174-81.

But Margaret in her turn pronounces her dreadful anathemas upon those who have wronged her. She cries out for King Edward's death because her king was murdered to make this Yorkist king. She begs God to let Queen Elizabeth die "neither mother, wife, nor England's queen" that justice may prevail and her own loss of child, husband, and kingdom be paid for. For all those who stood by when her son was murdered:

> God I pray Him,
> That none of you may live his natural age,
> But by some unlook'd accident cut off!

And her prayers are answered, even her prayer for the young Edward V:

> Edward thy son, that now is Prince of Wales,
> For Edward my son, that was Prince of Wales,
> Die in his youth by like untimely violence!

Her raucous demands for justice shock us, and the execution of that justice horrifies us, but they contribute to the pattern of the play.

In his turn God's evil executioner of his justice must feel the vengeance of the King of kings, and when he does, we see the working out of yet more of Margaret's awful curses:

> If heaven hath any grievous plague in store,
> Exceeding those that I can wish upon thee,
> O, let them keep it till thy sins be ripe,
> And then hurl down their indignation
> On thee, the troubler of the poor world's peace!
> The worm of conscience still begnaw thy soul!
> Thy friends suspect for traitors while thou livest,
> And take deep traitors for thy dearest friends!
> No sleep close up that deadly eye of thine,
> Unless it be while some tormenting dream
> Affrights thee with a hell of ugly devils![23]

Richard's device of closing the curse with her name before she can close it with his is unavailing, for Margaret's curses foretell

[23] I, iii, 196-227.

the manner of his punishment. His doom does not come upon him till his sins are ripe. Conscience gnaws his soul, and he never sleeps without horrible dreams. He distrusts his best friends and discards true advisers. He makes friends with traitors. His last night is a night of horror, and he meets his death ignominiously on foot, his horse having been killed under him in the course of the battle.

It is the God of the Old Testament that must be supposed to rule in such a moral order as Shakespeare here depicts, but it is a moral order. The justice is that of an eye for an eye, a Prince of Wales for a Prince of Wales. Prayers that are offered as curses by those with hatred in their hearts are answered by a divine justice without pity. The stage should indeed be hung with black for the presentation of this play. But it was a play that rounded out the cycle of history in which the crown was snatched from the House of Lancaster by unruly Yorkist hands, only to be lost by the third heir to the importunate Richmond. Holinshed explained:

And as it thus well appeared, that the house of Yorke shewed itselfe more bloudie in seeking to obteine the kingdome, than that of Lancaster in usurping it: so it came to passe, that the Lords vengeance appeared more heavie towards the same than towards the other, not ceassing till the whole issue male of the said Richard duke of Yorke was extinguished. For such is Gods justice, to leave no unrepentant wickednesse unpunished, as especiallie in this caitife Richard the third, not deserving so much as the name of a man, muche lesse of a king, most manifestlie appeareth.[24]

Thus Shakespeare pictured the dominating sins in the play as perjury and murder, sins against the moral order. He portrayed and analyzed the passion of ambition that caused Richard to sin and the passion of fear that at the same time punished him for his sins and forced him to wade still further in blood. He inserted non-historical scenes developing the Elizabethan philosophy of revenge. He used the supernatural to enhance the horror of the play and to contribute to the impression of a divine vengeance

[24]*Chronicles*, III, 761.

meting out punishment for sin. He showed God's revenge exacted through the agency of the evil Richard, who was nevertheless held to account for his evil-doing. He made use of pathos
in the death of the royal children. These are the common methods of Shakespearean tragedy, and they justify those who hold
Richard III to be a tragedy.

But on the other hand, Shakespeare's editors can also be justified for putting *Richard III* among the histories. Except for the
epilogue spoken by Richmond there are, of course, no great
speeches on political abstractions such as the later history plays
contained, or such as are to be found in *The True Tragedie of
Richard the Third*. Unlike *King John* and *Richard II* and *Henry
IV*, the play presents the usurpation of a throne and the punishment of the usurper without expounding the political sins involved. Yet Richard is, as Richmond says, a bloody tyrant and an
usurper, and his crimes constitute offenses against the common
weal for which the great King of kings takes vengeance. Thus
though Clarence and Hastings are the victims of Richard's private
vengeance, their deaths are made to emphasize the particular sin-
fulness of private vengeance executed, under the cloak of public
vengeance, by one who serves as God's vice-gerent. And the
pattern of sin and punishment is a political as well as a moral
pattern, for murder and perjury are motivated by political purposes. The God who demands vengeance is, furthermore, the
same God who presides as King of kings. In this play, as I have
said, we see where tragedy and history meet.

The Richard whom we know in Shakespeare's *Richard III*
both as the tragic villain and the historical usurper and tyrant is
the Richard whom Sir Thomas More gave to the world in a picture so convincing that none of the succeeding chroniclers could
banish it from his work. More's Richard III is, indeed, still the
Richard accepted by the multitude, and the apologists from Buc
onward who would give the devil his due have spoken to deaf
ears. More so foreshortened the events of the reigns of Edward
IV and Edward V as to make them but a setting for Richard III,
and Shakespeare has done likewise, but he has further distorted
the perspective by crowding the events of fourteen years into

eleven days, with certain intervals, according to Daniel's computation of dramatic time.[25] In itself the play covers almost the complete cycle from the seizing of the crown to its loss by the House of York, but the actual seizing of the crown is not portrayed on the stage. It is only recalled from its earlier presentation in *Henry VI*.

G. B. Churchill has so exhaustively studied the literary sources and parallels of *Richard III* that it would be a work of supererogation to repeat the process.[26] Churchill did not note, however, the significant fact that the *Mirror for Magistrates* isolated the chief events exhibited in Shakespeare's play, recording the working out of justice in each case. The relevant entries in the 1587 edition of the *Mirror* are as follows:

How George Plantagenet thyrd sonne of the Duke of Yorke, was by his brother King Edward wrongfully imprysoned, and by his brother Richard miserably murdered, the 11. of January. Anno 1478.

How King Edwarde the fourth, through his surfeting and untemperate life, sodaynly died in the middest of his prosperity. The 9. of Apriell, anno 1483.

How Sir Anthony Wodvill Lorde Rivers and Scales, governour of Prince Edward, was with his nephue Lord Richard Gray, and others, causles imprisoned, and cruelly murdered. Anno 1483.

How the Lord Hastings was betrayed, by trusting too much to his evill Councelour Catesby, and villanously murdered in the Towre of London, by Richard Duke of Glocester, the 13. of June. Anno 1483.

The Complaynt of Henry Stafford, Duke of Buckingham.

How Richard Plantagenet Duke of Glocester, murdered his brothers children, usurping the Crowne: and in the 3. yeare of his raigne, was most worthely deprived of life and Kingdome, in Basworth

---

[25] P. A. Daniel, "Time Analysis of the Plots of Shakespere's Plays: Part III. The Histories," in *The New Shakespere Society's Transactions*, 1877-79, pp. 257-346.

[26] G. B. Churchill, *Richard the Third up to Shakespeare* (Palaestra, X: Berlin, 1900).

plaine, by Henry Earle of Richmond, after called King Henry the seaventh: the 22. of August. 1485.

Later, not in chronological sequence, there is inserted another tragedy not developed by Shakespeare but, according to Churchill, the source of some of the modifications of history to be found in the play:

How Shores wife, King Edward the fourths Concubine, was by King Richard despoyled of all her goods, and forced to doe open penaunce.[27]

My interest in pointing out this arrangement of stories in the *Mirror* is, first, to note that, as in Shakespeare's play, Richard's victims, except the royal children, are represented as paying for their sins, Richard acting as the scourge of God, and that Richard himself "was most worthely deprived of life and Kingdome," even as Shakespeare showed his "deserved death." Second, I want to call attention to the fact that these *Mirror* stories were used to portray contemporary events and people, that while they were called tragedies, they were directed to political teaching.

Listing the various poetical and dramatic treatments of the story of Richard III written in Shakespeare's time, Churchill finds no evidence for Shakespeare's having used the well-known Latin play of *Richard Tertius* and but uncertain evidence for his use of *The True Tragedie of Richard the Third*.[28] Both plays portrayed Richard as a pattern of usurpation and tyranny. *The True Tragedie* has significance, however, not as a source but as a political play on Richard III which presumably antedated Shakespeare's.[29] It has many speeches dealing with the political theme of usurpation, and emphasis is given to the idea that Richmond is a lawful king who comes to free the people from a tyrant's yoke. There are such speeches as we expect in Shakespeare's play and do not find. Furthermore, Elizabeth, the daughter of Edward IV, is conspicuous in the play. She appears in the

[27]*Op. cit.*, pp. 530-31.

[28]An account of this play by Thomas Legge is given in E. K. Chambers, *Elizabethan Stage*, III, 407, and by Churchill, *op. cit.*

[29]Published in 1594.

opening scene as the peacemaker between Hastings and Marcus, who are the representatives of the contending factions at Edward's deathbed, and she is presented as a worthy grandmother-to-be of Queen Elizabeth, who is praised in the concluding speech of this play as she is in Shakespeare's. If Shakespeare was indebted to *The True Tragedie* for story details as critics suggest, he did not imitate its use of speeches on political themes.

Churchill's careful study of the sources and analogues of Shakespeare's *Richard III* is, of course, a literary study and takes no account of the treatment of Richard III in Elizabethan political polemics, where we must look if we are to understand the possible political implications of the play. Now, being against tyranny and usurpation is almost as safe as being against sin—in general. But being against a particular tyrant or would-be usurper is dangerous, as the poet Collingbourne, who suffered under Richard III, warned in the *Mirror for Magistrates:*

> But when these pelting poetes in theyr rymes
> Shall taunt, and jest, or paynt our wicked wurkes,
> And cause the people knowe, and curse our crymes,
> This ougly fault, no Tyrant lyves but urkes.[30]

For the most part the writers were, therefore, anonymous who used Richard III as the archetype by which they interpreted the designs and activities of certain contemporary figures, but the fact that they did so use him is important.

Among the earliest of the influential political libels of Elizabeth's reign was *A Treatise of Treasons against Queen Elizabeth*, published in 1572. Richard played a prominent role in the book, but since his treatment here bears upon the much-discussed topic of Richard's Machiavellianism, I must detour at this point to consider that subject briefly.

Edward Meyer's study of *Machiavelli and the Elizabethan Drama*, published in 1897,[31] inaugurated an era of skepticism in

---

[30]*Op. cit.*, p. 348, ll. 36-39.

[31](Literarhistorische forschungen: Weimar, 1897). See also L. Arnold Weissberger, "Machiavelli and Tudor England," *Political Science Quarterly*, XLII (1927), 589-607.

regard to any popular firsthand acquaintance with Machiavelli's *Prince* on the part of sixteenth-century Englishmen. It is generally agreed that Shakespeare's Richard III is a Machiavellian character, but whether Shakespeare knew the *Prince* and was influenced by it in drawing his villain-hero has been the subject of debate, most modern scholars agreeing that the character does not show any features which could not have been derived from history or from Marlowe. It has also been pointed out that Richard could, as he boasted, have been schoolmaster to Machiavelli. Meyer contended that the denouncing of Machiavelli was the result, not of familiarity with the teachings of the *Prince*, but of a secondhand acquaintance with that work through a book by Innocent Gentillet, generally known as the *Contre-Machiavel*. It was published in French in 1576, translated into English by Simon Paterike in 1577, but not published in its translated form until 1602. Meyer explained away earlier references to Machiavelli, saying that Ascham's "assumption that Machiavelli was known can only apply to scholars," and insisted that before the publication of Gentillet's work in 1576 he could find absolutely no references which show "the slightest tendency to misinterpret or denounce Machiavelli." Moreover, he asserted that in 1589 "Thomas Lodge introduced Machiavelli into the popular controversial literature of the day, with his immediately-suppressed pamphlet: 'A Reply to Stephen Gosson's Schoole of Abuse.'" I do not propose to enter into a discussion of the popularity of the *Prince* or of the influence of Machiavelli on English politics and politicians of the period, though all Meyer's pronouncements need to be reviewed. I only wish to show that most of his contentions can be challenged by referring to *A Treatise of Treasons*, published four years before the *Contre-Machiavel*. It is a political libel, definitely pro-Catholic and said by Camden to have been written in order to make Sir Nicholas Bacon and William Cecil, Lord Burghley, "odious to their Prince," the one being Lord Keeper of the Great Seal and the other Lord Treasurer of England.

The anonymous author professed two purposes: to disprove accusations against the Duke of Norfolk and Mary of Scotland,

and to prove the existence of treasons against Queen Elizabeth which were still undetected. He refers throughout his work to the two worthies against whom the book is directed as Machiavels and Catilines, using the terms together or interchangeably. This fact is of itself interesting because of the printer's ink that has been used by commentators on the line in *The True Tragedie* which reads

> And set the aspiring Catilin to schoole,

but which has been changed in the third part of *Henry VI* to read

> And set the mur'drous Machiavel to school.[32]

However, it is what he says about the Machiavel-Catilines that is of special concern to us here. These "Machiavellian Libertines," he charges, were responsible for having destroyed the old religion of the country by setting up a new one so that in effect they would leave no religion in the hearts of the people, and then he proceeds to definition:

And that is it, that I cal a Machiavellian State and Regiment: where Religion is put behind in the second and last place: where the civil Policie, I meane, is preferred before it, and not limited by any rules of Religion, but the Religion framed to serve the time and policy: . . . where it is free to slaunder, to belie, to forswear, . . . to invade, to depose, to imprison, to murther, and to commit every other outrage, never so barbarous (that promiseth to advaunce the present Policie in hand) without scruple, feare, or conscience of hel or heaven, of God, or Devil: and where no restraint, nor allurement is left in the heart of man, to bridle him from evil, nor to invite him to good: but for vaine fame only and feare of lay lawes, that reache no further than to this body and life: that cal I properly a Machiavellian State and Governance.[33]

[32]3 *Henry VI*, III, ii, 193.

[33]*Op. cit.*, fol. a5.

The *Treatise* abounds in literary and historical parallels, among others a long account of the Trojan-horse methods of the current Sinon, so that Richard's comparison of himself to Sinon in *Henry VI* is perhaps also noteworthy.[34] But the most extensive comparison is that described in a marginal note as "Comparisons betwene this Tragedie and that of K. Richard the third,"[35] which begins:

It would be to long a worke, to peruse in this maner al the pointes attemted against her [Queen Elizabeth] by these Machiavellians, that do breath and spire out their fatal malice towards her. To be therefore as brief as I can, I shal put you in mind of the last Tragedie of like nature and qualitie wrought among your selves, by K. Richard the third, as the Stories make mention: compassed by like fraudulent, impudent, and monstruous meanes, and ended with that Tyranical and blouddy successe, that this also threateneth and plainly portendeth.

The author professes surprise that the present queen is not as astute, in seeing that those who seize the Duke of Norfolk and imprison Mary Stuart intend harm ultimately to the queen herself, as was the earlier Queen Elizabeth, wife to Edward IV, in understanding that those who seized her kinsmen and put the little Duke of York in the power of his uncle intended harm ultimately to the young king, Edward V. The ultimate intentions of Richard III were not apparent in the initial events, he points out; likewise the devices of these Machiavellians are today leading to a conclusion not yet obvious. Then he gives twenty pages of text to listing parallels which I must perforce summarize briefly, though brevity means omitting many interesting details.

The first step in Richard's game was to create suspicion between Edward IV's party and his queen's kinsmen; the present plotters have created suspicion between Elizabeth and Mary and their respective friends.

Richard secured the destruction of important persons, notably the Duke of Clarence, under the pretense of preventing mis-

---

[34] *3 Henry VI*, III, ii, 190: "And, like a Sinon, take another Troy."

[35] *Op. cit.*, fols. 119-30.

chief; so have these men succeeded in making way with Norfolk, Guise, Huntley, Darnley, and others.

The kinsmen of Edward IV's queen were treated with kindness when first apprehended, as were the Duke of Norfolk, the Earls of Arundel and Pembroke, Lord Lumley, and the rest; but they were later executed. The rumors that the queen's kinsmen would destroy the king's kindred are comparable also to the outcropping of books and libels against these unfortunates today.

Edward's widow was defamed as an enemy to her husband's kindred and to the nobility and was accused of being a sorceress and a witch and was said by necromancy to have wasted the Protector's body; Mary, a widowed queen, is accused of being a harlot, of killing her husband, and of raising rebellions.

Edward IV was accused of being a bastard, and his sons were also announced to be bastards to debar them as heirs to the crown of England; writings, especially the book of John Hales, have pretended that because Mary was born in Scotland she could not inherit and have charged bastardy against Lady Margaret Lennox and her succession.

Richard succeeded in getting the younger son of Edward into his hands by pretending that his mother proposed to send him overseas; now it is said that Mary proposes to send her son (James) to Spain.

The Bishop of York, Lord Hastings, Lord Stanley, and others were unaware of the end purposed when they were instrumental in overthrowing the queen's kinsmen; these of the nobility today who have helped imprison the Bishop of Ross and the Earls of Arundel, Worcester, and Southampton should make sure that they are not serving a similar end.

The young king's faithful servants were weeded out few by few as the time of his destruction drew near; today the Queen of Scotland's faithful servants are removed few by few until now she has none about her able to resist any violence offered to her.

The "little babe" then said, "Though mine Uncle wil have my Kingdome, I would to God, he would let me have my life still;" so now the Queen of Scotland appeals but for her liberty and safety.

Compare the instruments of evil. There did not lack Shaws then among the clergy, or Sampsons now. There was a Catesby then, a Norton now, among the lawyers. There was then a Brakenbury who refused to become a slaughterman; now there is a Shrewsbury. But there was then a Tirrel to do the deed; now there is a knight to whom Shrewsbury may have to yield his prisoner.

As the purpose was then to root out the heirs male of Edward IV, so now if the descendants of Henry VIII are finished, the right successors are to be wasted and weeded away.

At this point the author of the *Treatise* stops particularized parallels but continues to show how the "captaine Catiline of this Conjuration" proposes, by arranging marriages and weeding out those who stand in his path, to see to it that he rules whoever is ruler of England, and that his succession "be Coosins to the croune, and annumbered among the noblest." The author adds ominously, "what more afterward, who wotteth yet."

Thus Richard was, at least by 1572, accepted as the archetype of Machiavellianism, his activities being made the pattern by which to interpret the doings of political aspirants. And he continued to be so used.

Probably the most scurrilous libels of Elizabeth's reign were directed against her favorite, the Earl of Leicester, and the most famous of the infamies hurled at him were those contained in a work of which I have already written, *The Copie of a Leter, wryten by a Master of Arte of Cambridge*, better known under its seventeenth-century title of *Leicester's Commonwealth*. The letter was published in 1584 in English and shortly afterward in a French translation bearing the more descriptive title *Discours de la vie abhominable, ruses, trahisons, murtres, impostures, empoisonnements, paillardises, atheismes, et autres tres iniques conversations, due quelle ià usè et usè journellement, le my Lord de Lecestre, Machiaveliste contra l'honneur de Dieu, la Maiestie de la Royne de'Angleterre, sa Princesse etc.* Since no adequate and unprejudiced biography of Leicester has ever been published, this libel has remained the basis for most of the accounts of his life up to the present day. Camden wrote that the libels against

Leicester disgracefully defamed him, "not without some un-truths," and he summed up the popular judgment of the earl by saying that "openly hee was accounted in the number of com-mendable men, but privily hee was ill spoken of by the most sort."[36] At any rate, the *Leter* but reaffirmed gossip that persisted from the early years of the reign about Leicester in spite of the most energetic measures taken by the queen and other author-ities, and it spread this old gossip with additions and interpreta-tions that drove the queen and the authorities to new but still unavailing attempts to suppress it. This all too popular libel represented Leicester, "Machiaveliste," like his father before him, as another Richard III.

The main charge directed against Leicester in this book is that, like his father, he is seeking to divert the crown of England from the true heirs to the heirs of another house, hoping ultimately to secure it to himself or to his heirs. It will be remembered that John Dudley, Duke of Northumberland, had succeeded in being made protector to young Edward VI after having manipulated the execution of Protector Somerset, Edward's uncle on his mother's side. He had then married his son Guilford to Lady Jane Grey, descended from Mary, the younger daughter of Henry VII; and on the same day he had married his daughter Katherine to Henry Hastings, son and heir of the Earl of Hunt-ington, descended on his mother's side from George, Duke of Clarence. Thinking he had secured the throne to his heirs what-ever might betide, the duke, according to the ugly rumors of the time, poisoned the young king and caused Lady Jane Grey to be proclaimed queen. The attempt to deprive the daughters of Henry VIII of the crown was paid for by the series of execu-tions which make somber pages in the history of the early days of Mary's reign. The affairs in which the Duke of Northumber-land had so largely figured were mirrored in tragedies of the reigns of Henry VI and Richard III in the *Mirror for Magis-trates*. Now the *Leter* proclaims that Robert Dudley, the Earl of Leicester, is following in his father's footsteps in trying to divert

[36]Camden, *Historie of . . . the Princesse Elizabeth*, Bk. III, p. 146. See also *Annales*, Bk. III, p. 288.

the crown from the true heirs (the Scotch line) to another house, that of Huntington. But it does not use the method of the *Treatise of Treasons* in comparing Leicester to Richard III; instead of concentrating parallels in one section of the book, it refers to them from time to time as occasion offers.

Leicester is dominated by ambition, the author asserts, and ambition always grows and is jealous. Leicester showed his ambition to become king or to have his heirs gain the crown first by trying to marry Elizabeth; then by attempting to have Elizabeth's natural issue instead of her lawful issue declared her successor (thus giving opportunity for him to foist off any illegitimate offspring of his own as hers); then by attempting to arrange a marriage with Mary of Scotland. Now he is attempting to advance the House of Huntington (his sister being married to the Earl of Huntington), or to marry his own son to Arabella Stuart and promote her claim.

Probably the most telling comparison between Leicester and Richard III dates from the early days of the reign when Leicester still hoped to marry Queen Elizabeth. In the course of the dialogue recorded in the *Leter* the Lawyer is made to say:

I have hearde men of good discourse affyrme, that the Duke of Northumberland had straunge devises in his head, for deceaving of Suffolk (who was nothing so fine as himself,) and for bringing the Crown to his own familie. And among other devises it is thought, that he had most certaine intention to marrie the Ladie Marie himself . . . and to have bestowed her Ma. that now is, upon some one of his children (yf it should have bene thought best to give her lyfe) . . .

The Scholar suggests that the duke already had a wife. Whereupon the Gentleman derides him:

. . . you question like a Scholar. As though my L. of Leycester had not a wyfe alive, when he first began to pretend mariage to the Q. Ma. Doe you not remember the storie of K. Richard the third, who at such tyme as he thought best for the establishing of his title: to marry his own nepce, that afterward was married to King Henrie the seventh, how he caused secretlie to be given abroode that his own wyfe was dead, whom all the world knew to be then alive and in good health, but yet soone afterward she was sene dead indeed.[37]

Here was the old story of the death of Amy Robsart again. Our most authentic version has come down to us in the Spanish State Papers in a letter referred to earlier in these pages, from Bishop Quadra to the Duchess of Parma. It was dated September 11, 1560, and reported a conversation that Quadra had with Cecil, who was so much disturbed by events that he was thinking of retiring:

He ended by saying that Robert was thinking of killing his wife, who was publicly announced to be ill, although she was quite well, and would take good care they did not poison her. He said surely God would never allow such a wicked thing to be done.

But Quadra continues:

The next day the Queen told me as she returned from hunting that Robert's wife was dead or nearly so, and asked me not to say anything about it.[38]

The strange death of Leicester's wife that followed his inauspicious prophecy so roused public indignation that Leicester's marriage to Queen Elizabeth was made forever impossible, historians have generally agreed, and it would be strange indeed had not Leicester's contemporaries commented on the likeness of Amy Robsart's death to that of Anne, queen to Richard the Third.

The author of the *Leter* argues, however, that though Leicester is pretending to support Huntington, there is old enmity between the earls, and

Hastings for ought I see, when he commeth to the scambling, is like to have no better luck by the Beare, then his auncestor had once by the Boare. Who using his help first in murdering the sonne and heire of K. Henrie the sixt, and after in destroying the faithful friendes and kinsmen of K. Edward the fift, for his easier way of usurpation: made an ende of him also in the Tower, at the very same day and

---

[37] *Op. cit.*, pp. 104-5.
[38] *Cal. S. P., Span.*, *1558-1567*, p. 175. See above, pp. 171-73.

houre, that the other were by his counsail destroied in Pontfract Castle.[39]

Nor would Leicester "be so improvident, as to make him his soveraign, who now is but his dependent," remembering what happened to the Duke of Buckingham who helped Richard III to the crown and to others who aided aspirants to their goal, since no king can satisfy these helpers or repay them sufficiently.

Nevertheless Leicester is now apparently supporting the House of Huntington and is ready to defend the title derived from the Duke of Clarence. The author adds:

they have an other fetch of K. Richard the thirde, whereby he would nedes prove, his elder brother king Edward to be a Bastard: and consequentlie his whole line aswel male as female to be void. Which devise though it be ridiculous, and was at the tyme when it was first invented: yet, as Richard found at that tyme a Doctor Shawe, that shamed not to publish and defend the same, at Paules Crosse in a Sermon: and John of Northumberland my L. of Leycesters father, founde out divers preachers in his tyme, to set up the title of Suffolk, and to debase the right of king Henries daughter . . .: so I dout not, but thes men would finde out also, both Shawes, Sandes, and others, to set out the title of Clarence, before the whole interest of K. Henrie the seventh and his posteritie, if occasion served.[40]

In order that Leicester may make clear the path for Huntington (or himself) to the crown, the Scotch line from Henry VII must be got out of the way:

You know, that Richard of Glocester had never bene able to have usurped as he did, if he had not first perswaded king Edward the fowerth to hate his own brother the Duke of Clarence, which Duke stood in the waye, betwene Richard and the thing, which he moste of al thinges coveted. That is, the possibility to the Crown, and so in this case is ther the lyke device to be observed.[41]

The nearness of the aspirants to the crown is dangerous to those who wear the crown. Henry IV did not mean to usurp the crown until he saw Richard II without an heir and Roger Mortimer slain in Ireland. Richard III did not mean to murder his

[39]*Op. cit.*, p. 106.
[40]*Ibid.*, p. 124.
[41]*Ibid.*, p. 160.

nephews until he saw his brother dead and his nephews in his hands. Henry VIII was so well aware of the menace that he thought it best to wipe out all the heirs of Clarence:

And yet now when one of the same house and line, of more habilitie and ambition, then ever anie of his auncestors were, maketh open title and claime to the Crown, with plotes, packes, and preparations to most manifest usurpation against al order, al law, and al rightful succession: and against a special statute provided in that behalf: yet is he permitted, borne out, favored, and friended therein.[42]

The author attributed certain of Leicester's stratagems to his following of Machiavelli, and Sir Philip Sidney, answering the *Leter* in defense of his uncle, took particular note of this fact:

as though I doubted that any would build belief upon such a dirty seat, only when he, to borrow a little of his inkhorn, when he plays the statist, wringing very unluckily some of Machiavel's axioms to serve his purpose, then indeed—then he triumphs.[43]

Sidney defended the good will of both Leicester and Huntington, but in spite of his defense the reputation of Leicester as a "rare artist" in poison was still current when Sir Robert Naunton wrote:

I may fear he was too well seen in the Aphorismes and principles of *Nicholas* the *Florentine*, and in the reaches of *Caesar Borgia*.[44]

And in 1592 another libel, directed against Cecil, was saying that Cecil had so often given to others the execution of his plans that their real author was not known, and was citing Leicester and Walsingham as examples. Of Leicester the author wrote:

The former of the twaine, for that he had in his youth, by overmuch attending his pleasures, neglected the observation of many secretes, which M. *Cecill* practized out of *Machiavill:* yet in the end, he did in a few yeares profit so much, and so recover his negligences past, as that he soone grew old in iniquitie: and left no mischief unattempted how abhominable so ever.[45]

[42]*Ibid.*, pp. 174-75.
[43]Sidney, *Miscellaneous Works*, ed. William Gray (Boston, 1860), p. 311.
[44]*Fragmenta Regalia* (1641), p. 15.
[45]*A Declaration of the True Causes of the Great Troubles, presupposed to be intended against the realme of England* (1592), pp. 52-53. All these libels are usually attributed to Robert Parsons.

But by 1592 libels of Leicester were out of date, for Leicester's son died in 1584, and he himself in 1588. Now the libels are turned particularly against Cecil, and the same charges that were made in the *Treatise of Treasons* twenty years before are renewed, with two additions: he has a hunchback son whom he is advancing, and he is trying to marry his grandson to Arabella Stuart in order to make him king in her right.[46] But there are no particular references to Richard III unless a remark attributed to the old Countess of Huntington may be so construed. She is reported to have warned of a prophecy that a man with two C's in his name would be the destruction of England and may have been parodying the warning which contributed to the downfall of the Duke of Clarence.[47] Be that as it may, the old charges against Cecil were renewed, and the parallels would hold as well as ever.

The specific and detailed comparison between Richard III and the members of Elizabeth's council prove that Richard was accepted as a Machiavellian before Gentillet's work was published, and that he continued to be associated with Machiavellianism. The comparison also proves that Richard was used as a mirror of usurpation and tyranny in Elizabethan England. Whether Shakespeare used him with any specific intent there is no evidence to decide. But there is ample evidence to prove that an Elizabethan audience would probably have current applications of history in mind.

Whether Shakespeare's *Richard III*, then, was rightly classed as one of the histories by the editors of the First Folio depends to a great extent upon Shakespeare's intention, for he did not make his play the vehicle for political moralizing, except rather casually in the last act. And even in this last act there arises the problem of the general moral versus the special political significance of the procession of ghosts which passed before Richard during his last terrifying night. The ghosts have been attributed to

[46]*Ibid.*, pp. 70-71.

[47]John Philopatris, *An Advertisement Written to a Secretarie of My L. Treasurers of Ingland* (1592), p. 39.

Senecan influence; they have been regarded as Shakespeare's interpretation of the workings of conscience, which the chronicles recorded; they have been attributed to the influence of the *Mirror for Magistrates* with its ghostly speakers. There were certainly many tales of the murdered returning to haunt their murderers in Shakespeare's day. But among such tales the most horrible were those relating to the death of Charles IX of France. The son of Catherine de Medici, he was at least technically responsible for the massacre of Saint Bartholomew's eve which had so shocked the Protestant world, and which was constantly recalled to Englishmen when Elizabeth proposed to marry first one and then another of Catherine's sons. Charles was said to have died horribly. His pores exuded blood. He dreamed of the massacred corpses which filled the streets of Paris. He had a hot fever, and the images of his victims passed before him. Such were the tales of the divine vengeance exacted from the sinner, who, according to the Protestant writers of Shakespeare's day, had sinned in accordance with the teachings of Machiavelli as Catherine de Medici had introduced them to France. If Shakespeare did have a Machiavellian Richard in mind, it would have been fitting to accord him a death copied from the death of the archrepresentative of Machiavellian evil.

To anyone who has read the chapter on *Henry V*, it will be apparent, I think, that Shakespeare used in brief the accepted pattern of battle in the last act of *Richard III* that he used in *Henry V*. Richmond accounts himself the captain of the Lord and his army God's "ministers of chastisement." His troops advance to the cry of "God and Saint George," certain that the Lord is with them. Richard resembles the French leaders in *Henry V* with his scorn of the enemy, "A sort of vagabonds, rascals, and runaways." Each of the leaders makes a formal oration to his army before the battle.

But it is not until Richmond's epilogue that we have a clear-cut political speech. It must be remembered that a renewal of the Wars of the Roses did not seem to the Elizabethans impossible. After the death of the Duke d'Alençon in 1584, it had been generally accepted that Elizabeth would not marry, and that the direct Tudor line would cease with her death. The author of the famous *Leter* expressed his fears

if once the chalenge of Huntington take place in our Realm. Which challenge being derived from the title of Clarence onlie, in the house of Yorke, before the union of the two great houses: rayseth up againe the olde contention, betwen the families of Yorke and Lancaster, wherein so much English blood was spilt in tymes past, and much more like to be poured out now, if the same contention should be set on foot againe. Seing that to the controversie of titles, would be added also the controversie of religion, which of all other differences is most dangerous.[48]

The same writer was still muddying the waters, however, when he published in 1594 his *Conference about the Next Succession to the Crowne of Ingland*. Surely Shakespeare was voicing the prayer of the men of good will in all England when he was writing the words with which Richmond closed the play:

> Abate the edge of traitors, gracious Lord,
> That would reduce these bloody days again
> And make poor England weep in streams of blood!
> Let them not live to taste this land's increase,
> That would with treason wound this fair land's peace!
> Now civil wounds are stopp'd, peace lives again:
> That she may long live here, God say amen!

And in that day it could not be without significance that he wrote also:

> O, now let Richmond and Elizabeth,
> The true succeeders of each royal house,
> By God's fair ordinance conjoin together!
> And let their heirs, God, if Thy will be so,
> Enrich the time to come with smooth-fac'd peace,
> With smiling plenty and fair prosperous days.

At least the partisans of the House of Lancaster could cry "Amen."

[48]*Op. cit.*, pp. 120-21.

INDEX

INDEX

INDEX

INDEX

339

INDEX

INDEX

INDEX

343

INDEX

INDEX

INDEX